The Best Self-Help and Self-Awareness Books

A Topic-by-Topic Guide to Quality Information

Stephen B. Fried, Ph.D.
Park College

G. Ann Schultis
Park College

American Library Association
Chicago and London
1995

The information in this book reflects professional knowledge of psychology and self-help. The recommendations and information are not intended as a substitute for diagnosis or therapy provided by psychologists, psychiatrists, and other mental health professionals. In addition, the recommendations are not intended as a substitute for professional legal or financial advice.

While extensive effort has gone into ensuring the reliability of all information appearing in this book, the publisher makes no warranty, express or implied, on the accuracy or reliability of the information, and does not assume and hereby disclaims any liability to any person for any loss or damage caused by errors or omissions in this publication.

Project editor: Kathryn P. Solt

Cover design: Richmond A. Jones

Text design: Dianne M. Rooney

Composed by Publishing Services, Inc.
in Palatino and Benguiat on Xyvision/Linotype L330

Printed on 50-pound Publishers Smooth, a pH-neutral stock, and bound in 12-point C1S RepKover Bind by McNaughton & Gunn, Inc.

The paper used in this publication meets the minimum requirements of American National Standard for Information Sciences—Permanence of Paper for Printed Library Materials, ANSI Z39.48-1992.∞

Library of Congress Cataloging-in-Publication Data

Fried, Stephen.
The best self-help and self-awareness books : a topic-by-topic guide to quality information / Stephen B. Fried, G. Ann Schultis.
p. cm.
Includes index.
ISBN 0-8389-0652-4 (alk. paper)
1. Self-help techniques—Abstracts. 2. Life skills—Abstracts. 3. Self-perception—Abstracts. I. Schultis, G. Ann. II. Title.
BF632.F7 1995
016.158—dc20 95-17644

Printed in the United States of America.

99 98 97 96 95 5 4 3 2 1

To our Park College faculty colleagues

To Connie

S.B.F.

To Mary Ellen and
the memory of
Ida and Richard Schultis

G.A.S.

CONTENTS

ABOUT THE AUTHORS

Stephen B. Fried

After obtaining a Ph.D in experimental social psychology from the University of Tennessee, Stephen Fried served ten years as a consultant, specializing in organization and staff development, team building, conflict resolution, and management coaching. In 1984 Dr. Fried came to Park College in Parkville, Missouri, where he serves as Professor and Chair, Department of Psychology. His teaching interests involve adult development and aging, social psychology, personality theory, the history of psychology, and American popular psychology. In 1988 the students of Park College selected Dr. Fried to be the recipient of the Zwingle Award, given annually to the outstanding faculty member, and in 1994, he was presented with the Governor's Award for Excellence in Teaching. He was selected to attend a National Science Foundation Summer Institute on Teaching the Psychology of Aging in 1992 and 1993.

Dr. Fried has received faculty development grants for his research and publishing activities, and as part of a Lilly Foundation grant, he is developing learning materials on diversity and aging. He has authored and coauthored numerous articles on a wide variety of topics, including the popularization of psychology, the psychology of aging, research methods, and team building. His articles have appeared in a wide assortment of scholarly and professional journals, such as the *American Psychologist, Teaching of Psychology, Psychological Reports, Clinical Management in Physical Therapy, Police Chief,* and *Caring* (the journal of the National Association for Home Care). Dr. Fried is the first author (with Dorothy Van Booven and Cynthia MacQuarrie) of *Older*

Adulthood: Learning Activities for Understanding Aging (1993), an active learning textbook used in both college classrooms and continuing education settings in the United States and abroad; he is also the author of *American Popular Psychology: An Interdisciplinary Research Guide* (1994). Professor Fried presents nationally on the popularization of psychology and the teaching of the psychology of aging to a variety of organizations, including the American Culture Association, the Association for Gerontology in Higher Education, and the Gerontological Society of America.

G. Ann Schultis

Ms. Schultis, Park College Assistant Professor, Library, received her B.A. in history from Cornell College, Mount Vernon, Iowa, her master's degree in library and information science from the University of Missouri-Columbia, and a master's degree in American social history from the University of Texas-San Antonio. Her professional experience has been in reference, library instruction, interlibrary loan, and access services at the University of Texas-San Antonio from 1976 to 1979, at the University of Texas-El Paso from 1979 to 1989, and in her present position of Reference Librarian at Park College since 1989. Her research interests include library instruction for adult students, library services for distance learning students, and the history of the American West with a specialization in Federal Indian policy. In the 1993–1994 academic year, she served as the Interim Chair of the History Department. She is a reviewer for the *Overland Journal* (Journal of the Oregon-California Trails Association) and has reviewed for *WLW Journal.*

ACKNOWLEDGMENTS

Without the assistance of our colleagues, friends, and families, this book could not have been completed. Many people gave large blocks of their time in assisting us with various phases of manuscript preparation. A number of our colleagues on the Park College faculty were particularly helpful. Dr. Joseph Blount, Professor John Lofflin, and Dr. G. Mack Winholtz read the entire manuscript and commented on both substance and style. We are particularly appreciative of John Lofflin's detailed comments. John is an exceptional journalist who writes and edits with great clarity.

Dr. Marvel Williamson, also a Park faculty member, commented on the chapters on sexuality and on coping with illness, disability, and death. Dr. Roger Chatten, a psychologist in private practice, critiqued the material on romance, love, marriage, and divorce and on psychological and substance-related disorders. Dr. Chandra Mehrotra, of the College of St. Scholastica, made useful suggestions for the chapter on aging. Dr. Neal Trent, of the U.S. Army and an adjunct faculty member at Park College, read and commented on the stress management chapter.

We wish to thank the Park College administration for their continuing encouragement and support of our scholarly endeavors. During the academic year of 1993–1994, we were awarded a Faculty Endowed Development Fund grant to assist in the completion of this book.

Thanks also to the interlibrary loan staffs of the following area libraries: Kansas City Missouri Public Library, Johnson County Kansas Public Library, Baker University, Benedictine College, Haskell Indian Nations University, Kansas City Kansas

Community College, the Metropolitan Community College Library System, Mid-Continent Public Library, Nazarene Theological Seminary, Rockhurst College, and William Jewell College. We also recognize Betty Vestal of the Park College Library for her assistance with interlibrary loan.

The editors of American Library Association Editions have demonstrated professionalism and common sense throughout the writing of this book. They have been very supportive from the time we conceived the idea for this book through its publication. Special thanks go to Herbert Bloom, Marlene Chamberlain, and Art Plotnik.

Our families and friends have aided us throughout the process. Steve Fried wishes to thank Drs. Theodore Albrecht and Mack Winholtz, for their encouragement; his children, Kurt, Kim, and Katherine, and most importantly, his wife and dearest friend, Connie Boswell. Connie's love and help made this project possible. Ann Schultis wishes to express her gratitude to her sister, Mary Ellen Schultis, her brother-in-law, Howard Collings, and three outstanding librarians, Drs. Harold Smith and Thomas W. Peterman, and Pamela K. Drayson.

For their innumerable contributions, we dedicate this book to the Park College faculty.

CHAPTER

1

How to Select High-Quality Self-Help Books

Readers are faced with a myriad of choices regarding which popular psychology books to select. Most bookstores have entire sections devoted to such popular psychology topics as parenting, relationships, and stress management. Libraries, too, devote much space to books on self-help. Some larger bookstores even have separate sections covering specific psychological topics, such as recovery and stress management.

Self-help psychology books are immensely popular in the United States.[1] These books may serve to provide "expert" verification of one's own beliefs or practices or may provide novel techniques for managing unruly children or coping with an inconsiderate boss. Self-help readers may also want confirmation that what they are feeling or doing is "normal." Readers may seek problem-solving strategies that can be used for self-improvement or they may search for coping strategies to help them adjust to changing circumstances often outside of their control, such as the losses associated with a divorce or the death of a loved one.

According to Steven Starker, self-help books are perceived by consumers to be a low-cost, highly accessible, mostly private, and possibly exciting form of assistance.[2] Although reading a book is clearly not a substitute for professional help, the price of self-help books is substantially less than the fee for just one session of psychotherapy. A $5 paperback may purport "to change your life," while reputable therapists, who may charge on the average $75 or $80 a session depending on the region of the country, are not allowed by virtue of professional codes of ethics to make such unrealistic claims.[3]

Popular psychology books are often accessible and available in libraries, supermarkets, bookstores, and even some convenience stores. Entering therapy involves securing a professional therapist through telephone calls, traveling to appointments as well as emotional and physical effort—all of which amount to a great deal of time. Starker suggests: "Once acquired, [the self-help book] makes few demands, awaiting the pleasure of the reader."[4] Reading psychology books is a private experience, with the only possible embarrassment being associated by some with the initial selection or purchase of the book. Finally, readers may feel a certain degree of excitement and belongingness, as a result of selecting and reading works read by millions of other fans of psychological bestsellers.

Although extremely popular, self-help psychology books are not without risks. Craighead and his associates discuss three negative consequences of some psychology self-help works:

1. Laypersons may label themselves as emotionally disturbed or suffering from some psychological disorder when neither is the case;
2. Ineffective programs are available while most consumers lack the necessary information to make a solid judgment regarding their efficacy; and
3. Readers may misdiagnose themselves and select popular books addressing one problem when their more significant concern may be entirely different.[5]

Gerald Rosen, who is a psychologist, self-help author, and critic of the excesses of popular psychology suggests that publishers and book reviewers rely more on data-based evaluations in deciding the merits of a particular book and in making various claims concerning its effectiveness in ameliorating various psychological maladies.[6] *Even though books may offer solid information, they are not an appropriate substitute for professional help. However, such popular works may be a highly useful adjunct to therapy. It is important that readers understand that they may misdiagnose themselves, resulting in reading the "wrong" books and following incorrect advice.*

Many health care professionals recommend self-help materials to their clients. In two studies Starker found a widespread practice among therapists and other care providers of prescribing specific books to some of their patients.[7] In one study Starker mailed surveys to psychologists, psychiatrists, and internists in the Portland and Seattle areas, and found that half of the psychologists believed their clients used popular self-help books often or very often. In this same study almost 90 percent of the psychologists, almost 60 percent of the psychiatrists, and about 85 percent of the internists prescribed popular works for their clients. On the basis of his findings, Starker concludes that "the self-help book has quietly established a niche in the practice of psychology, psychiatry, and internal medicine."[8]

Selection Criteria

How can the reader, health care professional, or librarian select the stronger psychology self-help books? What does one look for in a good popular psychology book? Key features include the author's background or credentials, areas of expertise and experience, the book's readability, the claims the author makes about the book's efficacy, its intended audience, and the publisher's reputation.

Look at the author's credentials. Turn to the book's cover, preface, or introduction for specific information about the author's basis of expertise, including his or her educational and professional experience. Self-help authors often fall into two not always distinct categories: *practitioners* and *fellow sufferers.*

Practitioners, for the most part, are psychologists, physicians (including psychiatrists), social workers, licensed professional counselors, and researchers who provide examples and solutions from their practices which readers may choose as a frame of reference for their individual concerns.

Fellow sufferers report that they have faced a particular problem like divorce or substance abuse and offer their experience as a model of how to affect positive change. *Readers are cautioned to analyze carefully the assertions of those authors who claim special knowledge because they maintain they are "victims" of dysfunctional families, low self-esteem, abusive marriages, or other assorted calamities. While it may be easier for the author and reader to form a special emotional pact as fellow sufferers, such life experience on the part of the author does not guarantee the validity of the information or advice. What may have worked for the author may not work for a particular reader, whose life circumstances and problems may be quite different.*

Examine closely the claims made on the book's cover and in the preface and introduction. Much of the self-help literature is published in paperback with eye-catching covers. The cover is often full of laudatory praise for the particular book. If such claims appear to be too good to be true, they probably are! This is particularly true of titles promising a quick fix, cure, or instant solution. Also, individuals whose comments of praise are quoted should be identified by name and institutional or professional affiliation.

Look in a self-help psychology book for problem-solving techniques that are based on professional experience and scientific evidence. Readers should take care when faced with claims solely based on "My method worked for me. I am sure it will work for you."

Good self-help books provide numerous examples as well as tested problem-solving techniques that readers can apply to their own situations. These techniques should be described clearly in detail, and the underlying therapeutic basis should be explained. For example, a book on parenting that includes a section on two-year olds may cite other child-development specialists on what might be a range of expected behaviors among the population of two-year-old children. If the author of such a work fails to use outside evidence and makes claims solely on his or her personal experience, the reader may be subject to the "because-I-said-so" syndrome. This can be dangerous when linked to exaggerated claims of the benefits one may derive from this approach (e.g., "It will change your life. You will be a whole new person."). The reader may end up using an unsound method that may have worked effectively for the author, but has no basis in or is even contrary to current psychological practice. In addition to basing recommended strategies on proven methods, good self-help books include a disclaimer and encourage the reader to seek professional assistance when needed.

Is the book intended for a *specific audience*? This is usually spelled out in the book's introduction. Most books in the category of psychological self-help are written for a broad-based group consisting of people who need help in a particular facet of life, people trying to alter or improve their life, and people wishing to solve problems on their own—this, then, is the basis for "self-help". Since this definition can apply to almost everyone, it is not surprising that the self-help market is booming. Some of the titles are targeted to a professional mental health audience, and these books often include empirical evidence as well as an extensive bibliography. Another ingredient of a quality psychology self-help book is a bibliography, which allows the reader to follow up on specific topics and examine the sources from which the author draws specific conclusions.

Scan several pages quickly. *Readability* should also be considered when purchasing a self-help book. While standing in the aisle of a library or bookstore browsing through the colorful covers and all the claims made about a particular book, look at the introduction, the table of contents, and flip through the first few chapters. Does the author write clearly and concisely? Is the purpose of the book spelled out? Are a variety of problem-solving techniques included? A self-help book that cannot be read with ease will be of little use as it sits on the shelf gathering dust!

Who published the book? Is it an established press known to the reader? A number of smaller presses specialize in self-help works. Consider the publisher's reputation in conjunction with the author's background, experience, and the basis for his or her authority. Typically, prior to the publication of a book, it is reviewed factually and stylistically by an editor and by experts in the field, in order to maximize accuracy and readability. Most publishers do this as a matter of course. The editors and expert reviewers are usually mentioned in the acknowledgments or in the book's preface or introduction. Some vanity presses, which require the author to pay to have a book published, print the book with no outside reviews. If the reader is unfamiliar with a particular publishing house, the book seller or the librarian may know its reputation. At larger bookstores, subject specialists select books in a particular area and are usually knowledgeable concerning publishers in their field. Libraries can also serve as a helpful source on publishers as well as on the best books about a particular topic. Reference librarians can often direct the reader to a title within the library's own collection or available through interlibrary loan. If these resources are not sufficient, then the reader can set out on a trip to a bookstore.

In summary, readers can use the following questions to select quality self-help psychology books:

1. *Is the cover free of claims regarding the effectiveness of the contents?*
2. *Is the purpose of the book clearly stated in the preface, introduction, or first chapter?*
3. *Is the author a mental health professional?*
4. *Does the author attempt to convey information regarding empirical support for the strategies contained in the book?*
5. *Does the book describe specific problem-solving strategies?*
6. *Does the author take into account individual differences among readers?*
7. *Is the writing clear and coherent?*
8. *Does the book contain a bibliography?*[9]

Overview

The remaining chapters in this sourcebook will survey a variety of psychological topics through narratives and complete, annotated bibliographies. A general discussion of pertinent findings from the scientific and professional literature will also form the basis for evaluating popular offerings for each topical area. These references will be cited numerically and listed as notes at the end of each chapter. Some of the most useful popular sources will be mentioned in the narrative section of each chapter. Following the general examination of each topic, the reader will be provided a selective list of what the authors consider to be among the best popular sources. The criteria for listing popular books include relevance, authority, empirical support, timeliness, availability, and comparison to similar works on the topic.

In using relevance as one of the criteria, the authors have selected books that discuss popular psychology topics in depth. Authority centers on the background and professional credentials of the writers of the self-help books; it also depends on the reputation of the publisher. While most popular psychology books are written for the general public, some of these works are based on research conducted by the writers or by others. Timeliness and availability refer to how recently the particular book was published and the relative ease with which readers can locate it. Books on a particular topic were reviewed and compared to other works, using the criteria described earlier in this chapter.

Popular psychology topics to be addressed include: (1) romance, love, marriage, and divorce; (2) sexuality; (3) parenting; (4) self-development; (5) stress management; (6) psychological and substance-related disorders; (7) coping with chronic illness, disability, and death; and (8) aging.

- The material on romance, love, marriage, and divorce will center on determining what an individual desires in a romantic partner, evaluating whether one is in love, determining the quality of a relationship, deciding on marriage, and developing a more satisfying marital relationship. This chapter also discusses the dynamics of ending a romantic relationship, grieving over the end of an involvement, and the impact of divorce on the couple as well as their children and in-laws.
- The chapter on sexuality will include discussions of understanding one's own sexuality, assessing personal sexual practices, modifying sexual behaviors, and guiding one's children regarding sexual issues. In addition to the criteria already listed, an additional content requirement was also used for this chapter. Books were selected for this section only if they included information on sexually transmitted diseases, such as HIV and AIDS, as well as information on safe sex.
- The chapter on parenting will cover the practical issues involved in raising children from infancy to adolescence: stages of child development, discipline, school behavior, and concerns germane to blended families.
- Information on self-development will cover a variety of personal development issues by distinguishing those aspects of the self which are more easily changed from those which are not. The chapter addresses gender issues, basic communica-

tion skills, assertiveness, and male-female communication, as well as meaning in life and happiness.

- In the next chapter stress management principles will be delineated by offering a framework for comprehending the basic physiology and psychology of stress, assessment of personal stress, and strategies for coping with common distressors.
- Psychological and substance-related disorders will be explored in another chapter centering on such concerns as anxiety disorders, substance-use disorders, eating disorders, mood disorders, and attention deficit hyperactivity disorder.
- The chapter on coping with chronic illness, disability, and death will explore the psychological effects of illness and disability on the individual and the family and will examine ways for people with chronic illness or disabilities to maximize their own life choices. This chapter will emphasize death as a final stage of life and the process of dying, as well as coping with the death of someone close.
- The final chapter on aging will include a description of the ordinary physical changes included in the aging process. Older adulthood will be viewed as a natural stage in the human life cycle, and the chapter will examine issues relevant to the relationships between older adults, their adult children, and their grandchildren.

Summary

This chapter included a discussion of criteria for use in selecting high-quality self-help psychology books. Subsequent chapters are devoted to: (1) romance, love, marriage, and divorce; (2) sexuality; (3) parenting; (4) self-development; (5) stress management; (6) psychological and substance-related disorders; (7) coping with chronic illness, disability, and death; and (8) aging. Each of the following chapters includes narratives as well as annotations of what we believe are the best popular books.

NOTES

1. *Publisher's Weekly* has listed several self-help titles in its review of longest-running hardcover and paperback bestsellers for 1993. In the

hardcover category: John Gray's *Men Are from Mars, Women Are from Venus* (36 weeks on the bestseller list), Deepak Chopra's *Ageless Body, Timeless Mind* (21 weeks*), and Marianne Williamson's *A Woman's Worth* (19 weeks*). In the paperback category: Stephen R. Covey's *7 Habits of Highly Effective People* (51 weeks*), and M. Scott Peck's *The Road Less Traveled* (22 weeks*). (An asterisk indicates that the title achieved the No. 1 spot on the list. Source: Paul Hilts, John Mutter, and Sally Taylor, "Books While U Wait," *Publisher's Weekly* 241 (Jan. 3, 1994): 56–57.)

2. Steven Starker, *Oracle at the Supermarket: The American Preoccupation with Self-Help Books* (New Brunswick, N.J.: Transaction, 1989), 5–6.

3. Jack Engler and Daniel Goleman, *The Consumer's Guide to Psychotherapy* (New York: Simon & Schuster, 1992), 163, 265.

4. Steven Starker, *Oracle at the Supermarket*, 5.

5. L. Craighead, K. McNamara, and J. Horan, "Perspectives on Self-Help and Bibliotherapy: You Are What You Read," in *Handbook of Counseling Psychology*, ed. Steven Brown and R. Lent (New York: Wiley, 1984), 878–929.

6. Gerald Rosen, "Guidelines for the Review of Do-It-Yourself Treatment Books," *Contemporary Psychology* 26 (Mar. 1981): 189–191; Gerald Rosen, "Self-Help Treatment Books and the Commercialization of Psychotherapy," *American Psychologist* 42 (Jan. 1987): 46–51.

7. Steven Starker, "Promises and Prescriptions: Self-Help Books in Mental Health and Medicine," *American Journal of Health Promotion* 1 (Fall 1986): 19–24, 68; Steven Starker, "Do-It-Yourself Therapy: The Prescription of Self-Help Books by Psychologists," *Psychotherapy* 25 (Spring 1988): 142–46.

8. Steven Starker, "Promises and Prescriptions," *American Journal of Health Promotion* 1 (Fall 1986): 24.

9. Stephen B. Fried, *American Popular Psychology: An Interdisciplinary Research Guide.* (New York: Garland, 1994), 194–95.

CHAPTER

2

Romance, Love, Marriage, and Divorce

Over the last two centuries, Americans have been instructed on "proper" strategies for romance, love, and marriage.[1] Much of the advice has been written for the consumption of women, who have been told repeatedly it is their responsibility to hold relationships together, that they attract the "wrong" men, and that they are "co-dependent."[2] In overwhelming numbers women continue to be the consumers of self-help books, particularly those concerning love-related subjects, and yet women are portrayed negatively in a great many of these popular books which purport to help them with their relationship problems.[3]

For some adults, the topics covered in this chapter conjure images of a perfect love, of a mate with wonderful and magical qualities who will love and adore them despite the reader's numerous imperfections. Here, romance, love, marriage, and divorce will be addressed as potentially positive aspects of life which require effort and the employment of practical problem-solving techniques. High-quality love relationships are mutual, realistic, and dynamic (e.g., they are forever changing). In addition, in the context of this chapter, both males and females will be considered as primary participants in romantic relations; neither gender will be given the lion's share of responsibility or blame when the relationship fails to provide what the participants deem appropriate. Although we will be centering on heterosexual relationships in this chapter, much of what is to be discussed, such as shyness, dating, romantic love, and mate selection, are applicable regardless of sexual orientation. Those readers interested in gaining more insight into the dynamics of gay and lesbian relationships should consult *Permanent Partners: Building Gay and Lesbian Relationships That Last* by Betty Berzon.

We want readers to know there is no known formula through which a reader can "learn the secrets of romance" or "the keys to a perfect marriage." Popular self-help books which make promises to that effect should be avoided. Books which purport to provide strategies for finding "Ms. or Mr. Right" will most likely prove disappointing to the reader. In an effort to assist the reader in understanding important issues surrounding romance, love, marriage, and divorce, this chapter will address the following topics: loneliness, shyness, dating, infatuation, types of love, committed relationships, cohabitation, marriage, remarriage, family therapy, and divorce.

Loneliness and Shyness

Everyone has experienced loneliness, which according to Robert and Jeanette Lauer, can be defined "as a feeling of being isolated from desired relationships."[4] Many people benefit from spending time alone, but that differs from a sense of loneliness, because such "alone time" is by choice, while loneliness relates to feelings of sadness because an individual is not in meaningful contact with others. Because feelings of loneliness are based on self-perception, people can be characterized as lonely if that is what they believe themselves to be. The Lauers contend loneliness is not based on a person's quantity of social contacts and relationships, but rather upon how the need for intimacy is fulfilled. So it is possible to have many friends, engage in activities with friends, and be involved in a romantic relationship (dating or marriage), and yet have ongoing feelings of loneliness.[5] Some people may experience chronic loneliness because of a lack of skill in forming or maintaining social and intimate relationships.[6] Furthermore, the Lauers conceive of loneliness as possibly leading to a downward spiral, so that if one's efforts to relieve feelings of loneliness are unsuccessful, the person may experience self-deprecation and sadness. If feelings of self-blame and the accompanying depression are not addressed effectively, the individual may develop physical symptoms, experience additional psychological problems, and be confronted with a continuing sense of loneliness.[7] In *Intimate Connections* David Burns provides strategies aimed at assisting readers in managing chronic loneliness through changing the ways they think about themselves and others. This cognitive restructuring is achieved by becoming aware of automatic negative thoughts, identifying distortions in thinking, and constructing more rational responses.

Some may feel lonely and consider themselves unable to change the situation because of their own profound shyness. As a behavioral characteristic, shyness typically begins in childhood, where it may be a consequence of temperament, a lack of social skills, rejection by other children, or a combination of these factors. Popularity in childhood appears to be a function of social competence, attractiveness, the child's expectations, as well as the response of the peer group. Unpopular children are judged more harshly for the same social behaviors as their more popular peers. Consequently, some children are rejected while others are neglected or ignored.[8] Because of isolation or rejection, some children and adolescents have fewer opportunities to develop social skills, which can contribute to shyness and lead to feelings of loneliness.

Promising forms of therapy, like social skills and assertiveness training, and cognitive therapy, assist those who experience difficulties with a wide range of behaviors involved in forming and maintaining relationships, such as greetings, the exchange of compliments, small talk, eye contact, and expressing warmth. Based upon individual requirements, clients may be taught how to ask others out on dates; this skill may be acquired through rehearsal, modeling, and reinforcement. Shy persons may benefit from cognitive therapy that centers on the client's false assumptions and beliefs about self and others.[9] Helpful suggestions for overcoming shyness can be found in *Shyness* by Philip Zimbardo.

Dating

In American society romantic relationships often develop in conjunction with dating. For long-married adults, thoughts of dating may bring back somewhat vague memories of high school proms, parties, drive-in restaurants, and movies, but for others who have dated more recently or are dating presently, perceptions may center around specific joys and anxieties of initiating and going out on dates. High school and college students are often surrounded by potential dating partners, although their own preferences and timidity may place limitations on social contacts. For many single and divorced adults, potential dating partners are met through work, friends, or organized groups. Stanford University professor Albert Bandura suggests that some of the most important happenings in life, like meeting the person we eventually date and marry, may occur as a matter of chance.[10] Bandura asks how many readers met someone important to them at a party that they decided to attend at the last minute due as a result of the insistence of a friend? All of the best planning for meeting our "true love" may be undone because we just happened to start talking to that attractive person seated next to us on the train while on the way home from work!

People date for a variety of reasons. Dating provides a structure through which two people can go out to dinner, movies, concerts, and other events, can share interests, have companionship, and possibly progress to affection and sex. In American society, many adults reluctant to dine at a restaurant or attend an event alone may feel more comfortable going with someone else, preferably with a date.

Several popular books provide suggestions for meeting dating partners through friends, work, athletic clubs, even at bars. Better books simply offer a bit of common sense. Dating persons who are previously unknown to the reader is potentially risky. For example, personal columns are ubiquitous, yet dangerous. Who will answer the advertisement? It could be almost anyone. Dating people with whom one works can present problems, whether a potential relationship develops or not. A certain awkwardness can follow if people continue to work together after dating one another. Meeting potential dating partners through mutual friends or through organizations like churches, synagogues, or interest groups (sports teams, hobby clubs, and so forth) can be effective. If two people meet through friends, the friends act as a filter screening potentially appropriate persons. An advantage of dating someone who belongs to the same social club or group is the opportunity to observe and interact with the person prior to initiating or agreeing to go out on a date with him or her.

Although some caution in dating is important, it is also important to go out and "have some fun." After all, going out on a first date does not mean that anything will develop beyond that first encounter. Readers who feel uncomfortable about initiating dates or unsure of appropriate behavior once on the date can consult Philip Zimbardo's *Shyness.* The author offers the following suggestions for making a date:

- Telephone for a date (many people are less anxious on the telephone than asking in person because they do not have to concerned about their body language);
- Identify yourself both by name and describe the circumstances under which you met (e.g., "This is Jim Metner. I sat next to you at the PTA meeting last week.");
- Make sure that the other person recognizes who you are;
- Offer a positive statement regarding the other person (e.g., "I really enjoyed talking with you after the meeting. I really had a great laugh. You have such a good sense of humor.");
- Request the date in very specific terms (e.g., "Would you like to go out to dinner with me on Saturday evening?");
- If the other person agrees to the date, both of you should decide on the restaurant and the time; and
- If the other person says no, you may want to ask for another evening, and if the response is still negative, then consider asking someone else out on a date.[11]

Just because one is turned down for a date, doesn't mean, according to Zimbardo, that the initiator is being rejected. A refusal may occur for many reasons that have nothing to do with the person requesting the date. The person who is asked for a date may refuse because of previous commitments, reasons of health, or because he or she has anxieties about dating.[12]

Jonathan Berent, in *Beyond Shyness: How to Conquer Social Anxieties,* offers pointers on handling rejection by cautioning readers not to overanalyze the situation, which only serves to elevate anxiety. In addition, Berent cautions those turned down for a date to "keep the feelings of disappointment specific to the rejection situation at hand," because they have been turned down by one person but not by everyone.[13] Philip Zimbardo also offers tips to the person who is asked out on a date but does not want to go. In this instance, the person is advised to be assertive and say no but to do so in a way which is not meant to be hurtful to the one making the request for the date. For information and useful sources on sexual behavior as it pertains to dating, see Chapter 3 of this book.

Infatuation

When we first meet someone whom we find attractive, we may begin to fantasize about that person, and possibly through dating or perhaps from a "safe" distance become infatuated. This infatuation centers on the perceived qualities of the other, since we may now view her or him through the "eyes of love," or at least what we label love. This stage of infatuation, which can last a few months or more, is exciting and a bit unnerving. One aspect of infatuation is an apparent inability to view the other person objectively. Later when one is past this phase, the other's limitations or eccentricities may become all too clear. Infatuation can be quite pleasant, if it is mutual and does not dominate one's life. When someone who is no longer in this state of desire and attention stops caring for the other person, or when the couple moves into a different stage of the relationship, then an individual may look back in amazement at how "silly" his or her behavior was. But it is important to note that feelings of joy and nervousness in the presence of a new love, as well as preoccupation with them is a normal part of what many persons experience as an early stage in the process of love. Unfortunately, if the relationship does not materialize, one might become depressed and experience a bit of sadness while ruminating over what might have been. These feelings of distress are normal, and for most such sadness will gradually dissipate with time and distance from the loss.

In other situations the persons involved experience a maturing relationship which continues to be nourished by a real joy in the presence of the other, perhaps the occasional sending or receiving of flowers for no particular reason and excitement when the two gaze into each other's eyes. Readers who wish to learn more about the role of romance and infatuation in long-term relationships are advised to consult two popular books: *Couples: Exploring and Understanding the Cycles of Intimate Relationships* by Barry Dym and Michael Glenn, and *Why Marriages Succeed or Fail* by John Gottman and Nan Silver.

Romantic Love

Thousands of poems, songs, paintings, and novels all attempt to describe the nature of romantic love. Some psychologists and representatives of neighboring disciplines have also tried to fashion an understanding of the topic. Robert Sternberg has constructed a triangular model of love which provides a clearcut way of viewing complex human relationships. According to Sternberg, love consists of three primary elements—intimacy, passion, and commitment.[14] In this model, intimacy is viewed as true concern about the needs of the other, respect, trust, sharing, and self-disclosure. Passion relates to sexual attraction and excitement in regard to the other person. The final component of the model, commitment, reflects a decision that one loves another as well as a choice to continue the relationship.

Based on various combinations of the three elements, Sternberg has suggested seven types of love: (1) liking (only intimacy); (2) infatuation (only passion); (3) empty love (only commitment without intimacy and passion); (4) romantic love (intimacy and passion without commitment); (5) companionate love (intimacy and commitment without passion); (6) fatuous love (passion and commitment without intimacy); and (7) consummate love (intimacy, passion, and commitment). Sternberg suggests that many kinds of love exist, and his model seems to fit reality.

Many adults, having been involved in several love relationships in the course of their lives, have found each one different. And, of course, the nature of love will undoubtedly change over time in the same relationship. *With the exception of pathological relationships (for example, a marriage in which partners physically or psychologically assault one another), one form of love is not better or worse than another form. Different persons, having differing needs, require varying relationships, so whatever works well for the two parties in fulfilling their requirements is the most satisfactory love relationship for them. Because individuals as well as couples change over time, it is highly unlikely both persons' needs will be met all the time.*

Violence in Relationships

Many couples experience violence in their romantic relationship. Typically, males are the ones who batter, and women are the ones who are battered. In *The Battered Woman* Lenore Walker discusses the emotional consequences when women are physically, verbally, and sexually abused by their mates. Walker delineates a three-phase cycle theory of violence. During the first phase, tension building, the victim employs psychological defenses in order to "protect" herself from an awareness of the severity of this situation. She may project blame for the violence on external factors, not on her mate. In her defense she may appear passive. Walker describes many battered women as trying to cope with the situation by covering for the batterer. They are afraid of the perpetrator and don't want the harassment to escalate.

As the tension-building phase continues, the batterer appears to be out of control. At this time the couple begins a second phase termed "the acute battering incident."[15] Walker writes,

> During phase two, the batterer fully accepts the fact that his rage is out of control, as does the battered woman. . . . His rage is so great that it blinds his control over his behavior.[16]

Typically the second phase lasts between two to twenty-four hours, but some women describe a period of a week or more. If police are contacted to intervene, the call for help is most likely to occur during or immediately after the incident.

A third phase follows the second and is characterized by contrition and kindness. The abuser asks for forgiveness. He attempts to convince the victim and himself that he means it. For many of these couples, the cycle repeats.[17] Walker suggests a number of strategies to reduce partner battering by eliminating sex-role stereotyping during child development, reducing the depiction of violence on television and in the movies, limiting the harshness in child discipline, and by increasing public understanding of "the victimization process of battered women."[18]

Walker also recommends the establishment of telephone hot lines and safe houses, both of which are available in some communities. *Women must be provided with safe environments. If women decide they need help in dealing with abuse, the community should and, in some cases, does provide short-term shelter, food as well as legal assistance. Some batterers have, through therapeutic intervention, learned to manage their rage, and some couples benefit from marital therapy.*

Committed Relationships

When two people spend more time with each other, they gradually define themselves and are defined by other persons in their lives as a couple. The longer they choose to stay together, the more likely is it that they will see themselves in a committed relationship. However, it is important to note that one of the persons may be much more committed to the relationship than the other. One or both may be more or less committed than they think. One or both are not committed, but do not leave out of either fear of the unknown, lack of a replacement, or a host of other factors.

Barry Dym and Michael Glenn have developed a model for charting the stages of committed love relationships. In their view couples transition through recurring "cycles of conflict and resolution," influenced by a "changing cultural narrative" that promotes standards and expectations by which the couple should behave.[19] Some couples conform very closely to the cultural narrative, doing everything expected of them, while other couples rebel as much as they dare from the societal pressures placed upon them.

Dym and Glenn suggest three stages in a couple's relationship: (1) expansion and promise; (2) contraction; and (3) resolution. The authors write, "The essential quality of early relationships is expansiveness. . . . We feel more capable and more available. . . . We are expressive, bold, and open."[20] Although expansion is characteristic of beginning relationships, it can occur a number of times in a committed relationship. Couples may reexperience expansion as they learn more about one another. Because expansion is one of "change and instability," the partners inevitability feel disappointment, fear, and concerns over control, leading to a stage of contraction and betrayal.[21] In this phase partners return to their old habits and ways of relating. Some people are disappointed when the "true" nature of their lover is revealed, while others are relieved to move beyond the early expansion, which is "exciting but exhausting."[22]

In contraction, some partners move into rigid, often stereotypical roles, without even talking about who is responsible for what specific duties. During this phase the flaws of the partner are magnified, and feelings of betrayal occur. However, the conflict endemic to this stage allows for further understanding and for openness about fears and concerns. According to Dym and Glenn: "Couples in contraction have three basic options. They can break up, they can remain stuck in contraction, or they can move into a new stage, resolution."[23]

In the third phase of the relationship, resolution, the couple develops a renewed sense of optimism through negotiation and compromise. Approaches taken during this phase reflect the unique character of the particular couple. This stage leads to a new contract centered on working out the major concerns. It is the nature of resolution not to last; couples are eventually thrust into a period of expansion as the cycle continues.

Marriage

In this section the following topics will be addressed: cohabitation, mate selection, the ingredients of a high-quality marriage, responsibilities within the marriage, communication, affection and sexuality, finances, children, maintaining a high-quality marriage, and remarriage.

Cohabitation

When a couple lives together without being married, they are said to cohabitate. Drawing on numerous research studies, psychologist Bernard Murstein has developed a taxonomy of different types of cohabitation:

- Linus blanket, in which one person is excessively dependent on the other;
- Emancipation, where one or both express a new-found freedom from parents;

- Convenience, in which living together is useful for such matters as helping to pay the rent but does not express a strong commitment;
- Affectionate-dating-going together (nonmonogamous), where the partners are romantically involved, but reserve the right to pursue other intimate relationships;
- Affectionate-dating-going together (monogamous), where partners are not to date others;
- Testing, where the partners use cohabitation as a way of measuring their success at living together;
- Temporary, in which due to various factors (for example, a lack of money), persons wish to marry, but must postpone marriage until a later time; and
- Permanent alternative to marriage, where the couple view themselves as married in everything but the legal sense.[24]

In regard to the legal ramifications of cohabitation, it is important to consider that while sometimes cohabitation may facilitate a breakup because a divorce is not required, the courts may view "the partners as having property obligations to each other, if one of them brings the matter to court."[25]

Mate Selection

The process of mate selection is shrouded in the myth that somewhere one may find the "perfect" love, the person with whom one was meant to spend his or her life, but no rational basis for such a belief exists. Since mate selection is to a large extent a rational process, a person who chooses to marry makes decisions based upon a set of criteria. Most individuals are not conscious of this rational process. According to Robert and Jeanette Lauer, the selection of a mate is a filtering process that proceeds through the following sequence:

- Start with all of marriageable age;
- Sort out persons of appropriate demographic and social characteristics;
- Sort out people with similar attitudes;
- Sort out persons with preferred physical attributes and similar personalities;

- Sort out persons with other similar and preferred characteristics; and
- Draw from a pool of potential mates.[26]

Randall Collins and Scott Coltrane, in reviewing research on mate selection, conclude that marital selection is quite predictable, because people tend to marry those similar to themselves in social class, race, religion, educational level, and degree of physical attractiveness. Two popular self-help books detailing practical and emotional issues inherent in mate selection are *How to Stop Looking for Someone Perfect and Find Someone to Love* and *A Fine Romance: The Passage of Courtship from Meeting to Marriage,* both by Judith Sills.

Ingredients of a High-Quality Marriage

Michael Emmons and Robert Alberti in their useful book, *Accepting Each Other: Individuality and Intimacy in Your Loving Relationship,* describe six dimensions of high-quality intimate relationships: attraction, communication, commitment, enjoyment, purpose, and trust. Attraction reflects the personal qualities, such as personality, appearance, and values, that drew the partners together in the first place. Communication, according to Emmons and Alberti, is the most important avenue for maintaining a solid relationship. Commitment is an assessment of the parties' desire to stay with the relationship. Enjoyment refers to the joyful, fun aspects of the association. Finally, trust suggests vulnerability, intimacy, and the willingness to place oneself in one's partner's hands. Additionally, Emmons and Alberti offer two other aspects of relationships: the qualities of each individual and the various environments (for example, economic, geographic, etc.) in which the relationship resides. These authors provide discussion of concrete suggestions for maximizing the quality of each of the elements.

John Gottman and Nan Silver describe the qualities of successful and unsuccessful marriages in *Why Marriages Succeed or Fail.* Their research leads to the clear notion "that a lasting marriage results from a couple's ability to resolve the conflicts that are inevitable in any relationship."[27] They delineate three approaches to conflict management in marriage: *validating,* in which partners acknowledge each other's point of view; *volatile,* in which partners engage in heated arguments that involve demeaning one another; and *avoidant,* in which partners go out of their way not to argue. All three styles may be successful. Each partner may feel good about dealing with a particular problem, though they differ dramatically in the strategies they employ. Also, stable couples are more adept at expressing themselves to each other. Gottman provides suggestions for couples who want to demonstrate more positive feelings. In addition, Gottman describes the many negative ramifications of criticism, contempt, defensiveness, and stonewalling.

Responsibilities within the Marriage

The concept of "his" and "her" marriage was formulated by Jesse Bernard to account for the differing perceptions and experiences that husbands and wives associate with their marriages.[28] A husband may feel satisfied if his meals are prepared and his laundry is done, while his mate may be highly dissatisfied if she's the one continually providing such services without adequate exchange. In this way one partner's marriage is literally different from the spouse's.

A marriage is, in part, a socioeconomic unit which depends upon financial resources, role obligations, and the accomplishment of a wide variety of tasks. Typically, married women work a "second shift," which begins when they come home after a day's work at a paying job.[29] Arlie Hochschild described the difference in position between many of these working women and their husbands as a "leisure gap," since the men enjoyed dramatically more free time than their wives. Only about 20 percent of the men in Hochschild's study participated equally in household responsibilities. Do findings like this lead to the conclusion that a return to single-career families will resolve this type of problem? No! Many couples both work because they have to do so in order to manage financially. Also, dual-career marriages are generally more successful, with partners reporting more satisfaction than those persons in single-career relationships.[30]

One key to marital success revolves around the equity that the partners perceive. In other words, if the tasks associated with the relationship are divided in a way that is felt to be fair, then the marital system tends to work. However, if the burden falls unfairly on one partner, that person may grow to resent the relatively smaller contribution of the other. No relationship is ever exactly equal, but many contemporary marital partners assume that they will both strive for a great degree of balance. As the marital relationship develops, many partners negotiate for who will cook what meals, clean the dishes, do the various housekeeping chores, change a baby's diapers, mow the lawn, pay the bills, take children to a medical appointment, and so forth. It is important that both partners feel that each of them is participating in the everyday responsibilities of the marriage. Interested readers will find the following titles helpful in discussing the issues involved in the dual-career marriage: *Successful Women, Angry Men: Backlash in the Two-Career Marriage* by Bebe Moore Campbell and *The Three Career Couple: Mastering the Fine Art of Juggling Work, Home, and Family* by Marcia Byalick and Linda Saslow.

Communication

Effective communication is a key element in building and maintaining a high-quality marriage or long-term relationship. Michael Broder in his helpful book, *The Art of Staying Together: A Couple's Guide to Intimacy and Respect,* describes twelve common ways in which marital partners interfere with the communication process. Broder labels these tactics as: (1) drowning in anger; (2) defensiveness; (3) blatant avoidance; (4) right issue, wrong time; (5) rigidity; (6) being too personal; (7) not letting go; (8) all or nothing; (9) allowing a lethal buildup; (10) top dog/underdog; (11) the forest for the trees; and (12) "You're all alike. . . ."[31]

In their popular book, *Accepting Each Other,* Michael Emmons and Robert Alberti provide a thorough discussion of speaking and listening skills as well as an examination of "intimacy-inhibiting communication habits."[32] In *Why Marriages Succeed or Fail,* John Gottman and Nan Silver provide useful strategies for calming oneself so that emotions do not block communication, ways of speaking and listening nondefensively, validating the feelings and opinions of the other person, and methods for overlearning communication skills so that they become almost automatic.[33]

Affection and Sexuality

In *Lucky in Love: The Secrets of Happy Couples and How Their Marriages Thrive,* Catherine Johnson describes the central role of affection and sexuality in the enduring relationship. After interviewing one hundred couples in long-term relationships, Johnson concludes that "an enduring sexual chemistry . . . proved to be very real. . . ."[34] Although partners may differ in the form and frequency of affection and sex, marriage is based, in part, on a physical attraction and a desire to be close.

Marital partners may express their affection in a variety of ways. Some couples openly display their feelings through frequent touches and kisses, while others who are less demonstrative may show their regard through smiles and compliments. It is important to the satisfaction of each partner that their particular needs for affection be addressed. Patterns of affection are typically established early in the relationship. However, in time some couples do tend to become less openly affectionate with one another. If a partner desires more direct signs of affection (e.g., kissing, hugging, and so forth), that concern needs to be expressed to one's partner, but levels of expressiveness and warmth and the ability to communicate such emotions vary from person to person.

In part, couples communicate their affection through sexual behavior. Michael Emmons and Robert Alberti advise couples to add more fun to their sex lives. Among their suggestions are: (1) take time for sex; (2) focus more on the process of sex than the results; (3) add romance to the sex; (4) tell each other what you enjoy; (5) have fun and don't take it so seriously.[35] Information as well as popular sources on sexual problems are covered in Chapter 3 on sexuality.

Finances

Marriages are both emotional and economic unions. A number of financial issues face couples. How do they spend their money? Does their income cover expenses? Does the couple have a budget from which they allocate money each month? Do they save and invest for the future? Are financial decisions made by one or both of the partners? Does the partner with the larger income have more control over financial decisions than the other person? The allocation of money is a reflection of values, and if the meaning of money differs greatly between partners, this signifies an area of conflict. For example, if one spouse spends money at a rate that exceeds or stretches their resources, while the other party worries continually about paying the bills, saving for emergencies, retirement, and putting money away for their children's college education, then marital conflict will ensue. It is vital that couples discuss their views on money, spending and saving patterns, and use of credit, prior to marriage. Compatibility in this area is important as to whether the marriage is successful or not. Readers who wish to learn more about practical financial matters should consult *Love and Money* by Sylvia Porter and *Couples and Money: Why Money Interferes with Love and What to Do about It* by Victoria Felton-Collins and her colleague Suzanne Blair Brown.

Children

For many marriages children bring great joy and a great deal of additional responsibility. Stan Katz and Aimee Liu, in their book, *False Love and Other Romantic Illusions: Why Love Goes Wrong and How to Make It Right,* discuss three common illusions regarding parenthood and marriage.[36] They describe the myth surrounding the notion that a "loving parent equals a loving partner."[37] The love of a parent is, hopefully, unconditional, while marital love is contingent on mutuality of feelings. Some exceptionally good parents have yet to experience a satisfactory marital relationship. Katz and Liu go on to discuss the illusion that a "true lover equals a willing partner."[38] Many persons, who despite being in a clearly satisfying love relationship, "are physically, financially, or emotionally unable to handle the job of raising a child."[39] Finally, the authors discuss the myth of: "Having a baby is a key to love."[40] Having a baby places many additional responsibilities and stresses on a marriage; as a result, a marriage beset with significant problems will be strained even more after the birth of a child, however wanted that child happens to be.

A great deal of evidence supports the notion that children place definite strains on a marriage.[41] Infants and toddlers demand a great degree of time and patience, but so do school-age children and adolescents. In summarizing the research on marital happiness, Randall Collins and Scott Coltrane observe that satisfaction is typically at its highest point early in the marriage, declines as the children are born, and dips to its lowest point when children are in adolescence. When children vacate the nest, marital happiness often begins to rise.[42] For couples who do not enjoy one another's company and whose marriages have been constructed around their offspring, a child's leaving home may be seen by their parents as negative, since they enjoyed their children and centered life around them.

Another concern for a great many parents involves an adult child who moves back "home," because of the financial and/or emotional problems associated with unemployment, underemployment, or divorce. Although customs regarding living with young adult children vary among subcultures, many persons would prefer that their children move out on their own. Both economics and fear may prevent the permanent launching of their offspring. Interested readers who wish to explore more specific issues and sources on parenting should consult Chapter 4.

Maintaining a High-Quality Marriage

No simple rules exist for a couple in the pursuit or sustenance of a quality marriage. Popular self-help books which offer a listing of specific steps to marital bliss are simplistic and will most likely disappoint the reader. Since marriages reflect the dynamic needs of two individuals, the relationship continually changes. Successful marriages are often different from one another. What they do seem to have in common is the tendency to employ effective communication in the resolution of conflict.

John Gottman and Nan Silver offer differing sets of advice depending on whether a couple is validating, volatile, or conflict-avoiding, and suggests that couples need to negotiate which of these three forms of stable marriage they prefer.[43] Issues upon which these styles are built include togetherness versus separateness, romance and companionship, honesty, persuasion, expressing emotion, traditional roles, and philosophy and beliefs.[44] Gottman and Silver believe that "productive disagreements" which are scheduled and structured are helpful, regardless of the type of marriage, but he also writes that in order to "foster stable marriages, couples need to continually celebrate those areas where they can come together. . . ."[45]

Remarriage

Around one-half of first marriages end in divorce and about two-thirds of those who divorce choose to remarry. Almost 60 percent of remarriages also end in divorce.[46] Those who marry for a second or third time face a great many of the same problems as they did with a first marriage, as well as additional concerns brought on by relationships and other concerns from the previous marriage. The success of a second or third marriage appears to be dependent upon several factors.[47] Have the partners worked through the grief, anger, and guilt that are naturally associated with the loss of a marriage? For some people that takes some time, professional counseling, or both. The amount of time necessary is based upon an individual's personality and the nature of the dissolution of the previous marriage. Many people develop self-confidence and new life skills from spending a period of time as a single person before moving into a new marriage. However, some persons may be so anxious about finding a mate that they proceed to a serious relationship before they have worked out their feelings over their previous marriage. Others may marry for financial security for themselves or for their children.

Remarriages are often comprised of children from previous marriages. As difficult as it is to be a parent, it may be more difficult to be a stepparent, since children typically have a "real" parent of the same gender as the new stepparent. Interested readers may wish to consult the section on stepparenting in Chapter 4 of this book. Attitudes of in-laws can have serious effects on any marriage. What if one's parents really adored one's previous spouse and view a new mate as a poor exchange? Finances often hamper remarriages. Partners may bring old debts, children, child support, and alimony payments to bear on the new couple's budget. Many remarrieds consider a prenuptial agreement to be a wise tool to handle potential financial conflicts. Louis H. Janda and Ellen MacCormick provide readers with a helpful guide on remarriage in *The Second Time Around: Why Some Second Marriages Fail While Others Succeed*.

Marriage and Family Therapy

Many marriages and families could benefit from psychological counseling. Some psychologists, psychiatrists, and psychiatric social workers specialize in assisting couples in improving communication, resolving conflicts, developing intimacy, building parenting skills, and aiding in other pertinent issues. Referrals for competent marriage and family therapists can be obtained through local psychological and medical societies, primary care physicians, and friends.

Research has demonstrated the efficacy of marriage and family therapy. Ronald Comer summarized the relevant literature and makes these points:

- Family therapy is as successful or more successful than other forms of psychological treatment;
- Success in family therapy is greatly enhanced if the father is involved in the process;
- Marital problems are better dealt with if marital partners are seen together in therapy rather than individually;
- Insufficient evidence exists regarding the effectiveness of one form of marital and family therapy over others;
- Short-term therapy appears to be as effective as therapy of longer duration; and
- No clear evidence has been presented that cotherapy (having two therapists present) is a more effective form of treatment.[48]

Common forms of therapy are described in *The Consumer's Guide to Psychotherapy* by Jack Engler and Daniel Goleman.

Divorce

Among the most painful aspects of human life is the demise of a love relationship, especially a long-term marriage. Breaking off from a loved or formerly loved partner often is part of an agonizing process. Typically, the parties vacillate between leaving and staying in the relationship, with the final decision to separate and divorce made by one or both partners after much "soul-searching." This section is devoted to a discussion of the psychological and social aspects of divorce.

In the latter part of the twentieth century, divorce has become so common that many persons go into their first marriage hoping that it will work, but realizing that it may not. After all, many of them, having previously experienced their parent's divorce, may not view marriage from an "until death do us part" perspective.

With women becoming gradually more and more independent economically, they are able increasingly to end emotionally unsatisfying marriages, and men, too, may view themselves as having greater life choices. It should also be noted that many of the laws surrounding divorce have changed. The requirement to find one partner at fault has been dropped in some states, leading to no-fault divorces. These factors have led to, as well as reflect, a lessening of the stigma of divorce in American society.[49]

A number of popular works address the difficult issues facing those in the throes of divorce. Some useful sources of information include: Genevieve Clapp's *Divorce and New Beginnings;* Lois Gold's *Between Love and Hate: A Guide to Civilized Divorce;* Marjorie Engel and Diana Gould's *The Divorce Decisions Workbook: A Planning and Action Guide;* Bruce Fisher's *Rebuilding: When Your Relationship Ends;* Christopher Hayes and associates' *Our Turn: The Good News about Women and Divorce;* and Abigail Trafford's *Crazy Time: Surviving and Building a New Life.*

Models of Divorce

Joseph Guttman describes several models for understanding the divorce process.[50] Included in Guttman's discussion are three models: (1) Wiseman's view of divorce as a process of mourning; (2) Bohannan's six stations of divorce; and (3) Kessler's analysis of the psychological process of divorce.

Relying upon crisis theory, Wiseman contends that coming to terms with divorce revolves around feelings of rejection and the requirement that both parties build new lives for themselves, while eventually being able to acknowledge the other.[51] Wiseman sees five stages in the mourning of a divorce: (1) denial; (2) loss and depression; (3) anger and ambivalence; (4) reorientation of lifestyle and identity; and (5) acceptance and a new level of functioning. During the first stage, denial, mates may believe that their marriage is fine in spite of serious dissatisfaction and conflict. Other couples may recognize difficulties, but choose to view them as the result of outside factors, such as problems with finances or children.

As couples realize they have serious conflict, they begin a process of loss and depression, which entails grief, sadness, loneliness, as well as difficulties in interpersonal communication. This depression is often rooted in anger, and anger often becomes a central emotion as the reality of divorce becomes more and more apparent. Because of differing legal and financial interests, marital parties are often cast as competing persons, which reinforces resentment and anger. During this phase, discussions are underway about contentious matters such as custody, visitation, child support, alimony, and dispersal of community property. If mates are able to deal effectively with their anger and ambivalence, their coping strategies are more likely to prove effective throughout the rest of the divorce process. During this phase, many couples express ambivalence regarding their own failure to solve the problems of the marriage, and some make some efforts toward reconciliation.

In the fourth stage, reorientation of lifestyle and identity, people faced with the actual divorce, are forced to construct a new identity and separate from their former mate. As part of their thrust toward getting on with their lives, newly divorced persons reassess their identities and a sense of self-esteem. Many people consider making occupational changes, because of economic need or to establish a new and better self. Others begin to use sexual relationships as a way of building up a badly bruised ego. Abigail Trafford refers to this period as the "crazy time," which "starts when you separate and usually lasts about two years. It's a time when your emotions take on a life of their own and you swing back and forth between wild euphoria and violent anger, ambivalence and deep depression, extreme timidity and rash actions."[52]

The fifth and final stage of Wiseman's model, referred to as acceptance and a new level of functioning, emerges when one is capable of turning aside enough of the anger to engage effectively in another long-term relationship. At this juncture, people are able to truly let go of the past and to transcend fears regarding the new love relationship. Bruce Fisher in his book, *Rebuilding* suggests that as a means of accepting losses the divorced person write letters (not to be sent) to the ex-spouse and to the relationship, in order to clarify that which one will truly miss as well as what one is pleased to leave behind.

Another way of viewing the process of divorce has been put forth by Paul Bohannan, who sees six simultaneous stations of divorce: (1) the emotional; (2) the legal; (3) the economic; (4) the coparental; (5) the community; and (6) the psychic. Even though these stations may occur simultaneously, concerns with one or more may vary greatly over time. With the emotional divorce, one or both mates decrease the emotional involvement in the marriage. Sometimes, the relationship appears to be less conflictual, but that is due to the withdrawal and denial of the partners.

The legal and economic divorces involve all the legal and financial ramifications of marriage and divorce. Legal and financial decisions made in conjunction with a divorce can have an everlasting impact on oneself and one's children, and these decisions are made during a time of tremendous emotional upheaval. For many divorced persons, especially women with young children, a dramatic decline in income follows the separation. Many divorced fathers become overburdened with child support and/or alimony payments. Couples who were "getting by" economically may experience poverty for the first time in their lives. *Appropriate legal guidance is essential so that an individual can make the best decisions regarding community property, child support, and so forth.*

In *Divorce and New Beginnings,* Genevieve Clapp devotes a chapter to "legal fundamentals," and in *The Divorce Decisions Workbook: A Planning and Action Guide,* Margorie Engel and Diana Gould provide hands-on activities for assessing financial and legal needs. For those couples capable of negotiating and mediating, Lois Gold's *Between Love and Hate: A Guide to Civilized Divorce* and Diane Newman's *Divorce Mediation: How to Cut the Cost and Stress of Divorce* may prove quite helpful. In mediation, a third party is used to assist a couple after they have decided to divorce as a method of avoiding litigation or after a divorce is finalized as a way of resolving conflicts that arise over finances, children, and so forth. *For some couples, mediation is not an appropriate option. Those spouses who endeavor to hide assets, are abusive, have serious psychological problems, or have trouble letting go of the relationship, would have difficulty with the mediation process.*[53]

The fourth station, the coparental divorce, underscores the fact that adults may divorce from one another, but, at least in theory, they do not divorce from their children. This aspect involves issues of custody, visitation, and parental involvement in decisions regarding the health, education, and welfare of offspring. Clearly divorce is extremely difficult for children. While divorce may be the best solution for parents, children's emotional needs for family and effective parenting do not change.[54] As part of a longitudinal study, Judith Wallerstein interviewed children both at the time of the divorce and ten years later, and found many viewing themselves as "survivors of tragedy."[55] Some research indicates that the psychological adjustment of the custodial parent is the best predictor of children's overall adjustment to divorce.[56] In reviewing the relevant research, Robert Emery concludes that "children from divorced but conflict-free homes have fewer behavior problems than children whose parents remain in an unhappy marriage," and that "children from high-conflict divorces have more adjustment difficulties than children from low-conflict divorces."[57]

For an excellent resource on how to effectively involve an ex-spouse in the parenting process, interested readers should consult *For the Sake of the Children: How to Share Your Children with Your Ex-Spouse in Spite of Your Anger* by Kris Kline and Stephen Pew. Additional information regarding children and divorce and single parenting can be found in Chapter 4 on parenting.

Bohannan terms the fifth station the community divorce. With divorce comes a severing of some of the ties with friends and in-laws. Mutual friends may feel awkward during the divorce process, not wishing to take sides. Some may feel threatened by divorced friends, especially if their own marriages are not firmly grounded. Some couples may not wish to socialize with one person, since their social relationships may exclusively involve other couples. Also, interests may change; the divorced friend is starting to date and further establish life as a "single." Also, for many divorced persons relationships with parents-in-law and their ex-spouse's siblings were closer than with their own family members. The loss or at least the distancing of these persons may prove immensely stressful and depressing. Many divorced persons develop new support systems through social, professional, and religious organizations. Christopher Hayes and his associates detail strategies for making new friends that have been employed successfully by middle-aged divorcees in their book *Our Turn: The Good News about Women and Divorce.*

According to Bohannan, the sixth station, the psychic divorce, refers to "the separation of self from the personality and the influence of the ex-spouse."[58] This station is important because it leads individuals toward growth and fulfillment, independent of their former mates. The process is difficult and may take several years for some persons; still others may never thoroughly integrate their new selves. Strategies addressing issues related to the psychic divorce are handled deftly by Genevieve

Clapp in *Divorce and New Beginnings*, Bruce Fisher in *Rebuilding: When Your Relationship Ends*, and Judith Wallerstein and Sandra Blakeslee in *Second Chances: Men, Women, and Children a Decade after Divorce*.

The third and final model to be discussed was developed by Kessler. Kessler sees six stages in the psychological aspects of divorce: (1) disillusionment; (2) erosion; (3) detachment; (4) physical separation; (5) mourning; (6) second adolescence; and exploration and hard work.[59] Every long-term relationship experiences some disillusionment, but for some couples this allows them to reevaluate their unrealistic and romanticized expectations of each other. In describing this stage, Joseph Guttman writes: "At first the disillusionment is inconsistent; . . . but with time, awareness and focus on the negative becomes concentrated. The person vacillates between idealization of the partner and total disappointment."[60]

If the partners are unable or unwilling to face these concerns, they move into erosion, which is the second emotional stage. This phase is characterized by feelings of anger and frustration, which were somewhat repressed during the first stage. Communication between the partners reflects effort to hurt or to avoid each other, though couples continue to be intertwined with each other. Sometimes one or both spouses engage in an extramarital relationship in an effort to meet emotional needs. The third stage, detachment, signals a lessening involvement in the marital relationship. Some partners transfer energies once placed in the marriage to work or hobbies. Efforts to avoid intimacy are not uncommon. Detached persons also contemplate what their life might be like following a divorce. Typically partners experience detachment at different times in the process, which further exacerbates concerns and conflicts. Detached partners struggle with their perceptions of the strengths and weaknesses of their marriages.

Kessler believes that the next stage, physical separation, is the most emotionally trying part of the process, since it is during this phase that people are forced to confront their anxiety and loneliness. Active spouses who initiate the separation may experience somewhat less stress because they have probably already detached from the marriage, and may have begun developing a new life through a new love relationship. However, some partners who initiate a divorce may have feelings of guilt, which is sometimes expressed as anger. Partners experience loneliness, but Kessler claims that "out of loneliness comes creativity, strong determination, courage, and deep commitment."[61] Both parties are forced to confront anxieties about the future.

During the next stage partners mourn the demise of their marriage. Mourning helps the former partners to work out some of their feelings regarding the profound loss of the love relationship. Both persons must deal with both good and bad memories of the other and of their time together. The process of mourning involves anger, depression, and sadness. Anger based on bitterness is negative, while anger related to frustrations regarding the construction of a new identity and new relationships may be quite helpful. Depression can reflect an internalization of anger. Kessler suggests that depression incapacitates, but sadness may lead to positive action.

After the divorce is worked through emotionally, persons may experience the next stage, a second adolescence, in which they are able to explore new life choices as well as feel excitement about future possibilities. Some people overreact to their newly found freedom, but, in time, most find some balance. Exploration and hard work is the label that Kessler gives to the final stage. During this phase people are able to set goals and work toward their achievement. In addition, people are more able to develop meaningful and lasting romantic relationships. The breadth and depth of emotion and pain typically associated with divorce should not be discounted. Most people who experience divorce feel anxious, guilty, depressed, and confused during some point in the process. Such feelings are normal. *Many people find brief psychotherapy to be helpful during this most difficult life crisis.*

Summary

In this chapter we have examined various issues surrounding romance, love, marriage, and divorce. Some adults experience great loneliness, which may be exacerbated by shyness and problems with social skills. However, many adults do date, finding it a meaningful way to enjoy a variety of activities as well as romance. Some forms of love may be reflected in committed relationships, and some lovers decide to cohabitate as an extension or reflection of their relationship. Those who choose to marry proceed through a conscious or at least subtle process of mate selection in hopes of choosing someone with whom they can experience a successful marriage.

Successful marriages involve an equitable sharing of responsibilities, good communication, affection and sex, effective financial management, and possibly child-rearing skills. High-quality remarriages reflect all of the above and more, depending on the circumstances of the couple. For married couples who perceive concerns with their relationship, marriage and family therapy may be helpful. A number of marriages end in divorce, which proves to be highly stressful and, for many, often the most difficult experience of their lives. Many who go through this transition suffer significant emotional, social, and financial loss.

RECOMMENDED TITLES

Loneliness and Shyness

Berent, Jonathan, and Amy Lemley. *Beyond Shyness: How to Conquer Social Anxieties.* New York: Simon & Schuster, 1993.

Psychotherapist Barent and coauthor Amy Lemley help the reader understand and identify the physical and emotional effects of shyness. The book outlines a five-step process for overcoming shyness that includes identifying anxiety symptoms and their impact on one's life; setting short- and long-term social goals; learning stress management techniques; learning or refining social skills; and expanding and refining one's social network. In each chapter questionnaires and exercises lead the reader through each of these steps. Since social anxiety plays a major role in how an individual interacts with others, the authors describe the characteristics involved in successful social interactions as well as those associated with poor or no social skills. In addition, age-specific behavior is outlined (e.g., shy children, preteens, and adolescents).

Burns, David D. *Intimate Connections: The New and Clinically Tested Program for Overcoming Loneliness Developed at the Presbyterian-University of Pennsylvania Medical Center.* New York: Morrow, 1985.

Readers will find a wide variety of practical techniques for overcoming loneliness, shyness, and social anxiety in this book.

Physician David Burns found that for many people loneliness is associated with low self-esteem. Using numerous questionnaires and exercises, the author helps readers identify loneliness, improve self-esteem, and enhance their social skills. The techniques suggested throughout the book have been tested at the Presbyterian-University of Pennsylvania Medical Center.

Cheek, Jonathan, Bronwyn Cheek, and Larry Rothstein. *Conquering Shyness: The Battle Anyone Can Win.* New York: Putnam, 1989.

In *Conquering Shyness* individuals can determine their shyness quotient. Do they feel shy all the time or only in certain situations? What happens to them physically and emotionally? By providing a series of relaxation techniques and sample conversations, Cheek and his coauthors demonstrate practical methods for readers to gain self-esteem and self-confidence by improving social skills at work and home, and in developing friendships and romantic relationships.

Zimbardo, Philip G. *Shyness.* New York: Jove, 1978.

In one of the earliest books on the social phenomenon of shyness, psychologist Philip Zimbardo describes shyness or social anxiety and the impact it can have on an individual's life. The author outlines levels or types of shyness. Some individuals may be uncomfortable and anxious in any setting. The degree and severity of this anxiety can vary from person to person, or may depend on a particular situation, such as speaking in public, a job interview, or meeting new people. Readers can identify other people who make them feel shy: those in authority, members of the opposite sex, or children. Situations can also cause social anxiety like being in large or small groups, relating one to one, asking for help, or being assertive. Zimbardo provides a practical guide for those who want to overcome social anxiety by helping them identify when they feel shy and what they can do to feel more at ease in any setting.

Dating

Broder, Michael S., and Edward B. Claflin. *Living Single after the Sexual Revolution: The Complete Guide to Enjoying Life on Your Own.* New York: Rawson Wade, 1988.

In this helpful guide Broder and his associate provide readers with social strategies for developing nonromantic relationships by making new friends, keeping old ones, and attending or hosting social occasions. In distinguishing between loneliness and being alone, the authors discuss strategies for dealing with loneliness. Romantic strategies which cover getting involved and nurturing a relationship are also explored. Additionally, readers are advised about the risks posed by sexually transmitted diseases including AIDS. The authors conclude with a section on taking care of oneself and family members.

Katz, Stan J., and Aimee E. Liu. *False Love and Other Romantic Illusions: Why Love Goes Wrong and How to Make It Right*. New York: Ticknor & Fields, 1988.

The authors contend that images of what they call false love abound in fairy tales, books, movies, and television. Many people find themselves swept up in finding only one true love, in being intensely attracted to their partner, and in finding someone who will meet all of their needs. These are only some of the components of false love. Psychologist Katz and coauthor Liu explain that when people try to find a partner based on these illusions, they are often disappointed when the relationship later dissolves.

The authors describe true love and how it compares to false and illusory love. A couple in "true love" share goals, commitment, respect, intimacy, and understand clearly the importance of mutual support and independence as both partners grow individually. Through the use of numerous examples, the authors show how couples can move from "false love" to "true love," once they realize the illusory nature of "false love." Finally, the last chapters give readers a summary of the steps to "true love."

Sills, Judith. *How to Stop Looking for Someone Perfect and Find Someone to Love.* New York: Ballantine, 1984.

In a straightforward guide psychologist Sills takes the reader through the steps involved in finding a mate, someone to spend the rest of one's life with. By defining and refining one's expectations and by learning what others have to offer, the individual is then ready to start the search process. The author provides a model for finding a mate. The person must be available both physically and emotionally. Can you accept this individual as a whole person, warts and all? Who is he with you? Who is she in the world at large? Does he or she provide security, companionship, and a shared sense of intimacy? What values do you hold in common (political, moral, and religious)?

By widening the pool of candidates and by being clear about what one requires, an individual can then take positive steps to finding a mate.

Sills, Judith. *A Fine Romance: The Passage of Courtship from Meeting to Marriage.* New York: Ballantine, 1987.

In a sequel to *How to Stop Looking for Someone Perfect and Find Someone to Love,* Sills, a psychologist, outlines the developmental flow of relationships based on her professional experience and on research about love, courtship, and marriage. By providing a road map through the relationship maze for the reader, the author dispels many of the myths associated with courtship. Finding Mr. or Ms. Right, the one perfect partner, or love will just happen along, are a few of these myths. Courtship moves through a series of stages that may progress toward intimacy, trust, and respect. Sills also identifies concerns that many people face, including fear of intimacy, rejection, and entrapment.

Sternberg, Robert, and Catherine Whitney. *Love the Way You Want It: Using Your Head in Matters of the Heart.* New York: Bantam, 1991.

The authors assert that romantic relationships are strengthened when the couple balances intimacy, passion, and commitment. These components are dynamic and can be changed if an imbalance exists. Readers are encouraged to make changes when necessary, to learn problem-solving techniques, and to identify masks that weaken the relationship. Looking below the masks, the authors reveal the underlying characteristics of each type, including the controller, the typecaster, the expert, and the conflict-avoider among others.

Violence in Relationships

Walker, Lenore E. *The Battered Woman.* New York: Perennial Library, published by Harper, 1979.

Walker, a psychologist, refutes many of the myths surrounding battered women, describes common characteristics of battered women, and examines coercive techniques batterers use. In these myths battered women are only a small percentage of the population; they are masochistic or crazy; and they are usually poor. Battered women often have low self-esteem and accept responsibility for the batterer's actions. Coercive techniques include verbal, physical, and sexual abuse, economic deprivation, and family discord. The author describes the cycle of violence that precipitates an attack as having three stages: a tension-building stage, an acute battering incident, and kindness and contrite loving behavior. Walker presents alternatives for battered women, including safe houses, legal and medical alternatives, and psychotherapy.

Committed Relationships

Beck, Aaron T. *Love Is Never Enough: How Couples Can Overcome Misunderstandings, Resolve Conflicts, and Solve Relationship Problems through Cognitive Therapy.* New York: Harper, 1988.

Beck examines the personal qualities needed for a strong relationship and the characteristics of a troubled relationship. The author encourages couples to identify their concerns through the use of questionnaires. These issues often include unrealistic expectations, poor communication, and biased interpretations. After identifying the issues, readers learn alternative strategies to address their concerns. Beck believes that couples can correct their self-defeating patterns of thinking and counterproductive habits, and improve communication. In applying this approach, couples concentrate on the positive aspects of their marriage by building on trust, loyalty, and respect, encouraging the tender, loving part of the relationship and strengthening the partnership.

Broder, Michael S. *The Art of Staying Together: A Couple's Guide to Intimacy and Respect.* New York: Hyperion, 1993.

Psychologist Michael Broder identifies two keys to successful relationships: passion and comfort. Passion, the emotional component, which usually brings the couple together, is accompanied by comfort, in which both partners trust and respect one another. The author also describes problematic relationships: the prebound, where one's partner is involved with someone else when the relationship begins; the one-sided, where one member of the couple makes all the effort to keep the relationship going; and the indifferent, where one partner may feel lonelier when the couple is together than when they are apart. Broder finds that successful couples recognize that an issue that affects one partner affects both as a couple, that they value the relationship because it fulfills the needs of both partners, and that they like, trust, and respect one another.

Dym, Barry, and Michael L. Glenn. *Couples: Exploring and Understanding the Cycles of Intimate Relationships.* New York: Harper Collins, 1993.

The authors, Dym, a psychologist, and Glenn, a psychiatrist describe what happens to couples over time. Unlike the works discussed in the dating section, this work is not a guide on how to meet people or to find a mate. Using couples from their practice as the basis for their model, they develop a basic pattern with each couple. Relationships proceed through three distinct stages: expansion and promise, contraction, and resolution. Although each stage has no set time limit, a couple may find themselves shifting from stage to stage over the life of the relationship. The stages are not automatically progressive in that couples can move from contraction into another expansion phase. The authors give many examples of common patterns in each stage. A question-and-answer chapter at the end of the book is also helpful.

Rubin, Lillian. *Intimate Strangers: Men and Women Together.* New York, Harper, 1983.

Rubin, a social psychologist, explores the changing roles for men and women and the impact these changes have on romantic relationships. Stereotypically, men worked and were responsible for maintaining the car, the lawn, and performing routine repair work in the home. Women were seen as homemakers and nurturers of children, and were responsible for all cooking and cleaning. As these stereotypes were challenged, the author describes how concepts of masculinity and femininity have been reshaped. Rubin reexamines changing role dependency in relationships. Rather than seeing dependency in terms of one partner being more dependent, the author finds that partners are moving toward interdependence, in which they rely on each other equally. In addition, the dynamics of intimacy and independence are also discussed.

Gay and Lesbian Relationships

Berzon, Betty. *Permanent Partners: Building Gay and Lesbian Relationships That Last.* New York: Dutton, 1988.

In *Permanent Partners* psychotherapist Betty Berzon reflects on both personal experience and professional practice with gay and lesbian couples in discussing the challenges facing homosexual couples today. Some of the issues are comparable to those facing heterosexual couples: establishing compatibility; improving communication; resolving conflict effectively; and dealing with changes in the relationship. Many of the issues are common to both gay and lesbian couples. Berzon believes that gay men can benefit from learning about lesbian issues and vice versa. These concerns include diagnosing the underlying issues of the relationship; the role of jealousy; sexual, financial, and legal matters; the role of families in the relationship; and having children.

Marriage

Byalick, Marcia, and Linda Saslow. *The Three Career Couple: Mastering the Fine Art of Juggling Work, Home, and Family.* Princeton, N.J.: Peterson's, 1993

Journalists Byalick and Saslow base their findings on their personal experiences, on those of eighty dual-career couples, and on that of experts in the field. Helpful tips on time and stress management for both partners are discussed. As two-career couples become the rule rather than the exception, both partners face the challenge of sharing equally in child rearing and dividing work at home. This book among others finds that couples who equally share housework responsibilities are in the more successful and stable marriages. Couples need to plan for unexpected crises by determining who will miss work to care for a sick child or take an aging parent to the doctor. Does this responsibility always fall on one partner? Is this by choice, by proximity, or by default? In the financial realm, decisions about finances, spending patterns, and developing a financial plan are outlined. Issues about career choices and relocation are also covered. Who is considered the primary breadwinner? Is this a permanent position or has it shifted from partner to partner over time? How are decisions about relocating made? Finally, the importance of making time for each other away from work and family responsibilities is stressed as well as finding time for oneself.

Campbell, Bebe Moore. *Successful Women, Angry Men: Backlash in the Two-Career Marriage.* New York: Random, 1986.

The 1960s and 1970s saw major shifts in traditional male and female sex roles in marriage toward a partnership between both partners in their careers, in child care, and in the equal division of housework. As couples married and made plans for the future, many agreed that their relationship would be a partnership of equals. Journalist and novelist Campbell explores what happened to these promises over time. Couples who openly expressed their desire for equality in all things often start out by sharing cooking and cleaning duties. As time passes and children come into the picture, the author finds that husbands begin to shift toward a more traditional view that their wives should take over most, if not all, child care and other domestic duties. As these responsibilities shift, resentment develops. As the phenomenon Campbell calls *backlash* evolves, misunderstandings by husbands and wives continue to build. The cumulative effect erodes the marriage further. Without a new understanding of what each partner is willing to do, the underlying strength of the relationship crumbles. Issues behind the backlash include what expectations, both stated and unstated, each person has; what career path each is on; and how supportive professionally each partner is. Campbell also discusses steps partners can take to overcome the backlash phenomenon and rebuild the relationship.

Emmons, Michael L., and Robert E. Alberti. *Accepting Each Other: Individuality and Intimacy in Your Loving Relationship.* San Luis Obispo, Calif.: Impact Pub., 1991.

Emmons and Alberti develop a model for relationships based on attraction, communication, commitment, enjoyment, purpose, and trust. Using the ACCEPT acronym for this model, the authors discuss each area in greater depth. Each relationship is seen as dynamic and ever-changing. In each section common elements found in the early, middle, and later stages of a relationship are outlined with recommendations of how relationships can be improved. As practicing psychologists, the authors include examples from their practices. The book is full of helpful written exercises readers can do to analyze their current relationship or future relationships.

Felton-Collins, Victoria, and Suzanne Blair Brown. *Couples and Money: Why Money Interferes with Love and What to Do about It.* New York: Bantam, 1990.

As a psychologist and certified financial planner, Felton-Collins and her associate Suzanne Blair Brown focus on the psychological issues surrounding money. The authors state that each individual brings a set of values or hidden investments about money to the relationship. In a series of questionnaires and examples, readers can identify their own attitudes about money. Are they hedgers who see money as a source of security, freewheelers who see money as a source of freedom, drivers who view money as a source of power, or relators who use money to enhance relationships? These attitudes are influenced by parental views, generational views, and past personal experience. By identifying one's psychological ties to money as well as those of one's partner, readers can use this guide to analyze their particular style and its impact on their financial well-being. The authors provide an alternative to budgeting called his/her cash flow management, which can be used for short- and long-term financial planning. Additionally, techniques to reduce reliance on credit and credit cards are included.

Gottman, John, and Nan Silver. *Why Marriages Succeed or Fail: What You Can Learn from the Breakthrough Research to Make Your Marriage Last.* New York: Simon & Schuster, 1994.

Psychologist Gottman and his associate Nan Silver base their findings on nearly twenty years of research encompassing the experiences of over two thousand couples. The authors find that marriages that last are those in which the couple is able to resolve conflicts as they arise in the relationship. Most couples fall into three conflict resolution types. In the validating marriage, couples compromise often and calmly work out their problems with solutions that satisfy both partners. In conflict-avoiding marriages, the partners agree to disagree but rarely confront their problems directly. In the volatile marriage, conflict erupts frequently with passions running high. The common denominator among all three types involves the balance between positive and negative interactions. Gottman and Silver state that couples, regardless of type, need to have at least five times as many positive as negative actions for the marriage to be stable. Through a series of questionnaires, readers can define what marriage type they have, how to identify problem areas, and how to overcome them. The authors call criticism, contempt, defensiveness, and stonewalling the "Four Horsemen of the Apocalypse" since each or a combination of all these factors can lead to marital dissolution. Using a series of dialogues, the authors demonstrate how the four horsemen can appear in conversation. Additionally, alternative positive responses are provided.

Johnson, Catherine. *Lucky in Love: The Secrets of Happy Couples and How Their Marriages Thrive.* New York: Viking, 1992.

This study of one hundred couples who had been married for seven or more years explores common characteristics of those who defined themselves as "happy." In this practical guide the author finds that at the outset couples felt comfortable with one another and had a shared sense of equality. Stable couples acknowledge that they are married at heart, that they have established daily routines, and that they have family rituals. Additionally, these couples have productive ways to deal with conflict when it arises. The impact of children, change, and tragedy on the couple is also discussed.

Levin, Laurie, and Laura Golden Bellotti. *You Can't Hurry Love: An Intimate Look at First Marriages after Forty.* New York: Dutton, 1992.

Although the authors, Levin, an anthropologist, and Belloti, a freelance writer, concentrate on a specific audience—single men and women forty and older at the time of their first marriage—they find that the individuals in their study face many of the same challenges as others looking for a positive love relationship. At the same time, these individuals find themselves facing stereotypes surrounding "old maids" and "confirmed bachelors." Common threads are woven in the stories of both men and women: keep dating, live life to the fullest as an individual and as a single person, and clarify personal priorities and intentions. The authors look for common reasons why these individuals did not marry earlier. Careers, the antimarriage sentiments expressed in the 60s and 70s, and living together in lieu of marriage, are among several reasons given. The importance of marriage as a precursor to starting a family was cited by both men and women in the study. After describing the characteristics of the people who marry late, the authors also discuss the major issues affecting most of the couples, including becoming a couple, becoming parents, handling family and financial issues, and managing careers.

Porter, Sylvia. *Love and Money.* New York: Morrow, 1985.

This guide, based on material from *Sylvia Porter's Personal Finance Magazine,* describes financial planning for singles, couples who live together, married couples, and separated or divorced couples. Psychological issues surrounding money are discussed at length as is the impact this can have on individuals and on the couple as they plan their future together. Porter advises couples to examine their personal values about money and to hold periodic planning meetings away from outside distractions. These meetings serve several purposes: to outline each person's view of money, to establish long- and short-term financial goals, and to plan how to meet these goals. The author encourages readers to review their financial balance sheet, noting all assets and liabilities as well as spending patterns and use of credit. This practical guide also includes information on cohabitation and prenuptial agreements, how to handle credit wisely, and planning for retirement. Using single, newly married, and long-term married couples, the author provides several useful budget makeovers.

Scarf, Maggie. *Intimate Partners: Patterns in Love and Marriage.* New York: Random, 1987.

At the basis of Scarf's book are two questions: What is intimacy, and what happens in intimate relationships? In answering these complex questions, the author explores with ease many of the issues involved in marriage today. By focusing in depth on five couples—how they met, what their family background had been and its influence on the present, how each couple resolved conflict and overcame challenges to the relationship—are all described. By interweaving each couple's interview material with her research, the author provides an excellent overview of a complex topic.

Viscott, David. *I Love You, Let's Work It Out.* New York: Simon & Schuster, 1987.

In a book aimed at committed or married couples, psychiatrist Viscott emphasizes the importance of commitment and communication to the stability of the relationship. Throughout the work the author encourages readers to keep a journal to note their feelings and reactions to commitment, communication, feelings, and conflicts. In some cases the partners are encouraged to share their journals with one another. Viscott divides individuals into several distinct types: dependent, controlling, competitive, and mature. Couples made up of these types are also described as are their conflict styles. Factors leading to infidelity and separation are also described.

Remarriage

Janda, Louis H., and Ellen MacCormack. *The Second Time Around: Why Some Second Marriages Fail While Others Succeed.* New York: Carol, 1991.

Psychologists Janda and MacCormack describe what factors make a second marriage successful. Not surprisingly, they are many of the same ones that make a first marriage succeed: compatibility, coming from similar backgrounds, having the ability to resolve conflicts, and having the attributes that one is seeking in a potential mate. In a second marriage additional factors play a role, with financial concerns and stepchildren being the primary ones. Relationships with ex-spouses and other family members must be resolved as well.

Marriage and Family Therapy

Engler, Jack, and Daniel Goleman. *The Consumer's Guide to Psychotherapy.* New York: Simon & Schuster, 1992.

Psychologists Engler and Goleman provide an insightful examination of the therapy process. In the first part of the book, readers are introduced to the issues involved in psychotherapy: when to consider it, how to select a therapist, and what therapeutic approaches are available. In addition, the authors include checklists that can be used to identify favorable, questionable, and unacceptable practices on the part of the therapist. Financial and ethical issues involved in the therapist-patient relationship are also discussed.

In the second part of the book, the therapy guide describes which types of therapy are most effective in treating problems commonly seen by mental health professionals. These include problems in everyday living, emotional and behavioral problems of childhood and adolescence, and psychiatric disorders. In each instance the problem is outlined as are treatment recommendations and what one should expect in treatment.

Divorce

Clapp, Genevieve. *Divorce and New Beginnings: An Authoritative Guide to Recovery and Growth, Solo Parenting, and Stepfamilies.* New York: Wiley, 1992.

In addressing both the legal and financial aspects of divorce, this straightforward book describes the patterns found in many divorces, and through the use of checklists suggests solutions to many of the common problems associated with divorce. The author describes some of the concerns of single parents, noncustodial parents, and stepparents. Using experiences from her own practice, from parents and children, and from research in family therapy, Clapp integrates all of this information into a handy guide. Appendixes include making lasting changes in one's life, practicing relaxation techniques, and a list of suggested readings.

Engel, Margorie L., and Diana D. Gould. *The Divorce Decisions Workbook: A Planning and Action Guide.* New York: McGraw-Hill, 1992.

In a helpful guide to divorce, the authors use checklists throughout to aid readers through the financial, legal, practical, and emotional aspects of the process. With fifty-five FORMulas™ ranging from a personal inventory to financial planning sheets, readers can use these inventories to organize their financial, legal, and emotional lives during this chaotic period.

Fisher, Bruce. *Rebuilding: When Your Relationship Ends.* San Luis Obispo, Impact Pub., 1989.

In *Rebuilding,* divorce therapist Fisher bases his approach on a series of building blocks. Although individual divorces may be unique, the author sees a pattern that develops as part of the divorce process. By comparing divorce to other types of loss—chronic illness, loss of a job, or the death of a loved one—Fisher describes the stages that accompany this type of crisis: denial, anger, bargaining, and acceptance. The author guides the readers through a series of fifteen sequential building blocks that can be used in rebuilding one's life: denial, loneliness, guilt/rejection, grief, and anger, among others. At the end of each building block readers are given a list of questions or concerns to consider. Journal keeping is a recommended technique in responding to the issues surrounding each block.

Gold, Lois. *Between Love and Hate: A Guide to Civilized Divorce.* New York: Plenum, 1992.

In recent decades as one of every two marriages ends in divorce, new methods to aid couples in ending their marriage have developed. Divorce mediation, which focuses on cooperation rather than competition and adversarial court cases, is one such method. The use of mediation involves negotiation, problem solving, and collaborative models. Through the use of exercises and questionnaires, readers can chart their progress through the mediation process.

Gold, whose private practice is in family therapy and divorce mediation, gives practical suggestions for reaching a constructive divorce. These suggestions involve taking responsibility for one's own behavior regardless of what the other partner does, separating emotions from decision making, and separating one's parental role from disputes with one's spouse. In addition, individuals need to accept responsibility for their contribution to the divorce, to understand their spouse's viewpoint, and to commit to reaching an equitable nonadversarial settlement. Sections on effective communication, selecting a mediator or attorney, and a resource list complete this sensible guide.

Hayes, Christopher L., Deborah Anderson, and Melinda Blau. *Our Turn: The Good News about Women and Divorce*. New York: Pocket Bks., 1993.

Our Turn, based on a study of women who were divorced after age forty, explores and explodes many of the myths associated with women who divorce at mid-life. In debunking myths that portrayed these women as lonely, fearful of aging, and unable to change, the authors found that women are more adaptable, that they take control of their lives, and that, contrary to popular belief, they do not dream of remarriage nor do they live through their children.

Additional findings revealed that the best predictor of post-divorce adjustment was not a woman's chronological age but her developmental age. Using a VCR metaphor, four patterns appeared: (1) pausers who put their life on hold by putting the family's needs first; (2) slow motions who took small steps toward independence; (3) rewinders who tend to rebel against the norm often through impulsive action; and (4) players who are independent women with a strong sense of identity. As do most divorce guides, this work discusses emotional turmoil, finances, letting go, and moving on. An appendix includes the study's methodology and questionnaire.

Johansen, Frances. *The Financial Guide to Divorce: Everything You Need to Know for Financial Strategies during (and after) Divorce.* 3d rev. ed., ed. Marcia Castaneda and Sally Marshall Corngold. Irvine, Calif.: United Resource Pr., 1990.

Certified financial planner Johansen outlines the key financial issues involved in divorce: spousal and child support, keeping or selling the home, dividing property, handling liquid and illiquid assets, pension funds, retirement, taxes, insurance, and living expenses. In short chapters the author lists the advantages and disadvantages inherent in various approaches to dividing property equitably.

Neumann, Diane. *Divorce Mediation: How to Cut the Cost and Stress of Divorce.* New York: Holt, 1989.

Divorce mediator Neumann answers the basic questions readers may raise surrounding divorce mediation: What is it, how does it work, can it work for me, why should it be used, how much will it cost, how does one find an attorney or mediator, and how is it different from traditional adversarial divorce? A sample mediation contract, a sample agreement with specifics, and a parenting schedule appear in the appendixes.

Trafford, Abigail. *Crazy Time: Surviving Divorce and Building a New Life.* New York: HarperCollins, 1992.

Journalist Trafford, health editor of the *Washington Post,* interviewed psychologists, psychiatrists, physicians, and hundreds of divorced men and women in this study. Tracking the process from the initial crisis and confrontation that leads to the end of the marriage, the emotional part of the divorce or the "crazy time," and the recovery, the author takes readers on a journey of discovery through the common threads of divorce.

In Trafford's analysis the underlying flaw in unhappy couples is a basic inequality in which one spouse dominates the other. The passive spouse role does not necessarily fall to women more than men. After the initial decision to separate and divorce is made, the phase Trafford calls "crazy time" ensues as the emotional roller coaster ride continues. This transition period begins at separation and can last as long as two years. It is characterized by elation and depression, anger and ambivalence, and rash actions followed by timidity.

The author also discusses how these patterns play themselves out for divorce seekers and divorce opposers. As the recovery phase starts, individuals begin to see that the marriage is over, that, as with any major loss, it should be mourned, and that they are forging a new identity. In recovery, the person often deals with a new often-lower standard of living, a new job or home, and changing relationships with family and friends. New relationships may develop and result in remarriage.

Wallerstein, Judith S., and Sandra Blakeslee. *Second Chances: Men, Women, and Children a Decade after Divorce.* New York: Ticknor & Fields, 1989.

The book details the long-term effects of divorce on parents and their children. Family members were interviewed at the time of the divorce and at one, five, ten, and fifteen year intervals. Wallerstein and her associate found long-term effects for all involved. In an in-depth analysis of three families representative of the most common patterns seen in divorce, the authors discovered that divorce is a wrenching experience for many adults and almost all children, that divorce is a part of a continuum in one's life and is only one of many experiences that contribute to a life, and that children feel the effects of divorce into young adulthood, particularly when they start forming relationships of their own.

Walther, Anne N. *Divorce Hangover: A Step-by-Step Prescription for Creating a Bright Future After Your Marriage Ends.* New York: Pocket Bks., 1991.

Concentrating on the emotional aspects of divorce, this work deals with many of the feelings associated with divorce: failure, guilt, loneliness, loss, pain, and anger. These feelings may linger long after the legal settlement is reached. Understanding that the divorce has a beginning, middle, and an end, Walther addresses the needs of readers who for whatever reason are unable to come to terms with the divorce and move on to the future. By offering effective strategies for readers to start and continue healing the emotional scars left by the divorce, the author's approach encourages the individual to recognize, to acknowledge, to accept, and most importantly to understand the emotional as well as financial costs involved. The final step includes moving beyond the pain of the past and concentrating on the future. While describing the symptoms of a "divorce hangover" and ways to remedy it, Walther uses a series of workbook exercises that aid the reader in realizing that divorce is not a permanent state of being and that it has an end.

Weiner-Davis, Michele. *Divorce Busting: A Revolutionary and Rapid Program for Staying Together.* New York: Summit, 1992.

In *Divorce Busting,* therapist Weiner-Davis encourages couples to build on the strengths of their relationship in resolving conflict. The author uses Solution-Oriented Brief Therapy, a therapeutic approach that focuses on future actions and emphasizes the individual's or the couple's strengths. Additionally, this approach stresses the importance of identifying possible solutions rather than on problems (e.g., "The trouble with you is. . . ." By the time couples reach the point of separation and divorce, the partners find few, if any, positive traits in one another. Couples are encouraged to recall situations when they enjoyed each other's company. These need not be romantic dinners but something as mundane as discussing what to have for dinner. By drawing attention away from the problems and moving toward what made them feel good about themselves and their marriage, the individuals can plan solutions with specific goals and actions. In setting short-term action-oriented goals, couples can make changes in a matter of months rather than years. The author includes information on selecting a therapist, on what to expect in this particular type of therapy, and on making and continuing positive changes. According to Weiner-Davis, this approach is designed for couples, but it can also be used by individual partners to improve their relationship.

NOTES

1. Barbara Ehrenreich and Diedre English, *For Her Own Good: 150 Years of Experts' Advice to Women* (Garden City, N.Y.: Anchor Pr./ Doubleday, 1978), 268–70.

2. Wendy Kaminer, *I'm Dysfunctional, You're Dysfunctional: The Recovery Movement and Other Self-Help Fashions* (New York: Vintage Bks., 1993, 14; Wendy Simonds, *Women and Self-help Culture* (New Brunswick, N.J.: Rutgers Univ. Pr., 1992), 1–18, 171–212.

3. Simonds, *Women and Self-help Culture,* 1–18; Susan Faludi, *Backlash: The Undeclared War against American Women* (New York: Anchor Bks., 1991), 1–2, 335–56.

4. Robert Lauer and Jeanette Lauer, *Marriage and Family: The Quest for Intimacy* (Dubuque, Iowa: W. C. Brown, 1991), 31.

5. Robert Lauer and Jeanette Lauer, *Marriage and Family,* 32.

6. Leticia Ann Peplau, "Loneliness Research: Basic Concepts and Findings," in *Social Support: Theory, Research and Application,* ed. Irving and Barbara Sarason (Boston: Martinus Nijhoff, 1985), 275.

7. Robert Lauer and Jeanette Lauer, *Marriage and Family,* 33–34.

8. Lois Hoffman, Scott Paris, and Elizabeth Hall, *Developmental Psychology Today,* 6th ed. (New York: McGraw-Hill, 1994), 252–55.

9. Ronald Comer, *Abnormal Psychology* (New York: Freeman, 1992), 236–37.

10. Albert Bandura, "The Psychology of Chance Encounters and Life Paths," *American Psychologist* 37, no. 7 (July 1982): 747–55.

11. Philip Zimbardo, *Shyness* (New York: Jove, 1978), 242–43.

12. Ibid., 243.

13. Jonathan Berent, *Beyond Shyness: How to Conquer Social Anxieties* (New York: Simon & Schuster, 1993), 183.

14. Robert Sternberg, "A Triangular Theory of Love," *Psychological Review* 93 (Apr. 1986), 119–35, 138.

15. Lenore E. Walker, *The Battered Woman* (New York: Perennial Library, 1979), 59.

16. Ibid., 60.

17. Ibid., 55–70.

18. Ibid., 187.

19. Barry Dym and Michael L. Glenn, *Couples: Exploring and Understanding the Cycle of Intimate Relationships* (New York: HarperCollins), 1993, 10, 28–47.

20. Ibid., 64.

21. Ibid., 81.

22. Ibid., 85.

23. Ibid., 109.

24. Bernard Murstein, *Paths to Marriage* (Newbury Park, Calif.: Sage, 1986), 91–92.

25. Randall Collins and Scott Coltrane, *Sociology of Marriage and the Family: Gender, Love, and Property* (Chicago: Nelson-Hall, 1991), 640.

26. Lauer and Lauer, *Marriage and Family,* 126.

27. John Gottman and Nan Silver, *Why Marriages Succeed or Fail,* (New York: Simon & Schuster, 1994), 28.

28. Jessie Bernard, *The Future of Marriage* (New York: World, 1972), 5.

29. Arlie Hochschild, *The Second Shift: Working Parents and the Revolution at Home* (New York: Viking, 1989), 3.

30. Collins and Coltrane, *Sociology of Marriage and the Family,* 402–406.

31. Michael Broder, *The Art of Staying Together: A Couple's Guide to Intimacy and Respect* (New York: Hyperion, 1993), 68–70.

32. Michael Emmons and Robert Alberti, *Accepting Each Other: Individuality and Intimacy in Your Loving Relationship* (San Luis Obispo, Calif.: Impact, 1991), 39–63.

33. Gottman and Silver, *Why Marriages Succeed or Fail,* 173–231.

34. Catherine Johnson, *Lucky in Love: The Secrets of Happy Couples and How Their Marriages Thrive* (New York: Viking, 1992), 156.

35. Emmons and Alberti, *Accepting Each Other,* 55–58.

36. Stan Katz and Aimee Liu, *False Love and Other Romantic Illusions: Why Love Goes Wrong and How to Make It Right* (New York: Ticknor & Fields, 1988), 115–30.

37. Ibid., 116.

38. Ibid., 121.

39. Ibid.

40. Ibid., 127.

41. Sara McClanahan and Julia Adams, "Parenthood and Psychological Well-Being," *Annual Review of Immunology* 5 (1987): 237–57.

42. Collins and Coltrane, *Sociology of Marriage and the Family,* 408.

43. Gottman and Silver, *Why Marriages Succeed or Fail,* 202–13.

44. Ibid., 203–204.

45. Ibid., 222–23.

46. Jeanne Belovitch, ed., *Making Remarriage Work* (Lexington, Mass.: Lexington Bks., 1987), xvi.

47. James Young, "Readiness for Remarriage," in Jeanne Belovitch, ed., *Making Remarriage Work,* 181–82.

48. Comer, *Abnormal Psychology,* 169.

49. Frank Furstenberg, Jr., and Andrew Cherlin, *Divided Families: What Happens to Children When Parents Part* (Cambridge, Mass.: Harvard Univ. Pr., 1991), 6–7.

50. Joseph Guttman, *Divorce in Psychosocial Perspective: Theory and Research* (Hillsdale, N.J.: Lawrence Erlbaum Assoc., 1993), 31–50.

51. Reva S. Wiseman, "Crisis Theory and the Process of Divorce," *Social Casework* 56, no. 4 (Apr. 1975): 205–12.

52. Abigail Trafford, *Crazy Time: Surviving Divorce and Building a New Life,* rev. ed. (New York: HarperPerennial, 1992), 65.

53. Genevieve Clapp, *Divorce and New Beginnings: An Authoritative Guide to Recovery and Growth, Solo Parenting, and Stepfamilies* (New York: Wiley, 1992), 30–39.

54. Judith S. Wallerstein and Sandra Blakeslee, *Second Chances: Men, Women, and Children a Decade after Divorce* (New York: Ticknor & Fields, 1989), 18.

55. Ibid., *Second Chances,* 23.

56. Neil Kalter and others, "Predictors of Children's Postdivorce Adjustment," *American Journal of Orthopsychiatry* 59 (Oct. 1989): 605–18.

57. Robert Emery, *Marriage, Divorce, and Children's Adjustment* (Newbury Park, Calif.: Sage, 1988), 94.

58. Paul Bohannan, *Divorce and After* (New York: Doubleday, 1968), 53.

59. Sheila Kessler, *The American Way of Divorce: Prescription for Change* (Chicago: Nelson-Hall, 1975), 20.

60. Guttman, *Divorce in Psychosocial Perspective,* 40.

61. Kessler, *The American Way of Divorce,* 32.

CHAPTER

3

Sexuality

Clearly one of the most intriguing and exciting aspects of intimate adult relationships is sexuality. Sexuality is shown not only in our physical desires and practices but also in the many ways in which we present ourselves, including styles of dress, hair, and conversation. Even when we are not sexually active, we project a certain sexuality. Though all human beings may be viewed as sexual persons, the various manifestations of that eroticism may differ with gender, sexual orientation, marital status, age, mood, and cultural context. Preferences for expression of affection and erotic feelings reflect individual biology, personality, and values.

Curtis Byer and Louis Shainberg view sexuality as "the sum of a person's sexual characteristics, behavior and tendencies; including biological, psychological, and cultural attributes."[1] Central to an understanding of human sexuality is the notion of a "sex print," a thumbprint of an individual's style of erotic expression: personal preferences for partners, activities and patterns of arousal.[2]

According to Martin Seligman, our sexuality consists of five layers: (1) sexual identity; (2) sexual orientation; (3) sexual preference; (4) sex role; and (5) sexual performance.[3] An examination of these layers will cover sexual and gender identity; sexual orientation; "normal" sexuality; values and sexuality; sexually transmitted diseases and AIDS; stages in the cycle of sexual response; "traps" in the response cycle; sexual dysfunctions; unusual sexual preferences; and sex therapy.

Sexual and Gender Identity

During childhood people develop both a sexual and a gender identity. Most children, by the age of two or three, are aware that they are physically a boy or a girl, but they are uncertain about the permanence of their gender (gender constancy) until around age four or five.[4] With puberty comes full confirmation of one's biological maleness or femaleness. Gender identity centers on a subjective sense of being psychologically male or female while sexual identity centers on physiological differences.[5]

Usually sexual identity and gender identity are consistent, but that is not always the case. Children with a gender identity disorder are not comfortable with their gender designation and desire to be members of the opposite sex. By adolescence this disorder usually disappears, but it can progress into transsexualism. A majority of adult transsexuals experienced a gender identity disorder in childhood, but most children with the identity disorder do not become transsexuals.[6] Transsexualism is relatively rare; about one in thirty thousand men and one in one hundred thousand women are thought to perceive themselves as trapped in the body of the wrong sex.[7] Jack Engler and Daniel Goleman suggest, "Both biological and psychosocial factors shape gender identity. The timing and levels of male and female hormones play a role. So do parental and cultural attitudes. . . . Gender identity isn't simply a by-product of sexual development. . . . Developing a psychological sense of maleness or femaleness . . . is a separate task and achievement."[8]

Sexual Orientation

The Continuum of Sexual Orientation

If one views sexual orientation along a continuum, people may fall somewhere between exclusive heterosexuality and exclusive homosexuality, according to psychologists Curtis Byer and Louis Shainberg, who define sexual orientation as "our sexual attraction to people of the same sex, opposite sex, or both sexes."[9] These authors suggest that there may be a difference between individuals' preferred sexual partners and their actual partners, perhaps due to social prohibition, like being raised in a religion which equates homosexuality with sin, or limitations of the environment, such as attending a unisex boarding school.[10] Adelaide and Kurt Haas report that about one-fifth of the adolescent population has engaged in behaviors that could be labeled homosexual, perhaps only a few times, and that this experimentation is not a good predictor of homosexuality in adulthood.[11]

While most American adults perceive themselves as heterosexual or attracted to members of the opposite sex, a significant minority can be characterized as bisexual or homosexual in their orientation. Drawing on a variety of studies, Byer and Shainberg estimate "that the prevalence of more or less exclusive homosexuality in the United States and similar Western cultures is between five and ten percent for adult males and from three to five percent for adult females. . . . The percentages of both sexes who are bisexual are thought to be about the same as those who are homosexual."[12] Such estimates may be incorrect, since some persons may not wish to divulge their sexual orientation even on confidential surveys, while others may not have clearly come to terms with their particular erotic preferences.

According to Jack Engler and Daniel Goleman, "sexual orientation is relative, not absolute."[13] Many heterosexuals have had homosexual experiences, fantasies, or both. Complicating the delineation of an individual's sexual orientation is the multifaceted nature of orientation, which is comprised of three aspects: affectional orientation, sexual fantasy orientation, and erotic orientation. Affectional orientation refers to the gender of those with whom we prefer to bond; sexual fantasy orientation is reflected by the gender of those about whom we fantasize; and erotic orientation denotes the gender of our sexual partners of choice. It is not uncommon for people to show variations in these elements of orientation. For example, while many lesbians and gay men are both emotionally and sexually attracted to same-sex persons, others, especially some younger gay men, may be attracted on an erotic level to men but on an emotional one to women.

Causes of Sexual Orientation

One of the more intriguing questions concerning human behavior relates to the causes of heterosexual and homosexual orientations. As of this writing, no specific causative factor has been found to be the key element in the development of a particular orientation. Biological theories involving genetic predisposition, prenatal hormones, or brain anatomy have been investigated and show promise. Psychoanalytic theories, once fashionable as an explanation, have come under widespread criticism among mental health professionals. These theories perceive weak fathers, strong mothers, and an inadequate resolution of the Oedipal complex (erotic feelings toward one's opposite-sex parent) as major variables in the development of a homosexual orientation. Other behavioral scientists attempt to explain the unfolding of sexual orientation as the result of social learning, through which the sexual object choice of the child and adolescent is molded through modeling of others and reinforcement.[14]

Homosexuality

From a clinical point of view, a homosexual orientation is not a greater problem than a heterosexual orientation.[15] Jack Engler and Daniel Goleman suggest:

> Homosexual men and women, like heterosexual men and women, have no inherent problems in their ability to love, to work, and to play. They are not impaired in any way by virtue of being homosexual.[16]

However, homosexuals may develop special problems related to societal attitudes. Some may take many years to accept their sexual orientation, experiencing a great deal of guilt and shame. Those persons fearing rejection by family members may seek to hide their sexual orientation. Also, because of the devastating effects of AIDS, many gays may be attempting to deal with the deaths of friends and lovers. *Most characteristically, homosexual men and women suffer from the same general problems facing heterosexuals: conflicts in relationships, problems with work, difficulties in life transitions, and so forth.*

One problem facing many gay and lesbian people and their parents involves the manner in which children explain their orientation to their parents. Robert Deisher provides specific suggestions for gays and lesbians and their parents. Among his points of advice for homosexuals are:

- Plan how you will explain your orientation to your parents;
- Prepare your parents to understand, perhaps by providing information for them to read;
- Communicate that you do not want this to change the quality of your relationship with them;
- Give them sufficient time to absorb this news; and
- Understand that accepting is not the same as approving, since some parents may learn to accept, but because of firmly entrenched values may not approve.

Deisher also provides tips for parents upon hearing of their child's orientation. Parents need to understand that their child's homosexuality is not a sudden development, and that the only change is the parents' new awareness of their offspring's sexual orientation. Also, parents are informed that the causal factors in homosexuality are unknown, and that they have no reason to feel guilty for something they did or did not do when their children were younger. For those parents having difficulty adjusting to their children's orientation, support groups, like Parents and Friends of Lesbians and Gays, are available in many communities.[17]

"Normal" Sexuality

Determining what is normal sexuality and what is not can present difficulties. Most people define normality using themselves as a point of reference. If people differ dramatically from us in sexual practices, we tend to view them as abnormal, but if their lifestyles and methods of sexual expression somewhat mirror our own, then by our standards they are normal.

Culture and historical context also determine what is seen as sexually appropriate and what is not. In some societies and during certain historical periods, some erotic behaviors have been reinforced while others have been discouraged. For example, while most people have masturbated (almost all men and around 75 percent of women), the practice continues to be condemned by some religious groups.[18] Some people found masturbating were incarcerated as mental patients in America at the beginning of the twentieth century because masturbation was thought to be symptomatic of a severe psychotic disorder.[19] *Masturbation does not cause psychological or physical dysfunction, and it only presents a problem when it develops into a compulsive behavior or is utilized in lieu of sexual activities with one's partner.*

Masturbation serves several functions. During adolescence people grow to understand their bodies and their sexuality through self-stimulation. People may masturbate in order to reduce tension, as a method to assist in falling asleep, or to deal with loneliness. Some persons enjoy combining masturbation with a variety of sexual fantasies. Through self-stimulation a person can discover specific sensations that can be communicated to a partner.[20] Finally, in an era of AIDS, masturbation may be the ultimate form of "safe sex." For a sensitive discussion of masturbation, interested readers could benefit from a chapter-long discussion appearing in *Right Brain Sex: Using Creative Visualization to Enhance Sexual Pleasure* by Carol Wells.

While masturbation is widespread as well as normal, so are a wide array of techniques for both partner arousal and orgasm. Preferred methods of kissing, use of the hands, and genital stimulation vary dramatically. A great many couples view intercourse as the ultimate sexual activity. Some prefer male-superior positions ("missionary"), but others choose female-superior ones (the most common style around the world), side-to-side, lateral, rear-entry, sitting, or a vast array of other coital techniques. While many couples prefer coitus, others would rather engage in some form of oral sex. The three basic forms of oral sex are: cunnilingus, fellatio, and mutual oral-genital stimulation. Cunnilingus involves oral genital stimulation of a female, while fellatio is the oral stimulation of a male. Of course, oral sex should be a matter of choice, and like other lovemaking strategies should be employed only if both partners are interested. *Some heterosexual and homosexual couples enjoy forms of anal stimulation. However, partners should be aware that anal intercourse is considered to be risky behavior regarding the contracting of AIDS.*[21]

Readers interested in learning about a variety of heterosexual activities may find Alex Comfort's *The New Joy of Sex: A Gourmet*

Guide to Lovemaking for the Nineties to be a source of a wide array of different erotic techniques and pleasures.

Values and Sexuality

Individual and cultural values impact sexual attitudes and behaviors. Human belief systems emerge from parental, peer, religious, media, and community influences. Gradually people develop a personal system of values that includes societal messages of the acceptability of various types of sexual practices. If individuals' value system differs from their erotic desires or behaviors, guilt may emerge and seriously impact feelings of self-worth, and possibly sexual satisfaction. For example, one may enjoy a certain erotic activity but may have been taught that anything other than "missionary"-style intercourse with a marital partner is morally wrong. Such dissonance between desires and early teachings may produce a great deal of personal conflict. *It is important that people only engage in a sexual activity when it is a matter of personal choice. A large part of what goes into adult behavior emanates from a well-defined value system. For many people, sexual values are consistent with their family and religious backgrounds, while others develop their own distinctively personal sexual value system in the process of adulthood.*

Sexually Transmitted Disease and Safe Sex

Sexually transmitted diseases affect all kinds of people. Millions of people participate in this "silent epidemic," unaware of their condition because they do not display any significant symptoms.[22] Many types of sexually transmitted diseases or STDs exist, including cervicitis, nongonococcal urethritis, hemophilus vaginalis, gonorrhea, syphilis, candidiasis, pubic lice, scabies, trichomonas vaginalis, lymphogranuloma venereum, venereal warts, Hepatitis B, genital herpes, and human immunodeficiency viruses (HIV I and HIV II), which cause acquired immune deficiency syndrome (AIDS).

With the rapid spread of HIV and AIDS among heterosexuals and gay men, "safe sex" becomes an imperative. The ultimate form of safety is abstinence, but for vast numbers of adults that is not likely. Two highly useful books describing safe sex practices are *The Complete Guide to Safer Sex,* edited by Ted McIlvenna of the Institute for Advanced Study of Human Sexuality, and *Dr. Ruth's Guide to Safer Sex* by Ruth Westheimer. McIlvenna and his associates list the following unsafe practices: (1) anal intercourse; (2) vaginal intercourse without a condom; (3) swallowing semen; (4) receiving semen vaginally; (5) unprotected oral-anal contact; (6) unprotected manual-anal intercourse; (7) unprotected manual-vaginal intercourse; and (8) sharing menstrual blood.[23]

Stages in the Sexual Response Cycle

The human sexual response progresses along a predictable pattern. William Masters, and Virginia Johnson describe the sexual response as a four-phase process: (1) excitement; (2) plateau; (3) orgasm; and (4) resolution. In their comprehensive book *Masters and Johnson on Sex and Human Loving,* Masters, Johnson, and Kolodny state that the separation of stages is arbitrary, that they vary among people, and are experienced differently by the same person at various times. Also, though the human response cycle typically proceeds in a consistent fashion, the amount of time spent in a stage may vary dramatically. For example, on some occasions excitement occurs quite quickly, while at other times it increases slowly over a period of hours.[24] Helen Singer Kaplan has developed a modification of the sexual response model delineated by Masters and Johnson. In Kaplan's view, the sexual response contains three phases: (1) sexual desire; (2) excitement; and (3) orgasm.[25]

Sexual Desire

Being influenced by both human psychology and physiology, erotic desire results from a combination of fantasy and hormonal level. A specific part of the brain, serving as the sexual center, is neurally connected to the brain's pleasure center as well as to the erection centers located in the lower spinal cord. Byer and Shainberg state:

> When stimulated these connections cause blood to flow into the erectile tissue in the genitals of both men and women. When sexual desire is high, erection and lubrication occur easily and quickly. . . . Sexual fantasy can be strengthened by

> the presence of mental images of a person who is sexually attractive to us. . . . Such fantasies activate the brain's sexual center.[26]

The hormone involved in both male and female sexual desire is testosterone, which is produced by women's ovaries and adrenal glands and men's testes and adrenals. Reduced testosterone lowers desire and affects male erection.[27]

The Excitement Phase

This phase is the result of sexual stimulation, which may be physical, psychological, or both. The following physiological changes are associated with the female during this phase of the cycle: vaginal lubrication beginning around ten to thirty seconds after the initiation of stimulation, expanding the inner part of the vagina; both the cervix and uterus move in an upward direction; the outer vaginal lips move apart and flatten; the inner lips enlarge in their diameter; the size of the clitoris increases; and usually the nipples become erect. As the excitement phase continues, veins in the breast tissue may become more apparent and for many women, breasts increase slightly in size.

For men several changes occur during this phase: the penis becomes erect, the testes are drawn in the direction of the body, the ridges of the scrotum start to become smoother, and some men experience the erection of their nipples. As this stage develops, the size of the testes increases slightly.[28]

The Plateau Phase

The plateau phase, characterized by a high degree of arousal, varies widely in duration. Women experience a swelling of the outer vagina, which serves to narrow the vaginal opening. Also, the clitoris is pulled against the pubic bone. Masters, Johnson, and Kolodny write:

> The inner lips enlarge dramatically as a result of engorgement with blood, doubling or even tripling in thickness . . . the inner lips push the outer lips apart, providing more immediate access to the opening of the vagina . . . vivid color changes develop in the inner lips.[29]

At a subsequent point in the plateau phase, the areola starts to swell. Breast size may increase dramatically for some women. About one-half to three-fourths of all women develop a "sex flush" either late in the excitement phase or during the beginning of the plateau phase. This flush, characterized by a reddish and spotty change of the color of the skin, starts in the upper part of the abdomen and spreads over the breasts, and can appear on many other areas of the body.

According to Masters and his associates: "During the male's plateau phase, the diameter of the head of the penis near the coronal ridge increases slightly."[30] The testes swell and rotate forward. During the plateau phase, a bit of clear fluid may appear from the male urethra, and it can occasionally contain live sperm. About one-fourth of all men experience the "sex flush" described previously.

For both men and women, this phase includes increased neuromuscular tension, especially in the areas of the thighs and the buttocks. The heart rate increases, breathing becomes more rapid, and blood pressure increases as well.

The Orgasmic Phase

Orgasm occurs as the body discharges the mounting sexual tension. Typically lasting only a few seconds, orgasm involves muscular contractions which result in physical relaxation. Interestingly, each orgasm is different; some are truly explosive, while others are mild. Both psychological elements, such as mood and relationship to one's partner, as well as physical factors like fatigue contribute to an orgasm's level of intensity.[31]

Masters and his associates describe the female orgasm this way:

> Orgasm . . . is marked by simultaneous rhythmic muscular contractions of the uterus, the outer third of the vagina . . ., and the anal sphincter. The first few contractions are intense and close together. . . . As orgasm continues, the contractions diminish in force and duration and occur at less regular intervals. . . . Orgasm is a total body response . . . muscles in many different body regions contract.[32] All female orgasms follow similar physiological patterns, regardless of the source of the stimulation, and all orgasms are of equal "worth," the value of which depends entirely on a women's particular preference.[33] Some prefer stimulation

through coitus, while others prefer oral or masturbatorial stimulation. While some females experience sequential orgasms, which occur as a series with brief intervals between each, only a few women have multiple orgasms, which occur without any break during a period of stimulation.[34]

The male orgasm is a two-stage process, an emission phase and a propulsion phase. During the emission phase, the urethral bulb expands with seminal fluid, the internal urethral sphincter, the ampulla of the vas deferens, the seminal vesicle, prostate gland, external urethral sphincter, and rectal sphincter all contract. In the propulsion phase, seminal fluid is released, contraction of the penile urethra and internal urethral sphincter, the rectal sphincter, and the muscles at the base of the penis occurs. Also, the external urethral sphincter relaxes.[35] There is conflicting data among sex researchers regarding the range of multiple orgasms among men.[36]

The Resolution Stage

In this final phase of the sexual response, men and women experience the following: (1) within about five minutes, muscle tension disappears; (2) sex flush dissipates quickly; (3) nipples lose erectness; (4) heart rate, blood pressure, and respiration return to their normal levels; and (5) perspiration may appear on many areas of the body.[37] For women, a number of changes in the vaginal area occur. The cervix and the vagina's upper walls drop into the seminal pool located on the floor of the vagina. The vagina returns to its prearousal state, as do the labia, clitoris, uterus, and breasts. Men typically lose erection rapidly to about one-half larger than the unstimulated size of their penis, and a rapid loss of vasocongestion in the scrotum and testes follows.[38]

One important difference in the male and female sexual response is the refractory period, a time following ejaculation during which men are incapable of further orgasm. This period can last between just a few minutes to more than twenty-four hours in the case of older adults.[39]

Aging and the Sexual Response

Age can impact various aspects of the sexual response. Women show less change in their sexual physiology than do men. In older women, breast size does not increase during arousal, and menopause is accompanied by a depletion of estrogen, causing the vaginal walls to thin, leading to dryness. For older women who do not continue to engage in continual sexual activity, vaginal secretions may decrease.[40]

Typically, men show more age-related changes in their sexual physiology. Usually, it takes longer for older men to develop an erection than younger men, and they may keep their erections for a longer period of time than younger men. The latter seems to be related to a reduction in the amount of seminal fluid. The refractory period lengthens with age. It is not uncommon of men over the age of fifty to have to wait between twelve and twenty-four hours following ejaculation to develop another erection.[41]

"Traps" in the Response Cycle

When considering sexual patterns, it is common practice to compare one's own bodily responses to a general description. *However, readers are strongly advised to consider these points. Everyone behaves differently! Just because an individual's body responds somewhat differently from the average, that is not necessarily an indication of a sexual problem. Sexual responses vary, depending on our feelings and physical condition. The phases of the sexual response cycle do not occur as distinct and separate events; the process has been divided in order to help explain its complexities. Some people fall into the trap of overemphasizing the mechanics, which may tend to increase performance anxiety or detachment. Intensity of pleasure varies greatly. The "earth doesn't necessarily move" each and every time. Finally, it is erroneous to evaluate one's sex life solely on the basis of the quantity and quality of orgasms.*[42]

Popular books written by sex therapists can explain various misconceptions about the sexual response. See, for example, Marty Klein's *Ask Me Anything: A Therapist Answers the Most Important Questions,* which offers easy-to-understand information that humanizes the nuances of the sexual response.

Common Myths about Sexuality

At the end of the twentieth century, many of us pride ourselves on our reliance on scientific fact and on our belief in sexual equality, yet common myths pervade our culture. Adherence to these myths (for example, that men are more sexual than women, or that following menopause women become asexual) can contribute to anguish, doubt, lowered self-esteem, conflict in relationships, and a lessening of sexual pleasure. Many people received little accurate information regarding sexuality when they were children or adolescents. Many parents and teachers were too ignorant, conflicted, or both to provide them with the necessary knowledge to develop a healthy adult sexuality. Too many people reach their adult sexuality with myths, which were communicated as facts by siblings, peers, and the media.

Sexual Dysfunctions

This section will address the lack of sexual desire, problems in arousal, orgasmic problems, and sexual pain disorders.

Lack of Desire

Clearly adults vary greatly in their preferred frequency of sexual expression. *Such preferences are purely a matter of choice. Some people want to have sexual relations every day; others are happy with monthly activity. There is not a correct amount of sexual activity. However, if partners differ in their preferred rate of sexual activity, conflict and frustration may result.*[43] According to Engler and Goleman:

> You or your partner may have . . . a lack of sexual desire if there has been a sharp drop in desire for more than just a few weeks or months. Many people go through periods when their desire wanes only to pick up again. . . . Typical causes of such temporary waning are personal losses such as the death of a loved one, or an increase in pressures at work. But a sudden, lasting drop may signal an ongoing marital conflict.[44]

Two forms of lack of desire are hypoactive sexual desire and sexual aversion. The former is characterized by an individual who functions effectively and may enjoy sexual activity, while the latter describes people who find sex to be quite unpleasant, even disgusting.[45] Sometimes lack of desire is the result of biological factors, such as lower levels of testosterone, medications (some antipsychotics, antidepressants, as well as some drugs utilized in the treatment of heart disease), and a variety of illnesses, including depression (see

Chapter 7 for a discussion of symptoms associated with depression).[46] Factors ranging from personal beliefs, increased stress, or a conflicted relationship, to previous molestation or assault may contribute to hypoactive sexual desire or sexual aversion.[47] Useful information on concerns about diminished sexual desire can be found in *Not Tonight, Dear: How to Reawaken Your Sexual Desire* by Anthony Pietropinto and Jacqueline Simenauer. Janet Wolfe has written an especially helpful book, *What to Do When He Has a Headache: Renewing Desire and Intimacy in Your Relationship,* which addresses sexual desire problems among males.

Problems with Arousal

In psychiatric language male erectile disorder refers to *impotence,* while frigidity is termed *female arousal disorder.* Jack Engler and Daniel Goleman view impotence as a continuing inability to develop an erection and/or to maintain an erection through the process of intercourse.[48] Current research indicates that erectile failure, which occurs in 8 to 10 percent of males, frequently results from a combination of biological and psychological factors.[49] Joseph LoPiccolo describes a study in which psychological factors were the cause of just ten of sixty-three cases of impotence, while organic factors alone led to only five of the cases.[50] Impotence can result from heart disease which can, through clogging of the arteries, limit the flow of blood into the penis. Almost half of all men with diabetes experience impotence, and spinal cord injuries and kidney disease can result in erectile failure. A number of medications may also cause erectile problems.[51] According to Engler and Goleman, if a man develops erections while dreaming or urinating, the cause of impotence is primarily psychological, not physical.[52]

Female arousal disorder is said to occur if erotic stimulation fails to produce sufficient vaginal lubrication or genital swelling or if there is a perceived lack of pleasure.[53] Typically this problem is psychological, frequently a reflection of a conflicted relationship although hormones may be involved as well.[54] Julia Heiman and Joseph LoPiccolo have written a useful book for women experiencing difficulties with arousal and orgasm, *Becoming Orgasmic: A Personal and Sexual Growth Program for Women,* and Bernie Zilbergeld offers insights and practical solutions for males experiencing problems with arousal, orgasm, and other concerns in his comprehensive book *The New Male Sexuality.*

Most males as well as females have occasional difficulties in becoming aroused, but this does not represent a problem unless it persists.[55]

Orgasmic Disorders

Two types of male orgasmic difficulties occur: premature or early ejaculation and inhibited male orgasm or retarded ejaculation. Premature ejaculation is very common, affecting at one time or another about 30 percent of the male population.[56] Masters, Johnson, and Kolodny "estimate that fifteen to twenty percent of American men have at least a moderate degree of difficulty controlling rapid ejaculation."[57] Typically those who have this problem engage in a variety of erotic activities, but lose control soon after penetrating the vagina. Interestingly, such early ejaculation may occur with some partners and not others, or only in certain situations with the same partner. Early ejaculation is usually the result of the male having not learned how to prolong the pleasure of sexual intercourse. Also, those who do not engage in sex very often are more prone to this problem. Performance anxiety seems to fuel the problem as does avoidance. But more importantly, this disorder enjoys an almost 100 percent rate of success if appropriate therapeutic procedures are used.[58]

Inhibited or retarded ejaculation, which can also be successfully treated, may have physical as well as psychological causes. Implicated as possible causal factors have been low levels of testosterone, a variety of neurological diseases, diabetes, various medications, as well as a host of psychological factors similar to those elements involved in erectile failure.[59] For a useful guide to problems associated with both male and female orgasm as well as other common concerns, readers may wish to consult Barbara Keeslings' *Sexual Pleasure: Reaching New Heights of Sexual Arousal and Intimacy.*

Inhibited female orgasm is more difficult to assess. According to Francoeur: "There is little agreement and much controversy about whether the inability to experience orgasm during vaginal intercourse constitutes a sexual problem."[60] Some women experience orgasm through manual or oral stimulation, but may have not the same results with penile-vaginal thrusting.

Current thinking reinforces the notion that "an orgasm is an orgasm is an orgasm." Women who enjoy orgasm through other means than intercourse are clearly normal, but some women want to achieve orgasm each time they engage in intercourse.[61]

Obviously, the most important factor is the woman's preference. Conflicting messages regarding females and female sexuality may contribute to orgasmic difficulties. Perhaps three in ten women have problems with orgasm.[62]

Sexual Pain Disorders

Dyspareunia, or painful intercourse, occurs in women and men. Recurrent genital pain association with intercourse is more common in women. The causes are often physical, but they may also be of a psychological nature. *Any woman experiencing pain should consult her gynecologist or other primary care physician.* The pain may be related to problems with lubrication associated with hormonal level or from irritation from contraceptive foam. Another problem, *vaginismus,* is usually the result of psychological factors. Vaginismus refers to vaginal spasms, which relate to a woman's anxiety concerning intercourse. This anxiety causes the female's brain to signal her vaginal muscles to resist the penetration of the penis.[63] For males, dyspareunia may be the result of a tight foreskin or from vascular problems.[64]

Unusual Sexual Preferences

Everyone has sexual preferences. Some adults become most excited if their partner is dressed a certain way, or they are excited by a certain region of their lover's body. These preferences are learned and can be traced to earlier experiences. But some preferences, which are atypical, are termed *paraphilias.* According to Jack Engler and Daniel Goleman:

> An unusual or bizarre sexual fantasy or activity only becomes abnormal when it is fixed, repetitive, and compulsive; it is a prerequisite for sexual excitement or orgasm; it is the predominant or preferred mode of sexual pleasure; or it causes harm.[65]

Many people who are quite normal have fantasies from time to time, but they are not obsessed with them. Those persons with paraphilic preferences may engage in behavior that is harmful to others, which may produce significant legal and psychological problems.[66]

Some of the more common paraphilias include (1) *fetishism*—involving inanimate objects (e.g., shoes or hats) or specific body parts (e.g., earlobes or feet); (2) *transvestism* or cross-dressing—the desire to dress up in the clothes of the opposite sex; (3) *pedophilia*—sexual gratification involving watching or participating in sex with children; (4) *exhibitionism*—fantasies or activities related to exposing genitals, with a desire to shock the observer (obscene phone callers demonstrate a form of this disorder); (5) *voyeurism*—the desire to observe people undressing or having sex without their knowledge; (6) *frotteurism*—fantasies and urges to rub against nonconsenting people; (7) *masochism*—desires and fantasies that involve individuals' own humiliation and pain; and (8) *sadism*—arousal related to inflicting physical or psychological pain upon others.[67] Most people with these unusual sexual preferences do not seek psychological help voluntarily, but such preferences may lead to serious difficulties with relationships as well as legal problems such as those involved with child sexual abuse.

Sex Therapy

Tremendous progress has been achieved in the field of sex therapy. Initiated by Masters and Johnson in the 1960s, therapy for sexual dysfunctions can deal effectively with most forms of dysfunction, with the rate of success between 70 and 95 percent and with little chance of relapse.[68] On the other hand, both sexual orientation and sexual preference are quite difficult to change. Orientation appears at the writing of this book to be largely biologically based and thus highly resistant to any therapeutic intervention.[69] Since sexual preferences, which are desired activities, are learned early and are reinforced through fantasy and masturbation, they are difficult, but not impossible to change.[70]

Present-day therapy aimed at alleviating sexual dysfunctions often combines cognitive and behavioral approaches. Typically therapy is short-term and consists of around fifteen or twenty weekly sessions.[71] Most sex therapists do not attempt to focus on assisting clients to analyze and change their personality, but instead center on developing communication skills and awareness of bodily pleasures. Joseph LoPiccolo describes the following components of most sex therapies: (1) assessment and understanding of the problem; (2)

provision of accurate sexual information; (3) efforts to alter certain problem attitudes and thoughts; (4) the elimination of both performance anxiety and the spectator role; (5) improvement of the communication between partners regarding sexual techniques; and (6) the alteration of destructive couple interactions.[72]

In most metropolitan areas of the United States, expertly trained sex therapists are available. Those mental health practitioners, certified by the American Association of Sex Educators, Counselors, and Therapists, have received specialized training.[73] *Competent sex therapists can help those who wish to eradicate a host of sexual dysfunctions. Readers with such concerns are strongly advised to seek appropriate help.*

Summary

Human sexuality represents one of the most potentially exciting and fulfilling aspects of adulthood. Some aspects of sexuality, particularly identity, orientation, and preference, are difficult, if not impossible, to change. However, sexual dysfunctions are particularly amenable to therapeutic intervention. What is considered to be "normal" in the arena of erotic desires and behavior is largely determined by individual values and societal norms, and sometimes those who engage in what may be considered unusual preferences develop guilt and may even have legal problems if their interests violate the rights of others. In an era replete with the spread of sexually transmitted diseases, especially AIDS, people can learn and employ "safe sex" practices. Finally, the professional practice of sex therapy has advanced to the point that the majority of people who participate in therapy for sexual dysfunctions enjoy marked improvement.

RECOMMENDED TITLES

"Normal" Sexuality

Comfort, Alex. *The New Joy of Sex: A Gourmet Guide to Lovemaking for the Nineties.* Rev. ed. New York: Crown, 1991.

In this revised edition of *The Joy of Sex,* psychologist Comfort addresses AIDS, other sexually transmitted diseases, and safer sex, in describing a variety of sexual techniques. In straightforward language the author emphasizes that couples can enjoy themselves by experimenting and by making changes in their sexual repertoire. This approach includes many methods for giving and receiving sexual pleasure without focusing on performance-driven intercourse. Using a cookbook format, he lists techniques under appetizers, sauces, main courses, and venues. Readers can skip around from one recipe to the next with ease. Photographs and line drawings graphically illustrate some of these positions.

Klein, Marty. *Ask Me Anything: A Sex Therapist Answers the Most Important Questions for the '90s.* New York: Fireside, published by Simon & Schuster, 1992.

Based on a question-and-answer format, sex therapist Klein discusses a wide range of issues surrounding sexuality. In the first section, the physical aspects of body image, menstruation and PMS, contraception, aging, sexual health, and sexually transmitted diseases are discussed. In the second section, the author explores desire, sexual techniques, play and experimentation, masturbation, orgasm, sex toys, and the ever-present "Am I normal?" In the third section, issues surrounding love and intimacy are described, ranging from turnoffs, sexual etiquette, communication, and sex roles to monogamy and affairs, spirituality, and homosexuality. The fourth section covers concerns readers may have relating to erection and ejaculation difficulties, fantasy, orgasm difficulties, desire conflicts, rape and date rape, and sex therapy. In the last section, the author includes a section on parenting (e.g., sex education, pregnancy, single parenting, and child abuse and incest).

Lloyd, Joan Elizabeth. *If It Feels Good: Using the Five Senses to Enhance Your Lovemaking.* New York: Warner, 1993.

Highlighting the importance of sight, smell, taste, touch, and sound and the role each plays in heightening sensual and sexual pleasure, Lloyd presents a series of erotic scenarios focusing on each sense. The author's theme centers on enhancing sexual play by appealing to one or more of the senses. Readers who are reluctant to discuss making changes in their lovemaking with their partners are advised to leave a bookmark in one of the fantasies for their partner to read later. The partner can respond by marking another story, and so on. The couple can then openly discuss what changes they would like to make. A discussion of AIDs, safer sex, and sexually transmitted diseases is also included.

Wells, Carol G. *Right Brain Sex: Using Creative Visualization to Enhance Sexual Pleasure.* New York: Prentice Hall, 1989.

The author describes effective visualization techniques that can be used to improve sexual pleasure. Rather than focusing on the general goal (e.g., "I want to have better sex."), Wells recommends that individuals identify what specific changes they want to make, concentrate their efforts there, and practice the visualization process. While many of the visualizations concentrate on the positive aspects of sexuality, some of them focus on improving specific areas of impotence, lack of desire, and premature ejaculation.

Zilbergeld, Bernie. *The New Male Sexuality.* New York: Bantam, 1992.

Many researchers in sexuality refer to the "Second Sexual Revolution" of the 1980s and 1990s, which is characterized by changes in women's expectations, in definitions of masculinity, and in concerns about AIDS and other sexually transmitted diseases. Zilbergeld explores these and other issues facing men. Overcoming myths surrounding male sexuality, the author discusses men and their emotional responses as well as men and their communication styles; he also takes up how to resolve specific problems like impotence.

Women are now considered equal partners in initiating, enjoying, and experimenting in sexual situations. The myths surrounding male sexuality fly in the face of the new sexuality for men. According to the author, men need to understand their own sexual likes and dislikes as well as those of their partner, to emphasize pleasure instead of performance, to resolve differences of opinion and conflicts with their partner quickly and effectively, and, finally, to communicate verbally and nonverbally about sex.

Sexually Transmitted Diseases and Safe Sex

McIlvenna, Ted, and others. *The Complete Guide to Safer Sex.* Rev. ed. Fort Lee, N.J.: Barricade Bks., 1992.

In this informative and forthright guide McIlvenna and his associates assert that "everyone has a right to a good sex life with safe sex techniques." By describing how the HIV virus that causes AIDS is spread and the role unsafe sex plays in the process, the authors examine which activities put individuals at risk and how to reduce risk factors. While informing readers about the risks of unsafe sex, the work emphasizes repeatedly that safe sex can be pleasurable. Use of condoms, spermicides, lubricants, and other preventive measures are discussed. Practical guidelines on telling children and adolescents about AIDS give specific age-appropriate examples. The authors outline in frank language a panoply of heterosexual, homosexual, and bisexual sexual practices and what is safe in each. Helpful dialogues about how to discuss safe sex with a partner are also provided, as are responses to partners who refuse to practice safe sex.

Westheimer, Ruth. *Dr. Ruth's Guide to Safer Sex.* New York: Warner, 1992.

Ruth Westheimer introduces readers to the reality of the HIV virus, AIDS, and other sexually transmitted diseases. Safer sex practices for men, women, and adolescents are described. In an open discussion of condoms, both male and female, the author encourages readers to practice safer sex at all times. Specific brands and their advantages and disadvantages are detailed. Masturbation, erotica (written and visual), and other techniques loosely defined as outercourse, are also included. In a chapter on the risks of unprotected sex, readers are given sample dialogues to use in discussing safer sex.

Stages in the Sexual Response Cycle

Masters, William H., Virginia E. Johnson, and Robert C. Kolodny. *Masters and Johnson on Sex and Human Loving.* 3d ed. Boston: Little, 1986.

In an extensive study of sexuality, Masters and his associates provide a thorough discussion of basic sexual anatomy, physiology, birth control, sexuality through a person's life, and gender roles. Describing findings from their own research and that of other sex researchers, the authors cover love and its development, intimacy and communication skills, sexual fantasies, and solitary sexual behavior. Heterosexuality, homosexuality and bisexuality as well as varieties of sexual behavior are explored in considerable detail. In addition, aberrant sexual acts (e.g., rape, incest, child sexual abuse) are examined. The authors conclude their study with an examination of sexual dysfunctions, disorders, and diseases.

Lack of Desire

Kreidman, Ellen. *How Can We Light a Fire When the Kids Are Driving Us Crazy?* New York: Villard Bks., 1993.

This book serves as a practical and sometimes whimsical guide for parents who find themselves torn between their children, their careers, and their marriage. The author suggests that parents can keep the romance that characterized the early days of their relationship alive by setting one evening a week as a date night when they go out without the children, other family members, or business associates. Every three months, a weekend getaway is recommended. Annually, a week-long vacation taken away from work, family, and home is also recommended. Parents often face barriers or make excuses for why they cannot go out (e.g., the nonavailability of a babysitter, lack of money, fatigue, or a lack of time). Kreidman provides creative solutions to each of these obstacles. In each chapter the author includes exercises on becoming a better parent and on becoming a better partner. The importance of open communication and effective conflict resolution are also stressed.

Pietropinto, Anthony, and Jacqueline Simenauer. *Not Tonight, Dear: How to Reawaken Your Sexual Desire.* New York: Doubleday, 1990.

Desire disorders serve as the focus for psychiatrist Pietropinto and his associate in this book. Lack of sexual desire is one of the most common concerns seen by sex therapists in recent years. The authors interview twenty-two psychiatrists and include research findings of many others in effective methods for improving sexual desire. By defining the different types of desire disorders and the causes behind each type, readers are introduced to the emotional and physiological aspects involved in each one. The results of this study show that both men and women seek help in this area. Desire diminishes for a variety of reasons: (1) false expectations; (2) changes in sex roles; (3) relationship problems; (4) personal problems; and (5) physical problems. Readers can evaluate their own desire levels by using the exercises included in the book.

Wolfe, Janet L. *What to Do When He Has a Headache: Renewing Desire and Intimacy in Your Relationship.* New York: Penguin, 1992.

Psychologist Wolfe concentrates on diminished sexual desire in men and how it can be remedied. Numerous reasons are given for lack of male sexual desire: changing sex roles, fear of intimacy, overwork and stress, lack of time, boredom, marital conflict, and fear of sexual dysfunction. Couples react to diminished male desire in different ways. Acceptance of having little or no sex may be one response if the relationship is satisfying overall for both individuals. The partner who thinks the lack of frequency is a problem can feel hurt, inadequate, or angry. These feelings, in turn, can weaken a strong relationship. In cases where the relationship, in general, and their sex life, in particular, is troubled, couples may find the desire discrepancy is only one of many problems resulting from poor communication or basic incompatibility. Readers are introduced to techniques which will help them change their overreactions to their partner's low interest; to psychological or physical conditions which may interfere with desire; to methods which may help their partner relate better emotionally; and to exercises which can enhance the sexual experience (e.g., relaxation and massage techniques). By helping readers identify activating events, the irrational beliefs that result, and the consequences of these beliefs on sexual desire, the author provides the reader with effective methods to combat the effects of the cycle. For example, although a bad day at work may be the activating event that results in low interest in sex, the partner may interpret the lack of interest personally ("He doesn't love me anymore"); this can have consequences if the other partner becomes distant and withdrawn as well.

Problems with Orgasm

Barbach, Lonnie Garfield. *For Each Other: Sharing Sexual Intimacy.* Landover, Md.: Anchor, 1982.

In *For Each Other,* Barbach continues the discussion of sexual problems first described in *For Yourself* (see annotation below). The focus shifts from female sexuality to include male sexuality as well. Beyond simple physiology, the author examines societal values that undergird sexual problems. These include role scripting (an assumption based on one gender initiating sex), relationship dynamics, and the emotional components of sexual response. Through observation, risk taking, and communication, the author provides a method for analyzing sexual problems and for identifying initial steps for change. Effective exercises for couples experiencing orgasmic difficulties with a partner, painful sex, or a lack of sexual desire are also outlined.

Barbach, Lonnie Garfield. *For Yourself: the Fulfillment of Female Sexuality.* New York: Signet, 1975.

Psychologist Barbach explores issues surrounding female sexuality on the basis of a program developed to help women understand the physiological and psychological aspects of orgasm. Working in therapeutic groups, preorgasmic women learn about the influence of societal values on their sexual practices. From the "good girls don't enjoy sex" myth combined with the "men know all about sex and how to please a women sexually" myth, women in these groups often believed that the failure to experience orgasm was entirely their fault. By debunking these myths and many other misconceptions about female sexuality, Barbach gives readers insight into the impact these myths have had on their sexual satisfaction. Readers are introduced to a series of exercises involving sensual touch, masturbation, and fantasy to orgasm. Partner exercises are also included. By citing the work of other researchers to strengthen the program, the author provides a practical and easy to implement a plan for women who would like to understand their sexuality more fully.

Heiman, Julia R., and Joseph LoPiccolo. *Becoming Orgasmic: A Sexual and Personal Growth Program for Women.* Rev. ed. New York: Prentice Hall, 1988.

Written for women who have difficulty reaching orgasm, the authors describe a series of exercises that familiarize the reader with her body, with the physiology of sexual response, with relaxation techniques, and with methods to enhance touching through massage, masturbation, use of a vibrator, and intercourse. Through these exercises the reader can learn how to become orgasmic by understanding her body and that of her partner. The authors emphasize the importance of pleasure rather than performance for both partners. Safer sex techniques are also explored.

Keesling, Barbara. *Sexual Pleasure: Reaching New Heights of Sexual Arousal and Intimacy.* Claremont, Calif.: Hunter House, 1993.

Sex therapist Keesling's approach focuses on first understanding and experiencing what is most enjoyable for the individual before exploring the partner's sexuality. Using massage, masturbation, and other relaxation techniques, the author encourages the reader to tune in to personal sensations at each stage of arousal and practice plateauing and peaking before orgasm. With the pleasure-centered approach, most of the exercises involve one partner giving and the other receiving pleasure, with each partner changing midway through the exercise. As part of the process, the receiving partner tells the giving partner what he or she enjoys as the exercise continues. Keesling advises readers to be tested for AIDS or to practice safer sex if necessary.

NOTES

1. Curtis Byer and Louis Shainberg, *Dimensions of Human Sexuality,* 3d ed. (Dubuque, Iowa: W. C. Brown, 1991), 616.

2. Jack Engler and Daniel Goleman, *The Consumer's Guide to Psychotherapy* (New York: Simon & Schuster, 1992), 513.

3. Martin E. P. Seligman, *What You Can Change and What You Can't: The Complete Guide to Successful Self-Improvement* (New York: Knopf, 1994), 147–49.

4. A. Huston, "Sex Typing," in *Handbook of Child Psychology: Vol. 4. Socialization, Personality, and Social Development,* ed. E. M. Hetherington (New York: Wiley, 1983), 387–467.

5. Engler and Goleman, *The Consumer's Guide to Psychotherapy,* 513.

6. Joseph LoPiccolo, "Sexual Disorders and Gender Identity Disorders," in Ronald Comer, *Abnormal Psychology* (New York: Freeman, 1992), 482.

7. Comer, *Abnormal Psychology,* 482.

8. Engler and Goleman, *The Consumer's Guide to Psychotherapy,* 513.

9. Byer and Shainberg, *Dimensions of Human Sexuality,* 346–47.

10. Ibid., 344.

11. Adelaide Haas and Kurt Haas, *Understanding Sexuality* (St. Louis: Times Mirror/Mosby, 1990), 342.

12. Byer and Shainberg, *Dimensions of Human Sexuality,* 345.

13. Engler and Goleman, *The Consumer's Guide to Psychotherapy,* 514.

14. Seligman, *What You Can Change and What You Can't,* 154–56; Byer and Shainberg, *Dimensions of Human Sexuality,* 346–49; Robert Francoeur, *Becoming a Sexual Person,* 2d ed. (New York: Macmillan, 1991), 445–46.

15. Engler and Goleman, *The Consumer's Guide to Psychotherapy,* 513.

16. Ibid., 513–14.

17. Robert Deisher, "When Parents Learn Their Child Is Homosexual," *Medical Aspects of Human Sexuality* 16, no. 6 (June 1982), 16U–16V.

18. Engler and Goleman, *The Consumer's Guide to Psychotherapy,* 515.

19. David Rosenham and Martin Seligman, *Abnormal Psychology,* 2d ed. (New York: Norton, 1989), 425.

20. Byer and Shainberg, *Dimensions of Human Sexuality,* 211.

21. Ibid., 216–30.

22. Francoeur, *Becoming a Sexual Person,* 328.

23. Ted McIlvenna and others, *The Complete Guide to Safer Sex*, 2d ed. (Fort Lee, N.J.: Barricade Bks., Inc., 1992), 62.

24. William Masters, Virginia Johnson, and Robert C. Kolodny, *Masters and Johnson on Sex and Human Loving* (Boston: Little, 1986), 59.

25. Helen Singer Kaplan, *Disorders of Sexual Desire* (New York: Brunner/Mazel, 1979), 9–23.

26. Byer and Shainberg, *Dimensions of Human Sexuality*, 178.

27. Ibid., 178–79.

28. Masters, Johnson, and Kolodny, *Masters and Johnson on Sex and Human Loving*, 60–64.

29. Ibid., 65.

30. Ibid., 66.

31. Ibid., 68.

32. Ibid., 69.

33. Ibid., 72.

34. Francoeur, *Becoming a Sexual Person*, 188–89.

35. Ibid.

36. Ibid., 190.

37. Ibid., 172.

38. Byer and Shainberg, *Dimensions of Human Sexuality*, 180–88.

39. Ibid., 190; Masters, Johnson, and Kolodny, *Masters and Johnson on Sex and Human Loving*, 75.

40. Stephen Fried, Dorothy Van Booven, and Cindy MacQuarrie, *Older Adulthood: Learning Activities for Understanding Aging*, (Baltimore: Health Professions Pr., 1993), 91–92.

41. Ibid., 92.

42. Byer and Shainberg, *Dimensions of Human Sexuality*, 188–89.

43. Engler and Goleman, *The Consumer's Guide to Psychotherapy*, 519–20.

44. Ibid., 519.

45. LoPiccolo in Comer, *Abnormal Psychology*, 460.

46. Engler and Goleman, *The Consumer's Guide to Psychotherapy*, 520.

47. LoPiccolo in Comer, *Abnormal Psychology*, 467.

48. Engler and Goleman, *The Consumer's Guide to Psychotherapy*, 523.

49. LoPiccolo in Comer, *Abnormal Psychology*, 463, 468.

50. Joseph LoPiccolo, "Post-modern Sex Therapy for Erectile Failure," in Raymond C. Rosen and Sheila R. Leiblum, eds., *Erectile Disorders: Diagnosis and Treatment* (New York: Guilford Pr., 1991), 171–97.

51. LoPiccolo in Comer, *Abnormal Psychology*, 468.

52. Engler and Goleman, *The Consumer's Guide to Psychotherapy*, 523.

53. LoPiccolo in Comer, *Abnormal Psychology*, 462.

54. Engler and Goleman, *The Consumer's Guide to Psychotherapy*, 523.

55. Ibid., 522.

56. Francoeur, *Becoming a Sexual Person*, 573.

57. Masters, Johnson, and Kolodny, *Masters and Johnson on Sex and Human Loving*, 467.

58. LoPiccolo in Comer, *Abnormal Psychology*, 470, 478; Masters, Johnson, and Kolodny, *Masters and Johnson on Sex and Human Loving*, 462–69.

59. LoPiccolo in Comer, *Abnormal Psychology*, 471.

60. Francoeur, *Becoming a Sexual Person*, 575.

61. LoPiccolo in Comer, *Abnormal Psychology*, 463.

62. Francoeur, *Becoming a Sexual Person*, 575.

63. Ibid., 576.

64. Ibid., 575.

65. Engler and Goleman, *The Consumer's Guide to Psychotherapy*, 527.

66. Ibid., 527–28.

67. Comer, *Abnormal Psychology*, 480–84.

68. Seligman, *What You Can Change and What You Can't*, 172.

69. Ibid., 154–57.

70. Ibid., 157–60.

71. LoPiccolo in Comer, *Abnormal Psychology*, 473.

72. Ibid., 473–75.

73. Francoeur, *Becoming a Sexual Person*, 569–70.

CHAPTER

4

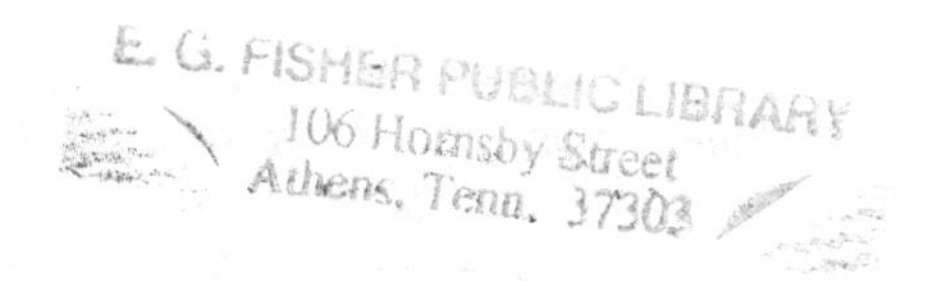

Parenting

For many people, one of the most potentially rewarding but difficult aspects of adulthood is parenting. Effective parenting is a learned process, based on a set of behavioral skills which vary with the ages and special circumstances of the children. Those responsible for child rearing may worry they are not up to the demands that comprise the role of mother or father, but much of what constitutes good parenting can be developed through experience, patience, and observation. Effective parenting will not ensure the development of happy and competent children, since "very good" parents may have children who are extremely difficult or who have psychological problems.[1]

Parents should also keep in mind that an approach that may work well with one child may not be an appropriate strategy with another. Every child and every parent are unique, so what works for a mom may not work for her husband, and what works for a timid older child may not fit the needs of a more assertive younger offspring.

Self-help books may provide important information regarding appropriate childhood behaviors based on developmental level or helpful pointers on dealing with problem areas like fighting between siblings or doing homework. Readers should keep in mind that every family and every parent-child relationship is different, so that knowledge gained from child rearing texts, should be taken as information that may or may not fit the specific needs of a given family unit. Also, readers are advised to seek the assistance of a child or family therapist if a child's behavioral or emotional responses have continuing negative effects on the child or the family.

The Uniqueness of Children

Each child is unique, born with his or her own physical and psychological characteristics and processes. According to Stanley Turecki and his associate, Leslie Tonner, in their book *The Difficult Child,* children display a temperament, an inborn behavioral style.[2] Drawing on the research of Alexander Thomas and Stella Chess, Turecki and Tonner describe the following nine aspects of temperament: activity level, distractibility, intensity, regularity, persistence, sensory threshold, approach/withdrawal, adaptability, and mood.[3] Parents may blame themselves or their children for an aspect of the child's behavior that reflects an aspect of temperament that can to some extent be modified. In many cases, however, temperament is a natural characteristic of the child. For example, children differ dramatically regarding their activity levels or ease of distractibility. Although parents may need to help children modify behaviors that reflect these aspects of temperament, a child may continue to be more or less active or distractable than is ideal. Although nurture can change a great deal about human beings, the power of nature and its impact on the individual child plays an equally important role in a child's development.

Elements of Effective Parenting

What are the key elements of effective parenting? Any discussion of the elements that provide a high-quality environment in which the child can develop needs to take into account both the quality of daily life of the child and her family and the goals of the parents. Books on this topic identify the following positive elements: raising a child with high self-esteem, providing structure, communicating values, and expressing affection. These elements suggest an effective parent is one who helps create a positive physical, psychological, and social environment, and who, through appropriate structure, affection, reinforcement, and example, guides the child toward gradually becoming more responsible. The success of this strategy depends on the child's values, interests, and abilities.

Most parents wish to raise children with high self-esteem who are able to master the skills necessary to function in the larger world. High self-esteem develops out of competence gained through reinforcement and experience. When parents provide an appropriate structure for a child's physical and emotional security, while at the same time encouraging age-appropriate exploration, children gradually learn that they are capable of handling themselves at school or at play, in their interactions with friends and with adults. Most children seem to thrive on praise based on their competent performance of a prized task.

Structure is necessary for safety, both physical and psychological. Children need clear boundaries reflected by parents fulfilling their basic responsibilities: providing nutritious meals at reasonable times; following schedules, including consistent bedtimes; and demonstrating consequences for behaviors. (For example, hitting one's sibling will result in being removed to the child's room for a period of "time-out"). James Windell defines time-out as "placing the child in a dull and non-stimulating area for a period of time following a misbehavior."[4] This is one of many strategies presented in books on parenting.

Whether they realize it or not, parents are continually communicating values to their children. Transmitting values is a key element in parenting. Thomas Gordon, in his highly useful book *P.E.T.: Parent Effectiveness Training,* asserts that parents teach values through the way they live. For example, parents who are highly materialistic in their lifestyle model that value for their children. Arguing with children regarding the youngster's overconcern with material things is futile, especially if parents are themselves driven to have all the latest and most expensive "things."

A key element of parenting is the expression of affection. Children need to be told and shown they are loved and prized. For some adults, expressing affection is difficult, but children need to know they are loved by their parent. As children go from elementary to middle school or junior high, they may become more self-conscious regarding parental affection, especially in public settings. But as these offspring mature, many will, in time, be responsive and delighted with parental hugs and exhortations of love.

Affection is often expressed through ongoing interaction with a child. Regular activities which are satisfying to both parent and child solidify the bonds between them. Playing ball, working on jigsaw puzzles, listening to music, and constructing forts with plastic logs may be positive for all concerned. If the play contains a competitive element, it is most useful to minimize the competitive aspects and focus on enjoyment. Highly competitive parents or children may be overconcerned with "winning" rather than being together and sharing an experience. Certainly parents are encouraged to teach their children how to master their environment and in that way to be competitive. However, if parents compete with their children, it may undermine feelings of self-worth and perceptions of competence and acceptance.

Children may develop interests and abilities through opportunities for a wide variety of experiences, and it is beneficial to provide children with the possibilities of an array of activities ranging from individual and team sports to regular visits to the local library. Typically, children are happiest when the activity is one of their own choosing, though tastes often develop out of opportunities selected by parents. As children develop, their own preferences gradually become clearer, and increasingly they may resist their parents attempts to impose particular activities upon them.

Another element of effective parenting is communication. Numerous parent-child conflicts result from ineffective communication, and many problems are made significantly worse as a result of inadequate styles of speaking and listening. As is the case with so many other behaviors, children learn how and how not to communicate from their parents. Because parents are the "adults" in relationships with their young children, it is the parents' responsibility to attempt to provide an environment that lends itself to the open expression of feelings. In their insightful and engaging book *How To Talk So Kids Will Listen and Listen So Kids Will Talk,* Adele Faber and Elaine Mazlish discuss numerous strategies for communicating with children in a constructive fashion. As an example of their helpful suggestions, Faber and

Mazlish tackle the concerns of children who fear the risks associated with failure. They counsel the concerned parent to not minimize the child's distress, to "be accepting of [the] child's mistakes and view them as an important part of the learning process," and to "be accepting of their own mistakes."[5]

Parental Issues during Pregnancy

The birth of children is often a time of great excitement and anticipation, but it can also be filled with concerns over the new responsibilities and constraints. Feelings of ambivalence toward one's "new" life and even depression are common in both mothers and fathers of newborns. In *Caring for Your Baby and Young Child: Birth to Age Five,* Steven Shelov and his associates discuss numerous issues confronting parents as they prepare for the arrival of their newborn. Shelov and his colleagues point out that mothers may ask (1) "Will the new baby come between me and an older child?" (2) "Will I be able to give the same intensity of love to the new child?" (3) "How can I avoid comparing one to another?" and (4) Will I be able to give the same intensity of love to the father?"[6]

Dads also experience concerns regarding newborns and are encouraged to become full participants in all aspects of child care. William Sears, in his brief guide entitled *Keys to Becoming a Father,* discusses "fathering the pre-born child."[7] Sears suggests that expectant fathers begin to bond with children before they are born by laying their hands on the "bulge" and talking to it. Some men may feel silly about talking to the "bulge," but these practices may bring the father closer to both the mother and the baby. In addition, Sears has included a number of tips for the pregnant father, such as "taking inventory" of the marital relationship before the baby arrives. *A new baby will not improve a deteriorating marriage; in fact, it will put much more strain on it.* Males who care for their mates are advised to demonstrate their affection throughout the pregnancy and after the delivery of the child. Also fathers are exhorted to "be sensitive," "respect the nesting instinct," and "show interest and involvement in the pregnancy."[8]

Older siblings, while being excited about the addition to the family of a new brother or sister, may, depending on their developmental level, be confused, frightened, or jealous of the baby. Change is difficult for the child, but the transition will be made smoother if parents discuss what will happen and are reassuring to the older sibling throughout the pregnancy.[9]

Infancy

As anyone who has ever taken care of a baby knows, the job is demanding. Frances Wells Burck in the highly useful book, *Babysense: A Practical and Supportive Guide to Baby Care,* includes a chapter entitled "Getting Control of Your Time and Your Life."[10] As a step in understanding what a caretaker does, Burck instructs the reader to carry a chart around for a day making "notes about what you are doing, including your feelings (pleased, harassed, tired, happy, angry. . . . Put an "A" next to any entry that has caused you anxiety. . . ."[11] Through this experiential vehicle, the parent may begin to understand the fragmentation of her day and those aspects of parenting that arouse feelings of anxiety. From this glimpse of a "typical" day, the parent may be able to establish priorities, which may aid in achieving a necessary balance and a lessening of worrying over what Burck considers trivial matters.

Those parents bringing home their first baby from the hospital may have many questions about the physical care of the newborn. In their book, *Taking Care of Your New Baby: A Guide to Infant Care,* Jeanne Driscoll and Marsha Walker provide specific information on the physical characteristics of the child: feeding, sleeping, eliminating, crying, and so forth. Other excellent sources of information on the physical aspects of infancy include the standard *Dr. Spock's Baby and Child Care* written by Benjamin Spock and Michael Rothenberg; *Your Baby & Child: From Birth to Age Five* by Penelope Leach; and *Caring for Your Baby and Young Child: Birth to Age Five,* edited by Steven Shelov and associates. Parents often must make a critical decision about breast feeding and bottle feeding. Penelope Leach includes excellent sections on the advantages and disadvantages of both methods in her book.[12]

Parents should monitor their infant's physical, intellectual, and emotional development and report any concerns to the child's pediatrician. However, keep in mind most children may be a little ahead or a little behind developmental milestones listed in parenting books, and most children will gravitate around the average.

In his highly readable book, *Little People: Guidelines for Commonsense Child Rearing,* Edward Christophersen suggests that parents talk to their babies while they are caring for them, "in normal adult speech, not baby talk, . . . the repetition of adult speech over the first several years can do wonders for the child's own speech development."[13] Christophersen offers concrete examples of how parents through their own behavior can encourage their infants to sleep through the night and can limit the amount of unnecessary crying.

Toddlerhood

Many parents find their children's toddlerhood to be most challenging. During this stage, "normal" children are actively exploring the world around them. The child's exploration is related to what the psychoanalyst Erik Erikson calls the conflict of autonomy versus shame and doubt.[14] Toddlers about fifteen to thirty-six months are struggling with the competing demands of wanting to be more independent from their parents, while at the same time feeling guilty about breaking these bonds. According to Laurence Steinberg and Jay Belsky, "children who gain a sense of self-control without loss of self-esteem have a lasting sense of autonomy and pride."[15] Burton L. White provides valuable insights into this age group in *The First Three Years of Life.*

Although toddlers' behavior can prove trying to even the most patient parents, their exploratory forays can become manageable. Edward Christophersen points out that many parents unknowingly encourage their young child's misbehavior by responding to the child as soon as she misbehaves, while ignoring the same child when she is well behaved. If the toddler is praised for behaving appropriately, she is more likely to behave in this way in the future.[16]

Effective disciplining of toddlers sets the stage for future socialization. In the highly useful book *Discipline: A Sourcebook of 50 Failsafe Techniques for Parents,* James Windell provides specific suggestions for the parents' first disciplinary techniques. Among the concrete methods Windell suggests are (1) teaching limits; (2) using distractions; (3) offering substitutes; (4) limiting access to various objects; (5) childproofing the home; (6) criticizing the behavior, not the child; (7) repeating the rules frequently; (8) avoiding abrupt changes; (9) offering assistance to children in frustrating situations; (10) anticipating and averting problems;

(11) offering choices to children; and (12) providing opportunities for children to make mistakes.[17]

Many parents find toilet training a difficult aspect of socializing the toddler. Steven Shelov and his associates suggest children are typically ready to begin the process of toilet training "between eighteen and twenty-four months, but it is also normal for it to occur a little later."[18] The authors advise that parents purchase a potty seat, place it either in the child's room or a nearby bathroom, and then proceed to prescribe a five-point strategy for successful training.[19]

Preschoolers

Preschoolers, those children from ages three to five, become less dependent on their parents, and will, if provided the opportunity, play more with other children. One of the positive aspects of increased interaction with peers is that many children of this age develop a gradual sense of empathy, which is an appreciation of another person's feelings. Those children who are not empathetic may be more disliked by their peers.[20] By learning to share and to play cooperatively, children at this stage develop their social skills.

During the preschool years children are learning how to do a wide variety of positive things, which certainly should be encouraged by parents. For example, three to four-year-olds can be taught to make their beds and take their dishes to the sink after eating.[21] *Many parents get upset with young children, when the child performs a task that is not at the same level or standard that the parent would perform the task. It is unrealistic to expect children who are learning how to complete a task to perform at an adult level. Such criticism also communicates that what the child does just isn't good enough to please the parent. Some parents complicate matters by doing chores for the child. For instance, if the child's bed making does not meet the parent's standards, they make up the bed for the child. This teaches the child to be sloppy at making the bed in order to get the parent to do it. Such manipulation often works because the parent reinforces it by continuing to do the child's assigned task.*

One common concern for parents of both toddlers and preschoolers is the tantrum, which is especially difficult to manage if it occurs in public. Children throw tantrums because tantrums work. In other words, many kids learn that if they jump up and down while screaming and crying, they can achieve a desired result. When children throw tantrums, they get the attention of adults. If adults provide the child with what he wants, they are unwittingly reinforcing the occurrence of the next tantrum. One method of discipline that may be effective in decreasing the number and severity of tantrums is time-out. Windell explains that time-out is quite humane, and that it should be applied either during or just after the tantrum or other misbehavior, so that the child will learn to associate the transgression with the punishment. Parents are instructed to explain the misdeed to the child and to point out the specific consequences. Windell suggests that the place where the child is put for a brief period of time-out "be uninviting, dull, and without entertainment value," and that "for a preschooler of four years, time-out should last about three to five minutes" or one minute multiplied by the child's age.[22]

Parents who are experiencing difficulty with young children's tantrums or other behavioral difficulties and want to learn more about behavior management strategies like time-out are advised to consult the popular works of Edward Christophersen, especially *Beyond Discipline: Parenting That Lasts a Lifetime* or *Little People: Guidelines for Common Sense Child Rearing,* or James Windell's *Discipline: A Sourcebook of 50 Failsafe Techniques for Parents,* or *Good Behavior: Over 1,200 Sensible Solutions to Your Child's Problems from Birth to Age Twelve* by Stephen Garber, Marianne Daniels Garber, and Robyn Freedman Spizman.

Some parents have a great deal of difficulty handling their own emotions and find even the most ordinary child behaviors difficult to manage. A number of these persons may abuse or neglect their own children. According to the Children's Defense Fund, nearly two million children are abused or neglected in the United States each year.[23] Several causes for the abuse and neglect have been suggested. Many abusing parents were themselves abused as children, although according to one insightful study only about a third of those who were abused become abusers themselves.[24]

Parents who abuse may have unrealistic expectations for their children's behavior and may become very upset when the child fails to meet these standards. It is likely that abusive parents abuse just one of their children, typically the one who is most vulnerable. Ironically, according to Laurence Steinberg and Jay Belsky, "premature, ill, or difficult children are at risk for abuse with certain kinds of parents."[25] Other factors which may be associated with abuse include stress, poverty, and substance abuse.[26]

Parents who believe themselves to be potentially abusive to their children should seek professional help as soon as possible. Counselors and therapists who specialize in this problem can be found through mental health centers as well as local societies of psychologists or physicians. Parents can learn effective parenting skills as well as ways to better manage their own emotions.

School-Age Children

In the present context, school-aged children are considered to be between the ages of five to twelve. During this period of development, children begin to focus on what Erik Erikson calls the issues of industry versus inferiority.[27] Children of school age are occupied with learning how to perform and complete a variety of gradually more complex tasks which, if they are successful, can lead them to feel a sense of industry. On the other hand, if children are unsuccessful in mastering a variety of tasks, they begin to develop inferiority feelings. Erikson and many other psychologists believe parents can assist their children by preparing them for the intellectual and social demands of school. Preschool or day-care experience, reading with children, and plenty of opportunities to play with peers can provide a strong basis for starting the school experience.

The experience of starting school, especially first grade because it lasts most of the day, may produce anxiety for children and their parents. Marguerite Kelly, writing in *The Mother's Almanac II: Your Child from Six to Twelve,* suggests parents and children tour a new school prior to the child's enrollment, which should help allay a variety of the child's concerns and will familiarize them with the setting in which they will be spending so much of their time.[28] It is normal for children to be somewhat frightened of the unknown and ponder such questions as: (1) Will I make friends? (2) Will I like my teacher? (3) Will my teacher like me? and (4) Will I do well in school?

Certainly, parents who are supportive of their child's school experience will find their offspring express more positive attitudes about going to school, doing homework, and dealing with school personnel, such as teachers and administrators. Involvement in the school through parent-teacher organizations and attendance at open houses, parent-teacher conferences, student recitals, athletic events, and any other activities centered on student performance, is extremely important for both the child and the parent. Because of work conflicts, some parents are prevented from the degree of involvement they would prefer. For parents unable to attend a long-anticipated event like a musical performance, a later screening of a videotape with a child may be of great benefit to both the parent and the child.

With each school year, children should be encouraged to become more and more independent. A child's sense of independence is linked with his self-esteem and sense of competence. Some well-meaning parents may become overinvolved in their children's lives. For example, these parents may prepare their son's or daughter's homework for them, or if their child forgets a needed book at school, the parents may be the ones to call other parents trying to locate another copy of the book. Another aspect of this type of overinvolvement is presented in David Elkind's *The Hurried Child: Growing Up Too Fast Too Soon* in which he describes the role parents, schools, and the media play in turning children into little adults.

It is important that children take responsibility for their own work. If a parent takes over the responsibility, the child will lose autonomy and her own sense of the responsibility for the work. Overinvolved parents may also try to live vicariously through their children's experiences and accomplishments. This does not work well for either the parent or the child. Most children will valiantly try to please their parents in an effort to make them happy. But that is fruitless, since it is difficult enough to make oneself happy.

One of the most common problems affecting school-aged children is underachievement, which can be seen as a significant difference between the child's intellectual ability and his school performance. *Most children want to be successful at school, and a style of underachievement may be an expression of a variety of concerns, including depression, boredom, attention-deficit disorder, and learning disabilities. Underachievement should be taken seriously and is a problem which can be addressed competently by child and family therapists. Psychologists may be especially helpful, since they will be prepared to give the child a series of intelligence and personality tests; these are essential for designing an effective treatment plan for implementation by both teachers and parents.* For specific suggestions on dealing with underachievement, readers may wish to consult *Ending the Homework Hassle: Understanding, Preventing, and Solving School Performance Problems* by John Rosemond. Ironically, underachievement is very common among gifted children. For an excellent sourcebook on issues related to the gifted child and underachievement, the interested reader is directed to *Guiding the Gifted Child: A Practical Source for Parents and Teachers* by James Webb and associates.

Adolescence

Adolescence is a period of profound physical, psychological, and social change. With puberty children are gradually transformed into "physical" adults. Many children as well as parents are concerned about what is "normal" physical development. For a highly readable account covering the physical aspects of adolescence, readers should consult *Caring for Your Adolescent: Ages 12 to 21* prepared by Donald Greydanus and associates. In this book written under the auspices of the American Academy of Pediatrics, the editors discuss the signs of puberty, normal versus abnormal physical development, growth, issues related to early and late onset of puberty, sexuality, nutrition, eating disorders, and other physiological topics.

Typically, children as they experience puberty develop a certain degree of self-consciousness and worry about their bodies. Parents can greatly assist their children by listening to their concerns and by supplying reassurance and simple facts about such matters as menstruation and genital growth. Since the pubescent child is predictably anxious about his or her body, parents should refrain from teasing their child about the physical transformation the child is undergoing. Teasing embarrasses the child and helps alienate the individual from the parent.

Since so many teenagers are concerned with their bodies and their appearance, it is understandable that eating disorders like anorexia nervosa and bulimia nervosa are most common at this time of life. These disorders appear in 1 to 4 percent of females and often occur between the ages of 14 and 18.[29] *Anorexia and bulimia are extremely serious and, if untreated, can lead to numerous medical problems and possibly death. It is essential that parents seek immediate treatment from a physician or psychologist specializing in these afflictions.* According to Ronald Comer, "the central features of anorexia nervosa are (1) a drive for thinness and a morbid fear of becoming overweight, (2) certain cognitive disturbances, (3) preoccupation with food, (4) personality and mood problems, and (5) medical dysfunctioning," while the picture for bulimia nervosa involves "recurrent episodes of binge eating, averaging at least two episodes a week of vomiting, use of laxatives or diuretics, strict dieting or fasting, or vigorous exercise in order to prevent weight gain."[30] Interested readers can consult Chapter 7 for more information on eating disorders.

Of course, one of the central aspects of puberty and adolescence is the sexual development of the individual. Parents are often filled with mixed feelings about their children's sexuality, and may, as a result of these contrasting emotions, send confusing messages. It is difficult for children to read their parents correctly when mom and dad romanticize their son's or daughter's social life, encouraging the latter to date before they are ready emotionally, while also expressing concern when they spend a great deal of time speaking on the telephone with each new love interest. *One important factor in determining how children view their sexuality relates to their parents. If a child sees the parents as comfortable with their own sexuality, the child will be influenced positively.*[31]

Adolescents also need accurate and timely information from their parents regarding sexual matters. By the time a child is in the throes of puberty, she has a great deal of information and much of it may be incorrect or incomplete. Discussions regarding sexual matters should begin at an earlier point, the time and content of which depends on the child's curiosity and maturity. Several excellent sources for parents to consult regarding adolescent sexuality are: *What Teenagers Want to Know about Sex: Questions and Answers* by the Boston Children's Hospital Staff and Robert P. Masland, *The Family Book about Sexuality* by Mary Calderone and Eric Johnson, and *Raising a Child Conservatively in a Sexually Permissive World* by Sol and Judith Gordon. The interested reader will find additional resource suggestions in Chapter 3 of this book.

A great many behaviors coming from adolescents are both annoying and distressing for many parents. Depending on their own personalities and values, parents may become frustrated with their children's mood swings, self-centeredness, materialistic practices, loud music, fads, friends, and so forth. *It is normal for parents to get highly annoyed with adolescents and for adolescents to become quite annoyed with their parents.* If life were perfect for the adolescent at home with his parents, he would have little reason to work toward a goal of becoming his own person, separate and independent from his parents. Therefore, a certain amount of conflict is natural and spurs the child toward adulthood.

Donald Greydanus and his associates discuss the challenges confronting parents of adolescents. These authors suggest that parents: (1) prepare for change; (2) prepare to be tested; (3) prepare for a period of rejection; (4) be flexible; (5) don't take everything seriously; (6) try to keep a sense of humor; (7) find time to listen; (8) examine their own changes; (9) become acquainted with the child's environment; and (10) when the time comes, cut the cord.[32] For a very sensible discussion of managing the joys and problems associated with raising adolescents, readers can consult *You Can Say No to Your Teenager and Other Strategies for Effective Parenting in the 1990s* by Jeanette Shalov and associates.

Adulthood

The parent role does not end simply because a child becomes a young adult. However, the parents of adult children typically play a less direct part in their lives. The level of involvement depends on the psychological needs and desires of parents and children, cultural values, and economics. Parents may provide certain kinds of assistance for their adult children, and they may also be recipients of services. For example, parents may offer child care and financial assistance following a divorce, while children may provide help in the area of home maintenance for their elders.[33]

Special Issues

In this section of the chapter, we shall examine the following topics: day care, adopted children, children with special needs, children and divorce, single parenting, stepparenting, and diversity.

Day Care

For the working parents of young children, one of the most difficult decisions involves the selection of appropriate child care. Even enlightened parents may feel guilty about turning over part of their child's care to other adults. However, research covering the effects of day care on children tends to support the experience as more positive than negative.[34] In *Child Care: A Parent's Guide,* Sonja Flating provides readers with an excellent self-test interested parents can use to identify personal needs in order to begin their search for appropriate child care. Under the auspices of the National Association of Child Care Resource and Referral Agencies, Judith Berezin has prepared *The Complete Guide to Choosing Child Care.* Included in Berezin's book are helpful chapters on children's developmental needs, in-home care, infant/toddler and early childhood facilities, care for school-age children, and summer camp.

Adopted Children

Many parents express concerns about special issues of parenting an adopted child. John Rosemond, in his *Parent Power! A Common-Sense Approach to Parenting in the 90's and Beyond,* suggests that parents of adopted children may go along with what he calls "The Adoption Myth", that is, "the mistaken belief that all problems that arise in the parent/child relationship are related in some way to the adoption."[35] It is imperative that parents tell their children that they were adopted, but the fact that the child was adopted should not dominate the relationship. Rosemond advises parents to tell the child of her adoption about the age of seven, by which time she will be able to understand the concept, but some children can comprehend the notion at an earlier age.[36]

People who adopt their children, in the vast majority of cases, love their children in the same ways that biological parents do, and children who are loved understand that. Many adopted children will be curious about their biological parents, potential health problems based on genetic inheritance, and about the circumstances which contributed to their being adopted. It is quite understandable why many young adults attempt to find and establish contact with a biological mother or father. Readers interested in further information on adoption can consult *Communicating with the Adopted Child* by Miriam Komar, *Making Sense of Adoption: A Parent's Guide* by Lois Ruskai Melina, and *How to Raise an Adopted Child: A Guide to Help Your Child Flourish from Infancy through Adolescence* by Judith Schaffer and Christina Lindstrom.

Transracial and international adoption has become more commonplace. Some persons view transracial adoption as a form of cultural genocide, but others stress an individual child's right to a loving family.[37] In *"Are Those Kids Yours?": American Families with Children Adopted from Other Countries,* Cheri Register details a host of concerns facing families who choose to adopt internationally and interracially.

Children with Special Needs

Under the best of circumstances, effective parenting is a difficult process. But a child with special needs, like one with developmental disabilities or a chronic illness, presents many additional parenting concerns. Many parents blame themselves when a child is born with physical or cognitive deficits, but such misplaced emotion only adds to the emotional strain. Parents are advised to assist their children in adapting to the world by teaching them to be as self-sufficient as possible. Peggy Finston in the readable book, *Parenting Plus: Raising Children with Special Health Needs,* offers practical tips to parents in developing strategies for fostering a sense of competence and independence. Interested readers may wish to consult our Chapter 8, which is devoted to the topic of coping with chronic illness, disability, and death.

Children and Divorce

When parents go through a divorce, all children are impacted, but the greatest stress is placed upon preschoolers. Because young children do not understand the dynamics of the situation, they may blame themselves, and they may fantasize that their parents will reconcile their differences. These children may feel particularly insecure, since they may worry that their parents may not love them anymore. After all, they may have been told that their parents have ceased to love each other.[38] Laurence Steinberg and Jay Belsky report research demonstrating that many of the negative effects of divorce upon young children may be caused "from the breakdown in effective parenting that generally accompanies the separation," and mention that usually "the greater the hostility involved in the breakup of the marriage, the poorer the parenting."[39] *It is very difficult for parents to continue to follow through with the structure involved in parenting when they are experiencing feelings of loss, anger, and sadness which often accompany the breakdown and breakup of a marriage.*

Because of their greater cognitive and adaptive skills, many older children, both school-aged and adolescent, seem to cope better than their younger siblings. Sometimes the effects of divorce on a child are not fully felt until much later when a young adult is contemplating his own plans for marriage and a family.[40] However, some older children do experience significant problems during and after the divorce. Steinberg and Belsky consider the following four factors to make a positive difference: (1) generally boys experience more difficulties, particularly if they live with their mother; (2) if the child continues to have a relationship with the father, the child will adapt more readily; (3) those children whose parents treat each other more positively following the divorce experience fewer problems; and (4) those children whose finances are not as negatively affected appear to cope better.[41]

Divorcing parents should refrain from speaking badly of the child's other parent in the child's presence. To hear a negative comment from a parent places the child in a difficult position. This also applies to parents in general. Although "Mom" and "Dad" may be divorced, they will always be "Mom" and "Dad." Separated and divorced parents can make the best of the situation if they use the best interests of their children as the basis for dealing with one another. This is often difficult because of the anger that they may feel toward one another. Many divorcing parents could benefit from several sessions with a therapist who specializes in such matters.

Interested readers might want to consult *Helping Your Child Succeed after Divorce* by Florence Bienenfield, *Vicki Lasky's Divorce Book for Parents: Helping Your Children Cope with Divorce and Its Aftermath* by Vicki Lasky, *Mister Rogers Talks with Families about Divorce* by Fred Rogers and Clare O'Brien, or *Helping Children Cope with Divorce* by Edward Teyber.

Single Parenting

With divorce may come single parenting. Although many single parents did not choose to marry before they started a family, a great many did. Some single parents find that for the first time they are responsible for the total care of the children. The particular problems confronting a single parent may relate to financial resources, work commitments, the ages and special needs of the children, and whether there is an ex-spouse or not. If there is an ex-spouse, the quality of the relationship with that individual and support from family and friends play a significant role in the single parent's life. The components of effective single parenting are the same as those of effective two-person parenting. The chief difference is that with single parenting, the stresses and strains are borne by one person. Joan Anderson has compiled a great many useful suggestions regarding many relevant topics in her book *The Single Mother's Book: A Practical Guide to Managing Your Children, Career, Home, Finances, and Everything Else.* Geoffrey Greif presents many of these same topics from the single fathers' perspective in *The Daddy Track and the Single Father.*

Stepparenting

Harold Bloomfield asserts that the most common family form of the next century will be the stepfamily.[42] The transition to becoming an effective stepfamily occurs gradually, often with many difficulties. According to Patricia Papernow, stepfamilies and their members may go through several developmental stages.[43] Fantasy is the first stage. Parents imagine that the healing will occur if the adult partners love each other, while children may still envision their parents reconciling differences and reconstituting their original family. During the immersion stage, the realities of the stepfamily become apparent, and family members may experience resentment as well as feelings of inadequacy. In the awareness stage stepparents become more conscious of their own feelings. With the mobilization stage family members more openly communicate their differences, and with the action stage new agreements among members are communicated. In the final stages of contact and resolution, intimate steprelationships may be forged and clear norms established.

Forming and maintaining stepfamily relationships can prove difficult. Problems surrounding strong feelings are reflected in statements from children like: "You're not my real dad," or "You're not my real mom." Differences in practices regarding discipline, money, and behavioral limits can produce conflict between partners as well as exacerbate tensions with children. Rivalries between stepsiblings are a natural outgrowth of the blending of two separate family units. Additionally, relationships with ex-spouses, whether they are positive or negative, impact the developing blended family. Interested readers should consult: *Making Peace in Your Stepfamily: Surviving and Thriving as Parents and Stepparents* by Harold Bloomfield and

Robert B. Kory; *The New American Family* by Mary Artlip and associates; *Stepfathering: Stepfathers' Advice on Creating a New Family* by Mark Bruce Rosin; and *The Good Stepmother: A Practical Guide* written by Karen Savage and Patricia Adams.

Diversity and Parenting

Depending on culture, race, religion, geographical region, or a host of other factors, parents may choose to raise their children in ways that are somewhat different from the larger population. A number of popular books addressing issues surrounding diversity and child rearing are available. For example, parents of African-American children may wish to consult *Different and Wonderful: Raising Black Children in a Race-Conscious Society* by Darlene and Derek Hopson and *Raising Black Children* by James Comer and Alvin Poussaint. Useful books covering parenting issues among other cultural groups can be found through the reader's local library.

Summary

Parenting is a very difficult undertaking, but it can be among the most richly rewarding aspects of an adult's life. A basic knowledge of the principles of effective parenting as well as a general knowledge of child development may prove helpful in building parenting skills. Those parents with adopted children, whose children have special needs, who are divorced or with stepchildren, or who are from a distinct cultural group may benefit from specialized information.

RECOMMENDED TITLES

General

Brazelton, T. Berry. *Families: Crisis and Caring.* Reading, Mass.: Addison-Wesley, 1989.

Pediatrician Brazelton explores a variety of crises and their effects on families. Death of a parent, illness of a child, divorce, stepparenting, parental rivalry, and adoption are included. Family members, parents, grandparents, and children are interviewed to examine how they reacted to the crisis and what changes have taken place. Each chapter outlines Brazelton's office visit, his home interview (most physicians rarely make house calls), and the issues involved. The book serves as a sourcebook for others facing similar issues.

Franck, Irene, and David Brownstone. *The Parent's Desk Reference.* New York: Prentice Hall, 1991.

The authors describe this book as "the ultimate family encyclopedia—from conception to college." The book is a high-quality reference source on a wide variety of topics, including pregnancy and childbirth; child development; nutrition and child care; genetic and other common disorders in childhood; educational, medical, and psychological concerns; and social services. It lists organizations affiliated with and books about specialized topics (e.g., adoption). Additional information on specific subjects may be found in checklists or information boxes on the same page. For example, in the section on choking, illustrations on how to clear an obstruction in an infant's or child's throat are provided.

Uniqueness of Children

Turecki, Stanley, and Leslie Tonner. *The Difficult Child.* Rev. ed. New York: Bantam, 1989.

In a thorough discussion of temperament and its role in a child's behavior, Turecki and Tonner, describe the innate characteristics of a difficult child: high activity, poor adaptability, and low sensory threshold, among others. Although these children are born with this temperament type, the authors outline helpful strategies for parents who can help their child become a better adjusted individual by using these techniques.

Effective Parenting

Faber, Adele, and Elaine Mazlish. *How to Talk So Kids Will Listen and Listen So Kids Will Talk.* New York: Avon, 1980.

The authors incorporate the skills of active listening, negotiating, and respecting others in their approach to parenting.

Each chapter is filled with role plays, exercises, and illustrations to explain a particular strategy. The primary focus is on the importance of acknowledging the youngster's feelings and developing the child's problem-solving skills. Faber and Mazlish also cover ineffective communication strategies: denying the child's feelings, blaming, or lecturing, among others. Techniques for communicating with children of all ages are outlined throughout the book.

Garber, Stephen W., Marianne Daniels Garber, and Robyn Freedman Spizman. *Good Behavior: Over 1,200 Sensible Solutions to Your Child's Problems from Birth to Age Twelve.* New York: Villard Bks., 1987.

In this practical guide the authors present general guidelines on changing a child's behavior, basic techniques of discipline, and ways to respond to specific problems. These basics include praising a child, ignoring the behavior, rewarding good behavior, using charts and time-outs. Subsequent chapters focus on specific types of behavior and effective strategies for changing them. Interested readers can consult the section that applies to a specific behavior (e.g., not helping with chores) or read extensively as other problematic behaviors are described. These behaviors range from morning problems, school and learning problems, and health-related problems, among others. The authors urge readers to consider professional help if a child demonstrates self-destructive behavior, destructive behavior toward others, or long-lasting problem behaviors.

Gordon, Thomas. *P.E.T. Parent Effectiveness Training: The Tested New Way to Raise Responsible Children.* Rev. ed. New York: New Amer. Lib., 1975.

Psychologist Gordon encourages parents to use active listening both in acknowledging children's feelings and in responding to them. "No lose" conflict resolution methods are described. Through the use of numerous examples, dialogues, and role plays, the author outlines the techniques of P.E.T. Effective and ineffective means of communication and discipline are discussed.

Nelsen, Jane. *Positive Discipline.* Fair Oaks, Calif.: Sunrise Pr., 1987.

The author encourages parents to teach their children self-discipline, responsibility, cooperation, and problem-solving skills. Nelsen presents several key concepts of positive discipline: show children that they are accepted and appreciated;

teach them problem-solving skills; and enlist their cooperation when trying to solve a problem. This is done by acknowledging the child's feelings, by relating a similar experience that the parent has had, by asking for their help in solving the current problem, and by asking the child how this situation could be avoided in the future.

Rosemond, John. *Parent Power! A Common-Sense Approach to Parenting in the '90s and Beyond.* Rev. ed. Kansas City, Mo.: Andrews & McMeel, 1990.

Although the section on adoption is only a small portion of this work, psychologist Rosemond offers an informative discussion as well as questions from adoptive or potential adoptive parents. The first section of the book deals with discipline while the second section describes common developmental issues from infancy to adolescence. The author details specific behavioral areas and then discusses questions received from parents. Rosemond makes use of numerous case studies to illustrate his points.

Salk, Lee. *Familyhood: Nurturing the Values That Matter.* New York: Simon & Schuster, 1992.

Famed psychologist Lee Salk combines his research with that of a national survey on family and family values to examine how families have changed. As part of the survey, individuals were asked to rank in order of importance those qualities that embodied family values. The top eight were: "providing emotional support to your family; respecting your parents; respecting other people for who they are; being responsible for your actions; being able to communicate your feelings to your family; having a happy marriage; respecting your children; and respecting authority."[44]

The author also reports on the changes in family structure that have occurred in the last generation. Nearly 75 percent of the survey respondents defined family as a group of people who love and care for each other; over 20 percent viewed family as persons related by blood, marriage, or adoption; only 3 percent regarded people living in one household as a family. Salk focuses the remaining discussion on how the eight qualities described earlier can be applied in child rearing and other aspects of family life.

Parental Issues during Pregnancy

Shelov, Steven P., and others. *Caring for Your Baby and Young Child: Birth to Age Five.* New York: Bantam, 1991.

Physician Shelov and his associates have written a comprehensive guide to infant and child care. Detailed line drawings highlight the informative text. Beginning with prenatal care, this guide provides details from selecting a pediatrician before the baby arrives to handling medical emergencies. The first part of the book covers developmental phases from newborns to preschoolers with sections on growth and development, basic care, family relationships, health issues, child care, and safety checks. The second part deals with common childhood ailments.

Infancy

Burck, Frances Wells. *Babysense: A Practical and Supportive Guide to Baby Care.* New rev. ed. New York: St. Martin's, 1991.

This book, about infant and toddler care covers many familiar topics: feeding, adjusting to the new baby, toilet training, child care, safety, and developmental stages among others. *Babysense* includes first person accounts from mothers and fathers as they reflect upon their experience. A consumer guide to selecting cribs, strollers, baby carriers, car seats, and baby clothes is also provided.

Christophersen, Edward. *Little People: Guidelines for Commonsense Child Rearing.* 3d ed. Kansas City, Mo.: Westport Publishing, 1988.

Christophersen sees the primary parental role as that of teacher rather than disciplinarian. The foundation of this approach is to give children positive attention when they are behaving well instead of negative attention as they misbehave. The author advocates the use of positive nonverbal cues, such as love pats, when children are "being good." Verbal praise often interrupts children and distracts them from what they are doing. The more the parents or caregivers "catch 'em being good" and pay attention to the children as they behave, the less likely children are to misbehave to receive attention. All of the techniques the author uses are reiterated in helpful summaries in the back of the book.

Driscoll, Jeanne, and Marsha Walker. *Taking Care of Your New Baby: A Guide to Infant Care.* Garden City Park, N.Y.: Avery, 1989.

The authors present a brief straightforward approach to baby care for first time parents. Preparing for the baby's arrival, deciding whether to breast feed or bottle feed, recovering from postpartum depression, and coping with the new responsibilities that go with a newborn are covered in depth. The father's role, the couple's changing relationship, and maintaining ties with family members and friends are described.

Leach, Penelope. *Babyhood: Stage by Stage, From Birth to Age Two: How Your Baby Develops Physically, Emotionally, Mentally.* 2d ed. rev. New York: Knopf, 1983.

Leach, a British psychologist, writes in a detailed yet straightforward manner about the first years of an infant's life. What parents can expect, what to do when the unexpected occurs, and how to handle emergencies are also discussed. While the book is written chronologically from birth to the age of two, one can use a thematic approach by reading the sections on feeding or language development at each developmental stage. The author also includes helpful summaries of each stage (e.g., at six months, at twelve months, etc.).

Leach, Penelope. *Your Baby and Child: From Birth to Age Five.* Rev. ed. New York: Knopf, 1989.

In a well-illustrated guide to a child's first five years, the reader finds that the descriptions of each developmental stage parallel one another with discussions of the child's feeding and growth patterns as well as her everyday care. Effective techniques for recognizing a baby's cries and comforting her are also included. In the chapters on toddlers, language development, and playing are emphasized. Toilet training methods are also detailed. A lengthy reference section on common childhood illnesses appears at the end of the book.

Sears, William. *Keys to Becoming a Father.* New York: Barron, 1991.

While much has been written about the mother-infant bond, this book focuses on fatherhood and establishing the father-infant bond. As a pediatrician and a father of seven children, the author illustrates nurturing techniques from his practice and his own experience. Each of the keys is only a few pages long so a new father could read a chapter in a few spare moments while taking care of his newborn. Tips on fathering toddlers, preschoolers, school-age children, and adolescents are also included.

Sears, William. *Keys to Calming the Fussy Baby.* New York: Barron, 1991.

In a brief but practical work, pediatrician William Sears gives readers a variety of techniques for coping with a fussy baby. The author contends that fussy or high-need babies are born with this temperament. The author describes different crying styles and the needs they reflect. Parents are advised to develop presleeping routines which help the high-need baby settle down. Colic and its medical basis are also discussed.

Spock, Benjamin, and Michael B. Rothenberg. *Dr. Spock's Baby and Child Care.* 6th ed. New York: Pocket Bks., 1992.

One of the most recognized child-rearing experts, Benjamin Spock, and his associate Michael Rothenberg have revised and updated the classic *Baby and Child Care.* In addition to the traditional topics covered in infant and child care books, (feeding, growth and development, and common health problems), the authors discuss contemporary issues, including sex, contraceptives, homosexuality, substance abuse, and AIDS.

Toddlerhood

Brazelton, T. Berry. *Toddlers and Parents: A Declaration of Independence.* Rev. ed. New York: Delta/Seymour Lawrence Book, 1989.

Noted pediatrician T. Berry Brazelton focuses on the psychosocial development of one to three-year-olds. As infants, these children were completely dependent on their parents for food, warmth, and shelter. As they move into toddlerhood, they begin to understand themselves as separate beings. They test newly found motor and language skills. In addition to these developmental skills, they experience new emotions. The author focuses on toddlers through photographs, examples from his practice, and helpful techniques parents and caregivers can use in living effectively with young children.

Brazelton, T. Berry. *Touchpoints: Your Child's Emotional and Behavioral Development.* Reading, Mass.: Addison-Wesley, 1992.

While each child is unique, each passes certain milestones in his or her psychological development. Pediatrician Brazelton describes these milestones and advises parents that often after the developmental step occurs, the child may regress. For example, when a child is learning to walk, he may take a few tentative steps as an experiment, and then return to crawling as his primary means of getting from place to place until he is ready to try again. As the author leads the reader through the behavioral map of "touchpoints," other common problems faced by toddlers and preschoolers are discussed, including bedwetting, separation, sibling rivalry, and school readiness. Brazelton emphasizes that each "touchpoint" is one more step by the child toward autonomy. Parental understanding of these advances and regressions can aid in smoothing the way to the next advance and in coping with the regression.

Lasky, Vicki. *Practical Parenting Tips: Over 1,500 Helpful Hints for the First Five Years.* Rev. ed. New York: Meadowbrook Pr., 1992.

In areas ranging from infant care to hygiene and health, the author provides sensible ideas for overcoming sibling rivalry, sharing toys, and traveling with small children by car or plane. Arranged by topic, the tips are often practical, ranging from how to remove gum from hair to building self-esteem in the family.

Lief, Nina R., and Rebecca M. Thomas. *The Third Year of Life.* The Early Childhood Development Center's Parenting Series. New York: Walker, 1991.

Child psychiatrist Lief and colleague Rebecca Thomas give the reader insights into the life of the three-year-old. What to expect, the importance of play, the developing personality, and discipline for this stage are described. Quotations from parents are used to illuminate each point. Changes in family structure and their effects are also considered. Suggested readings and a bibliography are included.

White, Burton L. *The First Three Years of Life.* 3d ed. New York: A Fireside Book, published by Simon & Schuster, 1990.

In a detailed yet practical description of child development, White, a child psychologist, explores all phases of a child's physical, social, and emotional life. Readers are introduced to each developmental stage with descriptions of what to expect, what not to expect, what to do, and, more importantly, what not to do. In each section the author discusses what toys and activities are fun for a toddler, and which ones should be avoided. Appropriate discipline methods, strategies to avoid spoiling a child, and techniques to combat sibling rivalry are also included in this informative book.

Windell, James. *Discipline: A Sourcebook of 50 Failsafe Techniques for Parents.* New York: Collier Bks., 1991.

Windell, a psychologist, points out the important distinction between discipline and punishment. Parents are recognized as teachers who, by their example and guidance, help their children be self-disciplined, productive members of the community, and have a strong sense of self. With these goals in mind, the author details the ten worst disciplinary techniques as well as techniques to encourage or discourage certain types of behavior.

School-Age Children

Elkind, David. *The Hurried Child: Growing Up Too Fast Too Soon.* Rev. ed. Reading, Mass.: Addison-Wesley, 1988.

Elkind finds fault with parents, schools, and the media for blurring the boundaries between childhood and adulthood. By expecting children to read, write, and do math at earlier and earlier ages, the author argues effectively that hurried children are stressed children. Playing a sport or a musical instrument for sheer enjoyment has been transformed by some parents into highly competitive organized sports or highly structured music lessons, in which the child is expected to hone her athletic skills or performance skills often at the expense of "playing." Media images from music, television, and fashion present a variety of confusing messages about violence, sexuality, and body image. The author argues that making children into little adults does considerable harm to them educationally and emotionally.

Kelly, Marguerite. *The Mother's Almanac II: Your Child from Six to Twelve.* New York: Doubleday, 1989.

The book is divided into three sections: the child, the family, and the world. In the first section, Kelly describes common characteristics of each age level: the physical, emotional, and spiritual points for development. Medical concerns are also discussed. In the family section, emphasis is placed on relationships, bonding, traditions, and stresses the family may face through divorce, illness, handicaps, child abuse, or death. In the world section, school, friendships, leisure time, and hobbies are covered. Resources for more information and a reading list are also included.

Laskin, David, and Kathleen O'Neill. *The Little Girl Book: Everything You Need to Know to Raise a Daughter Today.* New York: Ballantine, 1992.

Little girls and their development from infancy to adolescence are discussed. Socialization, how girls learn about femininity, gender roles, school, and sports are also included. The authors cite research on femininity, math anxiety, and computer usage among other topics which bolster the examples and case studies under discussion. In addition, information on sexual abuse and the challenge of single parenting make up the concluding chapters.

Webb, James T., Elizabeth A. Meckstroth, and Stephanie S. Tolan. *Guiding the Gifted Child: A Practical Source for Parents and Teachers.* Columbus. OH: Ohio Psychology Pub. Co., 1982.

Using a straightforward approach, the authors describe how parents and teachers can identify effective strategies for helping their gifted child. Each chapter opens with a discussion of the specific topic with questions commonly asked by parents, siblings, and teachers. Among the topics covered are identifying, motivating, and disciplining a gifted child. In addition, the importance of communication, stress management, and self-esteem are also explored. The authors debunk myths surrounding gifted children by contrasting the myths to checklists of common characteristics. Additional readings and a list of advocacy groups are provided.

Adolescence

Boston Children's Hospital and Robert P. Masland. *What Teenagers Want to Know about Sex.* Boston: Little, 1988.

In a straightforward question and answer format, this book approaches common concerns of most adolescents. Writing for teenagers, physician Masland and his colleagues discuss puberty, the human reproductive system, sexuality, sexual identity, masturbation, menstruation, contraception, abortion, sexually transmitted diseases, AIDS, sexual abuse, and substance abuse.

Calderone, Mary S., and Eric W. Johnson. *The Family Book about Sexuality.* Rev. ed. New York: Harper, 1989.

In a guide which focuses on adolescents and includes information about sexuality and related issues for persons of all ages, the authors provide an informative sourcebook which covers sexual development, human sexual response, and reproduction. In addition, a discussion of the importance of the family's role in a person's developing sexuality and in the equally important role in developing the individual's moral values. Sexual problems and sexually transmitted diseases are also described. Family planning and designing a sex education program are also covered. Readers who seek brief definitions can consult the A-Z Encyclopedia in the appendix. A bibliography of related books is also included.

Gordon, Sol, and Judith Gordon. *Raising a Child Conservatively in a Sexually Permissive World*. Rev. ed. New York: Simon, 1989.

The authors encourage parents to respond to questions about sex from children and adolescents as soon as the questions occur. Responses should be factual and given in language the child can understand. Commonly asked questions by each age group are provided as well as sample answers. By openly communicating with youngsters about sex from the beginning, the Gordons believe parents establish a pattern whereby children feel comfortable approaching them for information. When appropriate, parents can use these talks to discuss and reinforce their values. By setting and enforcing limits, the authors feel parents can educate their children and teens about sex without encouraging sexual behavior.

Greydanus, Donald E., and others. *Caring for Your Adolescent: Ages 12 to 21*. New York: Bantam, 1991.

The American Academy of Pediatrics sponsored this book as part of an ongoing series on child care. The book describes the physical, psychological, sexual, social, educational, and nutritional growth and development stages normally seen in this age group. Depression and eating disorders are covered in depth as are academic achievement issues.

Packer, Alex J. *Bringing Up Parents: The Teenager's Handbook*. Minneapolis: Free Spirit Publishing, 1992.

The author takes a decidedly lighter tone in using humor as the primary vehicle in delivering messages to adolescents about active listening, problem solving, and common problems teens face. Packer gives both parents and teens examples of phrases that will drive each other wild, and in so doing shows the reader the perspective of each person. An appendix discusses common areas of conflict between adolescents and their parents and suggests problem-solving techniques in the areas of money, phone use, friends, driving, curfews, sexual activity, and substance abuse.

Shalov, Jeanette, and others. *You Can Say No to Your Teenager: and Other Strategies for Effective Parenting in the 1990s*. Reading, Mass.: Addison-Wesley, 1991.

Written by five psychologists and counselors, this book provides a structure for parents to set limits by understanding their own values and expressing them to their adolescents. Because the teen years are known as a time for testing boundaries, Shalov and associates advise parents not to react to every situation but to set firm limits when necessary. The authors encourage the use of active listening and responding to the behavior rather than to the person.

Steinberg, Laurence, and Ann Levine. *You and Your Adolescent: A Parent's Guide for Ages 10–20.* New York: HarperPerennial, 1990.

The authors assert that many parents view the approaching adolescence of their child with great trepidation. Adolescence is usually no more trouble-filled than toddlerhood or other developmental stages. The book explores the normal physical and emotional development in adolescence, effective ways for parents to relate to their child, practical information about the concerns parents and teens have, and potential physical and emotional problems and their treatment. The first section describes effective parenting and communication strategies which can be used throughout adolescence. Steinberg and Levine divide the main portion of the book into early, middle, and late adolescent developmental stages. The authors emphasize that the connection between chronological age and a particular developmental stage in adolescence is relatively loose. For example, a ten-year-old may exhibit some characteristics of early adolescence, while a twelve-year-old does not. This does not imply that the twelve-year-old is somehow "late" or "behind." By understanding what to expect and what is "normal," the authors believe that parents and adolescents will be able to strengthen their relationship.

Warren, Andrea, and Jay Wiedenkeller. *Everybody's Doing It: How To Survive Your Teenagers' Sex Life (and Help Them Survive It, Too).* New York: Penguin, 1993.

Writer Andrea Warren and psychologist Jay Wiedenkeller write as concerned parents and as professionals. Parents are faced with surveys indicating that many teens are sexually active at earlier ages than in the past. The authors reflect on their experience as parents of two adolescent daughters, on the expertise of physicians and mental health professionals, and on their meetings with a variety of parental and adolescent support groups. What information should parents provide to teens? At what age? If they find their son or daughter is sexually active, how do they address safe sex and birth control? What about AIDS and other sexually transmitted diseases? What about gay and lesbian teens? In direct and straightforward language, the authors present stories of teens and their parents as well as those of physicians and mental health professionals.

Day Care

Berezin, Judith. *The Complete Guide to Choosing Child Care.* New York: Random, 1991.

Sponsored by the National Association of Child Care Resource and Referral Agencies in cooperation with Child Care, Inc., this guide provides a broad overview of child care and how to select a day-care center. The author describes key features to consider, types of child care, and how to evaluate a day-care center. The author also discusses safety concerns, licensing requirements, and available resources.

Flating, Sonja. *Child Care: A Parent's Guide.* New York: Facts on File, 1991.

The author advises parents to review what an ideal child care facility for their child would be. Common concerns include locating and evaluating day-care facilities and determining what type of care is best for the child. Flating addresses these issues and many other questions in this practical guide. A list of resources and state requirements for day-care centers and workers are provided in an appendix.

Adopted Children

Komar, Miriam. *Communicating with the Adopted Child.* New York: Walker, 1991.

Komar, a psychotherapist, identifies five styles of communication parents use with their adoptive children: (1) reflecting, where the parent acknowledges and accepts the child's feelings; (2) rational, in which a factual, truthful, straightforward style is used; (3) chosen baby, in which the child is reassured about how much the adoptive parents love her; (4) authoritarian, when the parent talks and the children listen; and (5) glorifying, where the adoptive parent always idealizes the birth parents.

The author recommends that the rational and reflecting styles can be used effectively in tandem, and the other styles may be used in specific situations. Telling the child about adoption is not a single occasion but an ongoing process. Komar describes how this communication changes over time as the child's level of understanding grows. Chapters on the child's self-esteem, her acceptance of her dual heritage, and on discipline issues are also included.

Melina, Lois Ruskai. *Making Sense of Adoption: A Parent's Guide.* New York: Harper, 1989.

This guide focuses on traditional adoption as well as those adopted through donor insemination or in vitro fertilization. Challenges facing parents include when to tell children about adoption, how to handle questions about birth parents, and what rights adopted children have. Each chapter includes an activity that the parents and children do together. A helpful bibliography of books on adoption for children appears in the appendix.

Register, Cheri. *"Are Those Kids Yours?": American Families with Children Adopted from Other Countries.* New York: Free Pr., 1991.

Register, an educational consultant and mother of two Korean children, writes of the ethical, psychological, and social issues involved in adoption with the focus on international adoption as well as the day-to-day experiences of adoptive families. The author interviewed families with adoptive children and children from the ages six to thirty who had been adopted. Through their experiences, the reader sees the complexities of international adoption, building a new family, and helping children with identity concerns.

Schaffer, Judith and Christina Lindstrom. *How to Raise an Adopted Child: A Guide to Help Your Child Flourish from Infancy through Adolescence.* New York: Copestone Pr., 1989.

In this guide psychiatrists Schaffer and Lindstrom provide information on what to expect of children at each age level. The authors add the impact adoption will have at each stage. After each chapter a series of question and answers pertinent to the particular age group are included. Throughout the work the authors advise readers on how to deal with strangers or family members and others who make insensitive or rude remarks about adoption in general or the adopted child. Sections on special needs children and transracial adoption complete the book.

Children with Special Needs

Finston, Peggy. *Parenting Plus: Raising Children with Special Health Needs.* New York: Dutton, 1990.

Physician Finston presents parents with guidelines for taking care of children with chronic or terminal illness. The author recommends that parents not blame themselves, that they identify the problem and learn how to live with it, and that they help their child learn how to help in the treatment process. Parents with special-needs children need to build teams of physicians and teachers who understand their child's condition and who can respond to it. Using case studies of children with a variety of illnesses, the author gives the reader insights into an assortment of challenges parents can face successfully.

Children and Divorce

Bienenfeld, Florence. *Helping Your Child Succeed after Divorce.* Claremont, Calif.: Hunter House, 1987.

While this text speaks for itself, the illustrations drawn by children of divorcing parents, graphically represent the pain and disruption felt by the children. The author proposes a system for parents to use while the family is changing; this involves creating a buffer zone between parental conflict and the child and creating a conflict-free zone for the child. Even though the very nature of divorce involves conflict, parents are advised to stop blaming themselves or their former spouse; to realize that children need both parents; to focus discussions with the former spouse on issues related to the child; to concentrate on the child's current and future needs; to work together to provide the child with a conflict-free environment; and to be civil to the former spouse in the child's presence and/or to refrain from making negative comments about him or her to the child. Additionally, sections on joint custody, rebuilding children's support systems, and how children see divorce are included.

Kline, Kris, and Stephen Pew. *For the Sake of the Children: How to Share Your Children with Your Ex-Spouse in Spite of Your Anger.* Rocklin, Calif.: Prima Publishing, 1992.

Since parents will share the care and nurturing of their children for years after the divorce, this book provides methods for former spouses to develop new ways of thinking, behaving, and communicating. Exercises take readers through strategies for breaking old habits, for developing nonblaming statements, and for including ex-spouses in school activities and family celebrations (graduations, weddings, etc.).

In addition, the authors describe how to maintain civil, if not cordial, communication with ex-in-laws, so that connections can be kept with the grandparents. Part of the parenting process for many ex-spouses includes a remarriage for one or both parents. Since joint custody and visitation schedules involve sharing the children, one of the major hurdles can be dealing with the new spouse. Sections on overcoming well-intentioned advice, reactions from children, and determining when to seek counseling complete this useful guide.

Krementz, Jill. *How It Feels When Parents Divorce.* New York: Knopf, 1984.

Photographer Krementz captures the experiences of nineteen children ranging in age from seven to sixteen years of age, in print and in photographs. For each child, photographs of the children alone and with their parents describe their reactions, recollections, and hopes for the future. In each case, the children are deeply affected by their experience. Some are relieved once the divorce occurs; others reflect on living with joint custody; and in a particularly harrowing instance a boy tells of being abducted by his mother and her boyfriend. He finally returns to his father after a private detective locates the boy in Florida. A number of children still hope that their parents will reunite.

Lasky, Vicki. *Vicki Lasky's Divorce Book for Parents: Helping Your Children Cope with Divorce and its Aftermath.* New York: NAL Bks., 1989.

This practical guide offers step-by-step strategies from first telling the children about the upcoming separation and divorce to the long-term adjustment that the children and their parents will eventually make. Lasky emphasizes the importance of stressing again and again that both parents love them. Children need to be reassured that they did not cause the divorce nor could they prevent it. Common problems faced by parents are described as are solutions. Throughout the book the author provides lists of age-appropriate books on divorce. While the primary focus is on helping the child cope with divorce, problems surrounding financial, legal, and custodial issues are also explored.

Rogers, Fred, and Clare O'Brien. *Mister Rogers Talks with Families about Divorce.* New York: Berkley, 1987.

Television's noted Mister Rogers and educational expert Clare O'Brien take families through the divorce process. While each family's experience is different, some common features are: telling the children and other family members about the divorce, examining the effects of separation on the parents and the children, and describing how the separation affects preschoolers, preteens, and adolescents. The authors offer strategies for helping children understand their feelings about the divorce: fear, guilt, relief and ambivalence, anger and denial, and confusion over loyalty to and affection for both parents. Especially stressful situations such as moving to a new home or celebrating the holidays are also discussed.

Teyber, Edward. *Helping Children Cope with Divorce.* New York: Lexington Bks., 1992.

Teyber, a psychologist, raises many of the common issues facing divorcing parents: breaking the news to the children, dealing with custody issues, arranging visitation schedules, and most importantly not using the children as mediators or as combatants in the divorce. Children often hold onto unrealistic hopes that somehow their parents will reconcile. By emphasizing that the marriage is over, parents can help children form a more realistic view of the family's future. Parents are also cautioned not to speak critically about their former spouse to the children. Youngsters may worry that since one parent has left them, they could also be abandoned by their custodial parent. In addition, they may feel that their loyalty is divided between their parents. Children may also find themselves treated as adults or surrogate parents. "Parentification" occurs when a parent continually relies on a child for emotional support as a listening post or as a confidant. The author emphasizes the importance of parents discussing their problems with adult friends or family members.

Single Parenting

Anderson, Joan. *The Single Mother's Book: A Practical Guide to Managing Your Children, Career, Home, Finances, and Everything Else.* Atlanta: Peachtree Pub., 1990.

Anderson, a former day-care center administrator, writes of her experience as a single mother and as a member of the Single Mother's Group at Vanderbilt University. The book covers redefining the family, dealing with the ex-husband and his family, handling legal issues, returning to work, child rearing concerns, home security, and rebuilding social connections among others. This practical guide is full of resource lists, role plays, and examples from other families.

Greif, Geoffrey L. *The Daddy Track and the Single Father: Coping with Kids, Housework, a Job, an Ex-Wife, a Social Life, and the Courts.* Lexington, Mass.: Lexington Bks., 1990.

Single fathers find themselves part of a growing trend as courts are awarding fathers sole custody or joint custody, and as widowers raise their children alone. The challenges these men face involve trying to balance responsibilities at home and at work, running a household, and serving as a sole parent when the noncustodial mother chooses to break with the family completely. Many of these men report the existence of a "daddy track" at work where they are torn between advancement at work and taking care of their children. Often these advances involve extensive travel or long hours. The author describes the myths surrounding single fatherhood and uses examples from his research to contradict many myths and to confirm others. In addition, strategies for getting along with noncustodial mothers, for dealing with the courts and child support, and for maintaining a social life are discussed at length. The author also examines the experience of fathers with joint custody and widowers.

Stepparenting

Artlip, Mary Ann, James A. Artlip, and Earl S. Saltzman. *The New American Family.* Lancaster, Pa.: Starburst Publ., 1993.

The authors provide examples from all over the United States of effective stepparenting techniques. Couples marrying a second time may have unrealistic expectations of how the families will "blend." The authors suggest that partners discuss issues relating to discipline, relations with ex-spouses, and custody arrangements. Stepsibling relationships may be difficult if children resent their stepparent or are jealous of one another. The book includes a number of suggestions which can alleviate some of these problems.

Bloomfield, Harold H., and Robert B. Kory. *Making Peace in Your Stepfamily: Surviving and Thriving as Parents and Stepparents.* New York: Hyperion, 1993.

By necessity the stepfamily is born of loss—the death of a former spouse or a divorce. As the families join, both the parents and children may still be coping with the pain and crises surrounding that loss. Adding to the "blended" family are issues of discipline, family roles, rules, and responsibilities as well as joint custody. Through exercises and examples, the authors lead the reader through the peacemaking approaches they advocate for effective stepparenting.

Rosin, Mark Bruce. *Stepfathering: Stepfathers' Advice on Creating a New Family.* New York: Simon & Schuster, 1987.

Based on his own experience and survey responses from fifty other stepfathers, Rosin explores in considerable detail the challenges that stepfathers face. While the wicked stepmother stereotype from fairy tales is well known, there is not an evil stepfather myth. While Rosin identifies ten common issues that stepfathers contend with, he advises readers that each stepfamily's experience is unique. These issues include the initial adjustment that family members make during courtship and after marriage, the ongoing adjustment that may continue for several years after the couple marries, as husband and wife find a balance in discipline. Stepfathers, in this study, discovered that their relationship with their children and stepchildren often blossomed as they spent time alone with the children. These men also reported the importance of private time with their partners. Whether the biological father actively participates in his children's lives or is completely absent, stepfathers need to acknowledge his presence in the family. Additional concerns include money matters and special skills needed when stepchildren reach adolescence.

Savage, Karen, and Patricia Adams. *The Good Stepmother: A Practical Guide.* New York: Crown, 1988.

On the basis of her own experience and as a family therapist working with stepfamilies, Savage and her colleague Patricia Adams outline common concerns of stepmothers. The authors review the steps involved in becoming a new family: before the wedding, coming home, and forming the new family. Money and relationships with ex-wives are discussed in detail, as are issues surrounding adolescence and sexual attraction between stepsiblings.

Diversity and Parenting

Comer, James P., and Alvin F. Poussaint. *Raising Black Children: Two Leading Psychiatrists Confront the Educational, Social and Emotional*

Problems Facing Black Children. Rev. ed. New York: Plume Bks. (distributed by Penguin), 1992.

The authors use a question-and-answer format to respond to parents who have concerns about children from infancy to adolescence. In addition to questions about growth, development, and discipline that apply to all children, the authors address questions about how children can deal with racial slurs and other injustices.

Hopson, Darlene Powell, and Derek S. Hopson. *Different and Wonderful: Raising Black Children in a Race-Conscious Society.* New York: Fireside Bks. (distributed by Simon & Schuster), 1990.

The authors encourage parents to talk frankly and openly about racism to their children. The primary focus is to develop child's self-esteem, model appropriate behavior, explore family history, and build an open communication system. The authors emphasize developing racial identity for the child at all age levels. Through exercises and examples, readers can see how this approach can apply to their situation.

NOTES

1. Stanley Turecki and Leslie Tonner, *The Difficult Child,* rev. ed. (New York: Bantam, 1989), 14–32.

2. Ibid., 16.

3. Alexander Thomas and Stella Chess, *Temperament and Development* (New York: Brunner/Mazel, 1977), 20–22.

4. James Windell, *Discipline: A Sourcebook of 50 Failsafe Techniques for Parents* (New York: Collier, 1991), 163.

5. Adele Faber and Elaine Mazlish, *How To Talk So Kids Will Listen and Listen So Kids Will Talk* (New York: Avon, 1980), 190.

6. Steven Shelov, and Others, *Caring for Your Baby and Young Child: Birth to Age Five* (New York: Bantam, 1991), 124–25.

7. William Sears, *Keys to Becoming a Father* (New York: Barron, 1991), 3–5.

8. Ibid., 6–8.

9. Shelov, *Caring for Your Baby,* 126–28.

10. Frances Wells Burck, *Babysense: A Practical Guide and Supportive Guide to Baby Care* (New York: St. Martin's, 1991), 157–62.

11. Burck, *Babysense,* 157.

12. Penelope Leach, *Your Baby and Child: From Birth to Age Five,* 2d ed. (New York: Knopf, 1989), 46–67.

13. Edward Christophersen, *Little People: Guidelines for Commonsense Child Rearing,* 3d ed. (Kansas City, Mo.: Westport Pub., 1988), 9.

14. Laurence Steinberg and Jay Belsky, *Infancy, Childhood, and Adolescence: Development in Context* (New York: McGraw-Hill, 1991), 211.

15. Ibid., 211.

16. Christophersen, *Little People,* 13, 16–18.

17. Windell, *Discipline,* 54–68.

18. Shelov, *Caring for Your Baby,* 309.

19. Ibid., 309–11.

20. Lois Hoffman, Scott Paris, and Elizabeth Hall, *Developmental Psychology Today,* 6th ed. (New York: McGraw-Hill, 1994), 208.

21. Christophersen, *Little People,* 39.

22. Windell, *Discipline,* 165.

23. Steinberg and Belsky, *Infancy, Childhood, and Adolescence,* 316.

24. Joyce Kaufman and Edward F. Ziglar, "Do Abused Children Become Abusive Parents?" *American Journal of Orthopsychiatry* 57 (Apr. 1987): 186–97.

25. Steinberg and Belsky, *Infancy, Childhood, and Adolescence,* 318.

26. Ibid., 316–19.

27. Richard Ryckman, *Theories of Personality,* 5th ed. (Pacific Grove, Calif.: Brooks/Cole, 1993), 191.

28. Marguerite Kelly, *The Mother's Almanac II: Your Child from Six to Twelve* (New York: Doubleday, 1989), 287.

29. Ronald Comer, *Abnormal Psychology* (New York: Freeman, 1992), 425.

30. Ibid., 399, 404.

31. Jeanette Shalov, and others, *You Can Say No to Your Teenager and Other Strategies for Effective Parenting in the 1990's* (Reading, Mass.: Addison-Wesley, 1991), 114.

32. Donald Greydanus, *Caring for Your Adolescent: Ages 12 to 21* (New York: Bantam, 1991), 6–12.

33. Stephen Fried, Dorothy Van Booven, and Cindy MacQuarrie, *Older Adulthood: Learning Activities for Understanding Aging* (Baltimore: Health Professions Pr., 1993), 105–23.

34. Hoffman, *Developmental Psychology Today,* 205–207.

35. John Rosemond, *Parent Power! A Common-Sense Approach to Parenting in the 90's and Beyond,* 2d ed. (Kansas City, Kans.: Andrews & McMeel, 1990), 321.

36. Ibid., 322.

37. Cheri Register, *"Are Those Kids Yours?": American Families with Children Adopted from Other Countries* (New York: Free Pr., 1991), xii.

38. Steinberg and Belsky, *Infancy, Childhood, and Adolescence,* 321–22.

39. Ibid., 323.

40. Ibid., 502.

41. Ibid., 411.

42. Harold Bloomfield, *Making Peace in Your Stepfamily: Surviving and Thriving as Parents and Stepparents* (New York: Hyperion, 1992), 3.

43. Patricia Papernow, *Becoming a Stepfamily: Patterns in Remarried Families* (San Francisco: Jossey-Bass, 1993), 12–17.

44. Lee Salk, *Familyhood: Nurturing the Values That Matter* (New York: Simon & Schuster, 1992), 24.

CHAPTER

5

Self-Development

This chapter is devoted to personal development concerns, distinguishing what can be most readily changed from that which are more difficult to alter. Topics will include the specific subjects of gender, communication (basics, assertiveness, anger and anger management, male-female), as well as more general material on life's meaning and personal happiness.

American popular self-help books covering self-development date back to the seventeenth and eighteenth centuries.[1] Puritan guidebooks like Cotton Mather's *Bonifacius: Essays to Do Good* instruct readers on how to prepare for the next life, while more secular works, such as Benjamin Franklin's *The Way to Wealth,* provide guidance in the pursuit of more earthly rewards.[2] Throughout the eighteenth and nineteenth centuries, clergy and successful businessmen wrote advice books directed at "elevating common men and women through prescriptions for improving personality by the use of such tactics as positive thinking and interpersonal manipulation."[3]

Because of a seemingly insatiable interest in personal development and the introduction of the paperback book in the late

1930s, Americans have been bombarded with such works since that time.[4] For example, few reading adults are unfamiliar with the writings of Dale Carnegie, whose *How to Win Friends and Influence People* was first published in 1937. By the 1960s mental health professionals were writing a number of popular self-development tomes like *Games People Play* by Eric Berne, *I'm OK—You're OK* by Thomas Harris, and *How to Be Your Own Best Friend* by Mildred Newman and Bernard Berkowitz. The emphasis on the "self" aspect of self-development reached an extreme in Robert Ringer's *Winning through Intimidation* (1975) and *Looking Out for #1* (1977).[5]

While an emphasis on individualism and materialism continues into the 1990s, a number of self-development books, particularly those written by religiously oriented writers, attempt to engage the reader in an analysis of issues related to personal meaning (e.g., M. Scott Peck's *The Road Less Traveled*). Many of the self-development books available today in libraries, bookstores, and supermarkets reflect similar strategies for achieving personal success and happiness through self-discipline, goal setting, and positive attitude.

Distinguishing What Can Be Changed from What Cannot

While American culture continues to emphasize the potential for individual change and development, the science of psychology instructs us that we may have less control over some personal factors than was previously thought. Martin E. P. Seligman, in *What You Can Change and What You Can't: The Complete Guide to Successful Self-Improvement,* describes numerous psychological and behavioral problems and offers evidence of their degree of changeability. Seligman contends our ability to change specific aspects of ourselves is related to "depth."[6] Depth reflects how deep or superficial what we want to change lies.

Three major tenets describe Seligman's approach to depth and change. First, he suggests the more a psychological element is biologically based, the less changeable it is. Second, Seligman believes: "The easier a belief underlying a problem is to confirm and the harder it is to disconfirm, the harder it will be to change."[7] For instance, Seligman provides the example of someone who believes that injustice and misery define the world. Such a belief is an overgeneralization, which is in part confirmed by watching or reading the news. With the availability of such "evidence," it is difficult to alter the belief.

Seligman adds a third tenet, the power of a belief. A belief has power to the extent that it is firmly embedded in us and aids in our understanding of the world. Powerful beliefs are central to us, like the belief in a particular form of government or religion. Other beliefs, like the one that "house cats are dangerous," are much less powerful. Therefore, Seligman states: "To the extent that the belief underlying a problem has high power, it will be hard to change; to the extent that it has low power, it will be easier to change."[8]

This theory of change can be applied to various issues of self-development. For example, according to Seligman anger has some biological base. General beliefs like "the world is unfair" are powerful, while more specific ones, such as "my brother-in-law is a slug" are of low power. While anger management strategies sometimes work better than at other times, anger does seem to be modifiable.[9]

Gender Issues

Major social and economic changes in America, notably alterations from the traditional two-parent, one-wage earner, middle-class family of the 1950s and 1960s to the dual-career, single parent, or single person lifestyle of the 1980s and 1990s, have affected gender roles and expectations profoundly. Many middle-aged men and women today grew up during an era circumscribed by "rules." Roles for men and women differed dramatically from those of today.

Gender Differences

Issues for women and men reflect the dramatic changes characterizing family and work life. While the roles of men and women have moved closer, some women and men have concerns emanating from their respective gender. Carol Tavris describes three common approaches to discussing gender differences: (1) "women are opposite and deficient"; (2) "women are opposite and superior"; and (3) "women are just like men."[10] The first of these approaches is reflected by our preoccupation with unwed adolescent mothers rather than unwed fathers. Contraception and abortion are frequently described as women's issues, but men are involved equally in matters of a sexual nature.[11] If women are described in comparison to men as if men are the norm, then, according to Tavris, "the male norm frames the very questions and solutions that investigators explore, and then creates the impression that women have 'problems' and 'deficiencies' if they differ from the norm."[12] For example, Tavris cites a study which found that women were more likely than men to show difficulty in forming a "separate sense of self." However, the results of this study could have been described in the following manner: "Men have more difficulty than women in forming and maintaining attachments."[13]

A second approach to viewing gender differences is to consider women as superior to men. Advocating this approach, Carol Gilligan suggests that women frame moral decisions with "a different voice."[14] She argues that women "tend to base moral decisions on principles of compassion and care."[15] Many psychologists refute Gilligan's findings, suggesting that adherents of such an approach have replaced a male bias with a female one.

For an enlightened discussion of the popular misapplications of Gilligan's theory, the reader can consult the chapter entitled "Beautiful Souls and Different Voices" in Carol Tavris' book, *The Mismeasure of Woman.*[16] A third way of comparing genders is simply to proclaim that no differences exist; but that approach does not reflect experience. As Tavris observes, the genders "differ in power and resources, life experiences, and reproductive processes."[17]

Women's Self-Development

Both genders continue to develop throughout the lifespan. In *Down from the Pedestal: Moving beyond Idealized Images of Womanhood,* Maxine Harris describes idealized images that shape perceptions of what a woman "should" be like.[18] Both women and men are impacted by such images held by family, relationships, and the culture.[19] Women are told of the lives of their foremothers, and influenced especially by their mothers' lives.[20] Harris argues that women utilize their mothers as gauges to measure their own lives and experiences.[21] But in addition, each time a woman enter a new "relationship, we see an idealized image reflected in the eyes of the other."[22]

Messages concerning women's images come from the immediate social circle as well as the larger culture. Defined ideas of women often suggest stereotypic visions that limit and assail women. Harris suggests that the stereotypic "Dumb Blonde," "Jewish American Princess," and "pregnant Soul Sister" abound in the popular culture and demean women, particularly ethnic women.[23]

During various historical periods, other idealized images have been propagated, including the "All-American Girl," the "True Women," and the "Lady of Leisure."[24] While emphasizing the insidious nature of image, Harris describes the "traps" which ensnarl the selfhood of young women as they encounter the models of the "Eternal Girl," the "Dutiful Daughter," the "Free Spirit," the "Charmer," and the "Lolita."[25] Women in midlife may feel restricted by images of the "Selfless Mother," the "Faithful Wife," the "Happy Homemaker," the "Super Mom," and the "Career Woman."[26] Older women may be categorized by images of the "Sweet Old Lady," the "Grandmother," the "Witch," the "Spinster," and the "Wise Woman."[27]

Harris thinks models of womanhood may make it more difficult for young women to progress fully along the life "themes of preparation, exploration, and receptivity," for middle-aged women to pursue "the themes of creation, transformation, nurturance, preservation, and balance," and for older women to embrace "integration, meaning, perspective, and remembrance."[28]

Another element which limits women's self-development is mother bashing, a common theme in many popular psychology books, used as a way of attempting to explain both women's and men's problems.[29] In the popular book *Don't Blame Mother: Mending the Mother-Daughter Relationship,* Paula Caplan describes mother blaming among psychological researchers and therapists, who themselves may have internalized various myths about mothers, and she offers concrete suggestions for mothers and daughters to mend their relationships. Interested readers may also wish to consult Harriet Lerner's *The Dance of Intimacy: A Woman's Guide to Courageous Acts of Change in Key Relationships.* Lerner devotes a chapter to "Our Mother/Her Mother/Our Self."[30]

Men's Self-Development

Men are also limited sometimes by the messages they receive from families, relationships, and the culture. Some men complain that others, both women and men, consider them "success objects."[31] According to Patrick Fanning and Matthew McKay, many men believe they are expected to earn a great deal of money, while working wives and mothers are "usually still expected to assume nearly all the psychological responsibility for their family's emotional well-being. But working husbands, even those whose wives outearn them, still assume all the psychological responsibility for their family's financial well-being."[32] It's a matter of social conditioning.

Men are instructed from early childhood that "real men" control their emotions, lest they be thought weak or "feminine." Men are taught from pubescence that they must initiate sex, even when they really don't want to pursue it. In their activity-based book *Being a Man: A Guide to the New Masculinity,* Patrick Fanning and Matthew McKay instruct male readers on understanding the relationship with their fathers, comprehending personal feelings and values, becoming a good friend, sexual partner, and father, as well as developing awareness and openness, and controlling anger.

Communication Skill Building

This section is devoted to a discussion of the basic principles of effective interpersonal communication, including a practical model, sending and receiving messages, and listening. The importance of nonverbal elements, assertiveness, and male-female communication will also be described. The discussion of assertiveness will address the meaning of assertiveness, "assertive rights," differentiating assertiveness from aggressiveness and nonassertiveness, coping with difficult persons, anger management, and assertiveness skill building. The material covering communication between men and women will highlight common problems and useful strategies for increasing understanding.

Basics of Effective Communication

There is a body of knowledge concerning the principal axioms of high-quality interpersonal communication. One popular model of interpersonal communication starts with a sender or source who intends to transmit a message that is comprised of symbols constructed to provide a specific meaning. Messages include words and/or nonverbal cues, like gestures and facial expressions. The sender encodes, that is, translates a message into symbols to be transmitted to a source. In addition, the source selects a channel through which the intended message travels, with the most prominent channel for interpersonal communication being face-to-face contact. The individual for whom the message is intended is the receiver, who engages in the process of decoding, that is, interpreting the various symbols. While engaging in the processes of encoding and decoding in face-to-face interaction, both sender and receiver are giving feedback to one another regarding the content and style of the message. Anything interfering or distorting a message is termed *noise*.[33]

Sending Messages

Matthew McKay, Martha Davis, and Patrick Fanning devote a chapter to expressing messages in their popular book, *Messages: The Communication Book*.[34] The authors describe specific strategies for communicating observations, thoughts, feelings, and needs. By delineating the differences among the four communication elements, McKay and his associates view observational statements as those based on an individual's experience. Thoughts, on the other hand, refer to inferences that are based on observations. For example, the statement "I dropped the encyclopedia on my foot," is an observation. But "It was clumsy of me to drop the encyclopedia on my foot," is a statement of thought. Thoughts may involve judgements of value, implying good and bad. Feeling statements involve affect. For instance, "I was embarrassed when I dropped the encyclopedia on my foot," communicates feelings. Statements of need concern that which would be of benefit to an individual. For example, "Could you help me put away the encyclopedia?" states a need. The authors assert that for many persons the expression of feelings is the most difficult aspect of the communication process.[35]

According to McKay, Davis, and Fanning, people sometimes communicate partial or contaminated messages. A message is partial if something significant is omitted, while contaminated messages provide information in a disguised form. McKay and his colleagues include the following as examples of contaminated messages: (1) "Why don't you act a little human for a change?" and (2) "I know what your problem is, you like to get paid but you don't like to work."[36] In the first message a value judgment is contaminated with a need, and in the second message a value judgement is contaminated with a feeling. Another mode of message contamination involves the expression of nonverbal signals, which alter or even contradict one's words. For example, facial expression of vocal tone can communicate anger or impatience, even though the speaker says, "Sure, I have time to talk to you."[37]

People can send messages interpersonally in several ways to minimize misunderstanding and maximize openness to the meaning of the messages. David and Frank Johnson provide several practical suggestions, including the following: (1) "Clearly 'own' your own messages by using first-person singular pronouns ('I,' 'my')"; (2) "Make your messages complete and specific"; (3) "Be redundant. Sending the same message more than once and using more than one channel of communication . . . will help the receiver understand your message"; (4) "Ask for feedback concerning the way in which messages are being received"; (5) "Make the message appropriate to the receiver's frame of reference," that is, use different words depending on whether the receiver is an adult, child, peer, and so forth; and (6) "Describe others' behavior without evaluating or interpreting."[38]

Listening

Frequently, people "pseudo-listen" when endeavoring to fulfill others' needs and not listen to the sender and her messages.[39] McKay, Davis, and Fanning assert that people are truly listening if they intend to do at least one of the following: (1) "Understand someone"; (2) "Enjoy someone"; (3) "Learn something"; or (4) "Give help or solace."[40]

McKay and his colleagues provide their readers with exercises intended to aid in assessing personal blocks to listening effectively. The authors discuss twelve blocks to listening: (1) "Comparing"; (2) "Mind reading"; (3) "Rehearsing"; (4) "Filtering"; (5) "Judging"; (6) "Dreaming"; (7) "Identifying"; (8) "Advising"; (9) "Sparring"; (10) "Being right"; (11) "Derailing"; and (12) "Placating."[41] In summarizing behaviors constituting good listening, the authors suggest the reader: (1) "Maintain good eye contact"; (2) "Lean slightly forward"; (3) "Reinforce the speaker by nodding or paraphrasing"; (4) "Clarify by asking questions"; (5) "Actively move away from distractions"; and (6) "Be committed, even if you are angry or upset, to understanding what was said."[42]

Nonverbal Communication

While it is essential that a receiver listen attentively to the sender's words, attention to nonverbal elements is also central to understanding. Interpersonal communication relies on a variety of nonverbal elements, such as physical distance, body movements, touch, and vocal style.

Physical Distance

The use and perception of space is referred to as *proxemics*.[43] Edward Hall describes four spatial zones reflecting the nature of the relationship and of the specific nature of an interpersonal transaction. The following spatial zones are generalized notions of nonverbal "rules" for Euro-Americans and may vary from one culture to another: (1) "intimate distance"—0 to 18 inches; (2) "personal distance"—1½ feet to 4 feet; (3) "social distance"—4 feet to 12 feet; and (4) "public distance"—12 feet and beyond.[44]

Typically, people try to reserve the intimate zone for interactions with their most significant others: lovers, children, and close friends. Personal distance denotes the appropriate spacing for many personal interactions, like those at a party. Social distance provides a framework for more interpersonal activity, such as a work setting. Public distance is often used for gatherings such as meetings and public addresses.[45]

Another spatial concept which has been applied to interpersonal communication is *territoriality*, described as an individual staking out an area or a set of objects.[46] While people seem to differ in their spatial needs, most persons do "mark" their areas or territories to signal that a space is owned or occupied. Common markers include the placing of one's coat on a chair to reserve it or a fence surrounding an individual's house.[47] A person may seem threatened when marked territory is entered without permission.

Body Movements

Body movements play a significant role in both the sending and receiving of interpersonal messages. One useful way of categorizing movements, or *kinesics*, as they are called by researchers, has been devised by Paul Ekman and Wallace Friesen.[48] The authors divide kinesics into five types: (1) emblems; (2) illustrators; (3) affect displays; (4) regulators; and (5) adapters.

Emblems are those movements which have a direct verbal translation such as the sign for "OK" or certain obscene gestures. Emblems are culturally and linguistically bound; the same movement means something else in a different country or accompanying a different spoken language. Sometimes movements describe or elaborate on the meaning of words. These illustrators are often out of our awareness and are much more universal than emblems.[49] Moving one's hands as one describes the mountains visited during a recent trip exemplifies the use of an illustrator.

The third category, affect displays, includes all the facial expressions of emotion. The form of affect display shows significant consistency across cultures, but the intensity of expression and the conditions and frequency of specific facial expressions vary from culture to culture.[50]

Readers interested in detecting deception and interpreting emotional expression may wish to consult Paul Ekman's popular book, *Telling Lies.* Nonverbal behaviors which monitor speaking or listening are termed regulators. Regulators include head nods, eye movements, leaning in a chair, and other signals aimed at letting the speaker or listener know whose turn it is to speak or to listen. Adaptors are unintentional movements which satisfy some personal need like scratching or stroking one's hair.

Touch

Another important nonverbal medium of communication is touch. Stanley Jones and Elaine Yarborough describe the following meanings of touch: (1) positive affect; (2) playfulness; (3) control; (4) ritual; and (5) task-relatedness.[51] Touch may suggest affection, nurturing, protection, inclusion, reassurance, sexual desire, or affectionate or aggressive play. However, touch can also be used to signal the other person to do something or to stop doing something.

According to Nancy Henley, touch may be an attempt to communicate male dominance over women.[52] With increased awareness some men are becoming cognizant of the possibility of touch being inappropriate or being misunderstood in many interpersonal interactions with women. Frequently, touch serves a ritualistic function, handshakes, for example. Finally, the completion of a task, like assisting others with their coat, may necessitate a certain degree of touch. Certainly the use and meanings associated with touch vary with gender, age, and the culture.

Vocal Style

A final category of nonverbal communication is vocal style, or *paralanguage,* which pertains to all the elements of speech except the words that are being used. Paralinguistic factors include pitch, resonance, articulation, tempo, volume, and rhythm.[53] Matthew McKay and his associates in *Messages: The Communication Book* offer suggestions for readers who wish to modify their paralinguistic styles. These authors direct the interested reader to tape record their voice and to wait at least twenty-four hours prior to listening to themselves to maximize objectivity. Readers are directed to ask themselves the following questions as they listen to the recording: (1) "Does your voice reflect what you want to say?"; (2) "Is your voice congruent with the words you speak?"; and (3) "Is there something about your voice that you dislike?"[54] Those readers who discover that they wish to modify their vocal style are instructed to practice speaking on tape, while altering their voice to reflect the desired changes.[55]

Assertiveness

Nonverbal elements of communication, such as vocal style, physical distance, gesture, posture, facial expression, as well as eye contact are significant ingredients of assertive communication. In *Your Perfect Right: A Guide to Assertive Living,* Robert Alberti and Michael Emmons offer the following definition of assertiveness: "Assertiveness behavior promotes equality in human relationships, enabling us to act in our own best interests, to stand up for ourselves without undue anxiety, to express honest feelings comfortably, to exercise personal rights without denying the rights of others."[56]

Assertive Rights

Everyone has or should have a set of basic rights. However, people may have been taught to disregard or minimize their legitimate rights in some aspect of their lives. Martha Davis,

Matthew McKay, and Elizabeth Robbins Eshelman in their book *The Relaxation and Stress Reduction Workbook,* provide readers with a set of corresponding "legitimate rights."[57] For example, Davis and her associates say the assumption that it is "selfish to put your needs before others' needs" is mistaken. The authors counter that people have a right to sometimes put themselves first.[58] In a highly useful self-help book, *When I Say No, I Feel Guilty,* Manuel Smith offers ten assertive rights, including "You have the right to judge whether you are responsible for finding solutions to other people's problems," and "You have the right to change your mind."[59] It is Smith's contention that other individuals may attempt to manipulate us, but that all of us are, in the final analysis, the "ultimate judges" of our own behavior.[60]

Differentiating Assertiveness, Aggressiveness, and Nonassertiveness

Robert Alberti and Michael Emmons distinguish three styles of communication: assertiveness, aggressiveness, and nonassertiveness.[61] These authors describe the possible feelings and consequences for the sender whose communication is assertive, aggressive, or nonassertive, and the typical results for the receivers of such messages.[62] With assertive behavior, the sender is more likely to behave in a self-enhancing manner, but if she is aggressive, that self-enhancement is achieved at the receiver's expense. On the other hand, if one displays nonassertiveness, that is clearly self-denying. While the assertive communicator chooses for self, the aggressive one chooses for others, and the nonassertive communicator allows others to choose for him. Persons who send assertive messages may be more likely to accomplish their desired goals than their nonassertive peers. Aggressive persons may achieve their goals also, but it may well be to the detriment of another person. Receivers of messages may react very differently depending on whether communications are presented assertively, aggressively, or nonassertively. Alberti and Emmons describe the receiver of assertive messages as more likely to feel enhanced, but the person who is on the receiving end of aggressive behavior may feel defensive or hurt, and the recipient of nonassertiveness may build up anger or guilt in response to the self-denying style of the sender.[63] It is important to note that no one is always assertive, but in reality, everyone may display aggressiveness or nonassertiveness in certain specific situations.[64]

Anger and Anger Management

For most persons it is difficult to behave assertively when experiencing intense anger. On the basis of past learning and experience, many individuals display aggressiveness either directly or indirectly (passive-aggressiveness) or act nonassertively. Carol Tavris in her challenging popular book, *Anger: The Misunderstood Emotion*, presents three powerful myths surrounding anger. The first myth is stated as "Aggression is the instinctive catharsis for anger."[65] According to Tavris, there are some "people for whom aggression is not cathartic," and who "feel guilty about expressing hostility."[66] Tavris cites a number of research studies which lead to the conclusion that ventilating anger may have quite the opposite effect than being cathartic. For some individuals in some settings, getting angry simply leads to greater expression of anger. This may be the case in families where yelling precedes physical violence.[67]

Another myth concerning anger is: "Talking out anger gets rid of it—or at least makes you feel less angry."[68] Tavris suggests that instead of reducing anger, talking about it may, in fact, rehearse it, because describing one's hostility can contribute to building up emotional arousal and lead to a greater degree of anger.[69]

Those interested in exploring anger felt by women are invited to read *The Dance of Anger: A Woman's Guide to Changing the Patterns of Intimate Relationships* by Harriet Lerner. Lerner suggests strategies that women may wish to employ in confronting and working through the anger that accompanies many relationships.

Assertiveness is one of several helpful strategies for managing anger in self and others. Robert Alberti and Michael Emmons, in *Your Perfect Right: A Guide to Assertive Living*, describe a number of constructive approaches to handling anger. Among the suggestions provided by these authors are: (1) understand that individuals are responsible for their own feelings; (2) it is possible to express anger in an assertive fashion; (3) it is important to recognize triggers for personal anger and not set oneself up; and (4) learn and apply assertiveness and stress management techniques.[70]

Alberti and Emmons present a strategy for an adult in dealing with another adult who "is furious and directing their full hostility at you," by suggesting the following steps: (1) "Allow the angry person to vent the strong feelings"; (2) "Respond only with acceptance at first ('It's obvious that you're really upset about this')"; (3) "Take a deep breath, and try to stay as calm as possible"; (4) "Offer to discuss a solution later—giving the person time to cool off . . ."; (5) "Take another deep breath"; (6) "Arrange a specific time to pursue this matter"; and (7) "Keep in mind that no immediate solution is likely."[71] *This strategy is designed for dealing with the anger of people known to us to be nonviolent. Allowing people to vent their anger if they might couple it with physical or verbal abuse may place an individual in harm's way.*

Assertiveness Skill Building

Most people appear to be capable of changing their level of assertiveness in given situations. If readers find their behavior is at times relatively nonassertive or aggressive, they may wish to apply various assertive techniques. Two books with concrete suggestions for behavioral changes are: Alberti and Emmons' *Your Perfect Right: A Guide to Assertive Living* and Manuel Smith's *When I Say No, I Feel Guilty.*

Alberti and Emmons suggest seventeen specific steps for increasing assertiveness. Included among the seventeen steps are: (1) "Observe your own behavior"; (2) "Keep track of your assertiveness"; (3) "Set realistic goals for yourself"; (4) "Concentrate on a particular situation"; (5) "Review your responses"; (6) "Observe an effective model"; (7) "Consider alternative responses"; (8) "Imagine yourself handling the situation"; (9) "Try it out"; (10) "Get feedback"; and (11) "Set up social reinforcement."[72]

The authors encourage readers to try out new behaviors in role-playing with friends or others before using them in real life settings. Role-playing provides a safe environment in which to practice assertiveness.[73] Manuel Smith describes several specific communication tactics to be employed in certain situations. For instance, Smith advises readers to use the "broken record" technique when asserting their position. When applying this strategy, persons are to calmly repeat over and over again their position without getting angry or wavering.[74] Smith finds this technique particularly helpful in dealing with representatives of bureaucracies (e.g., attempting to correct an error in a bill from a utility company). Also, Smith offers several techniques for use in handling criticism. Many persons are uncomfortable in giving and receiving that which can be perceived as negative. Smith describes "fogging" as:

> a skill that teaches acceptance of manipulative criticism by calmly acknowledging to your critic the probability that there may be some truth in what he says, yet allows you to remain your own judge of what you do.[75]

People who receive what they feel is manipulative criticism are instructed to reply "as if the [critic] were a 'fog bank.' . . . Inevitably, we give up trying to alter the persistent, independent, nonmanipulable fog and leave it alone."[76] Another technique that can be offered in response to criticism is "negative inquiry," through which the receiver is seeking additional information if it is beneficial or exhausting the sender if the message turns out to be manipulative.[77] For example, if a spouse is critical of his or her mate's selection of clothes, the one who is criticized may continue to respond with variations of "What is it about my clothes that you don't like?" and "What is that you don't find attractive about my jacket?" If the criticism is well founded, it can be communicated, but if has no basis in fact, it can be dismissed.

Another valuable technique Smith describes is "negative assertion." This technique allows an individual to admit a mistake when hearing valid criticism without the necessity of apologizing and groveling. In this way one agrees that one has erred, but without the accompanying feelings of defensiveness.[78] Stanlee Phelps and Nancy Austin describe specific assertiveness strategies for application by women in their self-help book, *The Assertive Woman*. Techniques for use in work, family, and love relationships are discussed in detail.

Male-Female Communication

In her popular book *You Just Don't Understand: Women and Men in Conversation,* Deborah Tannen asserts that the differing conversational styles of the genders is a key factor contributing to the misunderstandings between men and women. According to Tannen, men utilize "report-talk" while women use "rapport-talk." In the final paragraph of the book, Tannen proclaims:

> If you understand gender differences in what I call conversational style, you may not be able to prevent disagreements from arising, but you stand a better chance of preventing them from spiraling out of control.[79]

In *The Mismeasure of Woman* Carol Tavris includes a chapter entitled "Speaking of Gender" in which she argues that the differences observed in male and female conversational styles are not based on gender, but rather on the distribution of power.[80] Citing research from linguistics and psychology, Tavris thinks that styles of conversation depend more on the power balance or imbalance between two parties than on their particular genders.[81] While Tannen's book may offer insights to interested readers, those same readers should understand that many social scientists and linguists see real limitations with Tannen's basic premise. Readers interested in male-female communication may also wish to consult Harriet Lerner's book, *The Dance of Anger: A Woman's Guide to Changing the Patterns of Intimate Relationships.*

Meaning and Happiness

In this chapter, previous sections devoted to communication issues relate to the management of behavioral styles. This final section on meaning and happiness centers on the more fundamental life questions addressed in the self-help psychology literature. About twenty years ago, when one of the authors of this book was giving a public lecture on interpersonal communication, a member of the audience asked a variation of the following question: "What is happiness?" An answer to the question was naively offered, satisfying neither the audience member nor the speaker. *As people seek to uncover life's meaning as well as personal happiness, they often find that a number of popular books, many with a definite religious orientation, aim to aid readers in this most difficult journey. Given the individualized nature of meaning and happiness, self-help psychology books addressing these topics may disappoint readers who are searching for particular answers reflecting their own personal circumstances.*

The Search for Meaning

Each of us in our own way seeks to figure out a purpose in living. Some gain structure and possible answers to questions surrounding the meaning of life through a formal religion, a personalized belief system, work, relationships, community service, or a combination of these factors. Existential psychiatrists and psychologists like Viktor Frankl and Rollo May assert that the central issue in mental health is a meaningful or authentic existence. Those who espouse an existential perspective often discuss the following: (1) "existence and essence"; (2) "choice, freedom, and courage"; (3) "meaning, value, and obligation"; and (4) "existential anxiety and the encounter with nothingness."[82] Even though each person is born in a specified existence in a particular society, a particular family, and a particular physical body, that individual still can determine the type of person she is to become. People are free to some extent to make choices, many of which require courage, and every person must seek satisfying personal values. When persons are unable to find meaning either through inaction or by settling for an "inauthentic" life (for example, taking up an occupation that is unsatisfying but lucrative), they may feel "existential anxiety," which is caused by a fear of "nonbeing" or "nothingness." The existentialists suggest that death is the ultimate symbol of nonbeing, and that in order to truly find meaning in life, an individual must face nothingness through living a life filled with personal meaning.[83] Readers interested in the existential perspective are encouraged to read Viktor Frankl's *Man's Search for Meaning: An Introduction to Logotherapy.*

Self-Efficacy and the Illusion of Control

One very promising concept for understanding meaning and happiness is termed *self-efficacy,* which involves persons' belief that they can effectively perform a specified activity.[84] If people perceive that they have control over their successes because their accomplishments have come about through internal causes, they may be somewhat better prepared to manage the various traumas which interfere with human happiness.[85] In her popular book *Positive Illusions: Creative Self-Deception and the Healthy Mind,* Shelley Taylor writes:

> Most people say they are happy most of the time. . . . Moreover, positive illusions about one's personal qualities, degree of control, and likely future appear to promote happiness. People who believe that they have a lot of control in their lives and who believe that the future will bring them

even more happiness are happier by their own reports than people who lack these perceptions.[86]

The illusion promoted by optimism appears to have many positive effects. Martin E. P. Seligman devotes a chapter to "Optimistic Life" in his useful book *Learned Optimism*.[87] One key technique for conquering disturbing beliefs that impede optimism is called *disputation*.[88] As an example, Seligman describes a graduate student returning to school at midlife who receives a lower than desired grade on a first exam. The student believes that she must be "stupid," "too old," and so forth. As a consequence, the student feels "dejected and useless." By engaging in disputation, the woman considers that she may be "blowing things out of proportion."[89] Furthermore, she attributes her lack of success on the initial exam to her work and family commitments, and reasons that age is not a key issue in this instance. As a result of the disputation, she begins to feel better about both herself and her performance on the exam.

Flow

An intriguing concept which has been linked to meaning and happiness is termed flow. In *Flow: The Psychology of Optimal Experience*, Mihaly Csikszentmihalyi suggests some activities are intrinsically satisfying, and that when a person is engaged in performing them, a subjective experience called flow may occur.[90] While experiences of flow differ markedly, they do exhibit two common themes. First of all, "flow involves a focused and ordered state of consciousness," and second, it "involves an equivalent ratio of skills to challenges."[91] The latter theme reflects the fear or anxiety which may occur if an individual's level of skill is no match for the challenge; if on the other hand, the task is no real challenge for a person with superior skills, that individual may experience boredom.[92] When people experience flow, they are pleasantly lost in the process of what they are doing. Certainly those people whose jobs afford them the frequent experience of flow have found a high degree of happiness in their work.

Summary

This chapter encompassed a variety of self-development topics. It addressed the notion of distinguishing what people can change most easily about themselves from what they cannot; gender concerns, particularly gender differences and women's and men's self-development; communication skill building, including the basic elements of interpersonal communication, assertiveness, anger and its management; and male-female communication, as well as meaning and happiness.

Even though subjects related to self-development are immensely popular, it is difficult to find high-quality self-help psychology books on relevant subjects that meet the criteria delineated in Chapter 1. The clear exception to this statement is in the area of assertiveness, where a number of excellent sources exist. Several highly popular books address happiness and meaning, but a great many approach the subject from a particular religious perspective, thus excluding readers from other spiritual or value orientations.

RECOMMENDED TITLES

Distinguishing What Can Be Changed from What Cannot

Seligman, Martin E. P. *What You Can Change and What You Can't: The Complete Guide to Successful Self-Improvement*. New York: Knopf, 1994.

Psychologist Seligman explores the conflict between biological psychiatry, which contends that genetic predisposition and brain chemistry underlie most disorders (making them difficult, if not impossible, to change), and the self-improvement movement, which asserts that all behavior can be changed. In this examination the author describes what individuals can change, which types of interventions are most effective, and what cannot be changed. Conditions that can be changed with considerable success are outlined.

In describing what cannot be changed, Seligman concludes that dieting over time rarely ever works, and that changing sexual identity and sexual orientation are extremely difficult, if not impossible, to do. He asserts that treatment programs for alcoholism are no better than the natural course of recovery, and that adult personality problems are not improved by reliving childhood trauma. This title is also annotated in Chapter 7 on psychological disorders.

Gender Differences

Tavris, Carol. *The Mismeasure of Woman.* New York: Simon & Schuster, 1992.

Social psychologist Tavris examines the consequences of comparing men and women from a developmental perspective. As part of the comparison, Tavris argues that men are considered the norm, while women are different. In one line of thinking, men are seen as normal and women, being opposite, are viewed as deficient. In another view, men are normal, women are opposite from men, but are viewed as superior to men. In yet another, men are normal and women are or should be like them. Tavris asserts that nothing about men and women is essentially different in terms of personality traits, abilities, dreams, and desires.

Women's Self-Development

Caplan, Paula J. *Don't Blame Mother: Mending the Mother-Daughter Relationship.* New York: Harper, 1989.

The roots of the mother-daughter rift are explored in depth. The author sees that mother blaming still exists in psychiatric and psychological practice. The images of the Good Mother, the Bad Mother, and the Wicked Witch provide stereotypes and an additional basis for misunderstanding. In situations involving a mother who is cold and distant to her daughter, the daughter who believes the myth of the Good Mother sees the lack of affection as evidence that she is unlovable. Caplan explores ways that mothers and daughters can reduce the pain surrounding their relationships in the past. By looking past the stereotypes and their impact, such women can understand the barriers between them and how myths have hampered their relationship.

Harris, Maxine. *Down from the Pedestal: Moving beyond Idealized Images of Womanhood.* New York: Doubleday, 1994.

Harris, a clinical psychologist, finds that women are often trapped by trying to live a life based on idealized images. By adhering to these images, women may sacrifice their own individuality, while trying to fit the mold as the Good Mother, the Faithful Wife, or the Wise Old Woman. The author describes the images of young womanhood, midlife women, and older women, and the impact living these images has on women at each life stage. Harris asserts that women can break away from these images by exploring the themes surrounding their individual lives. By applying a thematic approach, women can view their lives on a continuum that allows for individual choice rather than adherence to a particular image. The theme of young womanhood is one of exploration as one tries new relationships, goes to college, and lives on one's own for the first time. In midlife, the theme is one of nurturance and creativity, as women raise children, counsel employees, and help their aging parents. In older women, integration, reflection, and contemplation are themes.

Lerner, Harriet Goldhor. *The Dance of Intimacy: A Woman's Guide to Courageous Acts of Change in Key Relationships.* New York: Perennial Library/Harper, 1989.

Lerner's view of intimacy and the role it plays in individual lives stresses the importance of self-focus, open communication, and a respect for differences in others. It also stresses the importance of staying emotionally connected to others during periods of anxiety. Self-focus involves realizing that changing the behavior of another person is something that only that person can do. In building intimacy, the individual reflects on her own values, perspectives, and beliefs, and is able to express these ideas. In doing so, the person builds the foundation for a more solid self, which serves as the basis for intimacy.

Men's Self-Development

Fanning, Patrick, and Matthew McKay. *Being A Man: A Guide to the New Masculinity.* Oakland, Calif.: New Harbinger, 1993.

The authors work from several basic assumptions: that men are as good as women, that differences exist between genders, and, most important, that the many similarities between men and women provide more chances for collaboration and cooperation than for conflict. Fanning and McKay stress the importance of the relationship between father and son, since the father usually is the first teacher of what masculinity is.

The next section covers the inner life, integrity, and work life. Relationships of all kinds are also examined: male friendship, committed relationships, marriage, and fatherhood. In a section on expressing one's emotions, the authors discuss clarifying and expressing feelings, being assertive, and controlling anger. A closing chapter on health issues for men completes this practical guide.

Basics of Effective Communication

Sending Messages

Ekman, Paul. *Telling Lies: Clues to Deceit in the Marketplace, Politics, and Marriage.* New York: Norton, 1985.

In his original studies of psychiatric patients, Ekman explored verbal or nonverbal clues given when an individual lies. This was especially crucial when treating suicidal patients. One such patient had lied to her doctor to get a weekend pass only to admit to him later that she was still suicidal and had planned to commit suicide when she was out of the hospital. Upon reviewing the videotape of this patient, Ekman and his colleagues observed several visual cues. As the study continued, the author was able to detect visual cues, other nonverbal behavior, and changes in speech patterns as indicators of lying.

A number of examples from politics, criminal cases, and the author's own studies examine why people lie, how it is done, and how it can be detected. Ekman also includes a chapter on the polygraph machine or "lie detector," which the author views as only an indicator of how an individual responds to stress rather than indicating whether an individual is lying.

McKay, Matthew, Martha Davis, and Patrick Fanning. *Messages: The Communication Book.* Oakland, Calif.: New Harbinger, 1983.

The authors emphasize communication skills rather than communication theory throughout this practical guide. Basic skills include active listening, self-disclosure (communicating information about oneself to another), and expressing ideas, thoughts, and feelings effectively. McKay and his associates describe the importance of body language, voice quality and tone, and clear and concise language in building communication skills. A separate section concentrates on developing conflict resolution skills: assertiveness, fair fighting, and negotiation. Discussions conclude by concentrating on social, family, and public speaking skills.

Assertiveness

Alberti, Robert, and Michael Emmons. *Your Perfect Right: A Guide to Assertive Living.* 5th ed. San Luis Obispo, Calif.: Impact Pub., 1986.

By defining assertive behavior, the authors present the reader with the key features of this communication style. These include acting in one's own best interests, standing up for one's self, expressing feelings honestly, and recognizing the rights of others. The difference between assertive, nonassertive, and aggressive behavior is also discussed as are the components of assertive behavior, which consist of physical closeness, gestures, facial expression, voice tone, inflection, and volume, smooth speech, timing of the message, listening, thinking, and the content of the message. The authors also explore barriers to assertive behavior. Methods for developing assertive behavior skills are presented as well as recommendations for using the new skill at work, in romantic relationships, and with angry people.

Davis, Martha, Elizabeth Robbins Eschelman, and Matthew McKay. *The Relaxation and Stress Reduction Workbook.* Richmond, Calif.: New Harbinger, 1982.

Assertiveness training is but one of many stress reduction techniques described in this practical guide. The authors present a step-by-step approach to assertiveness by identifying three styles of interpersonal behavior—aggressive, passive, and assertive; reviewing situations where one can use assertiveness; describing problem scenes; and using assertive behavior in these problem scenes. Readers also learn assertive body language. The last step involves strategies which can be used if the person ignores an assertive request or responds aggressively.

Phelps, Stanlee, and Nancy Austin. *The Assertive Woman: A New Look.* 2d ed. San Luis Obispo, Calif.: Impact Pub., 1987.

In *The Assertive Woman* the authors identify four behavioral styles: passive, aggressive, indirectly aggressive, and assertive. Attitudes or myths which inhibit women from becoming assertive are explored, including the following: women should be seen and not heard, should not rock the boat, and should not ask for what they want out of fear of being seen as selfish. The authors examine a model for learning assertive behavior, which includes a description or modeling of the behavior, practicing the new behavior, reinforcing the desired behavior, and receiving accurate and rapid feedback.

According to the authors, women are particularly susceptible to the Compassion Trap. Because of women's traditional role as caretakers, nurturers, and mothers, women may be asked more often to take on these responsibilities without help from other family members. Specific strategies for facing the Compassion Trap are outlined.

Smith, Manuel J. *When I Say No, I Feel Guilty: How to Cope—Using the Skills of Systematic Assertive Therapy*. New York: Bantam, 1975.

Smith outlines a series of ten assertive rights and provides readers with strategies to maintain these rights. Persistence and other approaches for making assertive requests are described. Assertive responses to criticism, to consumer conflicts (e.g., shoddy service), to work conflicts, and to relationship conflicts are also covered.

Anger and the Anger Management

Lerner, Harriet Goldhor. *The Dance of Anger: A Woman's Guide to Changing the Patterns of Intimate Relationships*. New York: Perennial Library, Harper, 1985.

Lerner focuses on the issues of women and anger. In defining the "Nice Lady" stereotype, the author finds women are expected to keep angry feelings to themselves to avoid open conflict. Additionally, women avoid making forthright statements about their feelings if these statements would make the other person uncomfortable or would expose differences. The goal of the book is to help readers identify sources of women's anger and to learn to take action by clarifying their own beliefs, learning communication skills, and by anticipating reactions of others when the person responds directly. Lerner asserts that women, in dealing with anger, feel that they must choose between having a relationship and having a self. The author contends that is possible to have both.

McKay, Matthew, Peter D. Rogers, Judith McKay, and edited by Kirk Johnson. *When Anger Hurts: Quieting the Storm Within*. Oakland, Calif.: New Harbinger, 1989.

McKay and his associates provide readers with a practical guide to understanding anger, its physical and emotional costs, and its benefits. Using the methods set out by the authors, individuals can develop their ability to control destructive anger venting, reduce the frequency and intensity of physiological response, change beliefs that result in chronic anger, identify and cope with stress, and learn to communicate without anger. This approach focuses on anger toward others. The authors examine the myths, costs, and skills needed to cope with anger. In addition, anger in the home is discussed.

Tavris, Carol. *Anger: The Misunderstood Emotion*. New York: Touchstone Bks., published by Simon & Schuster, 1982.

In a thoughtful and insightful analysis, Tavris explores what anger is and is not. By defining anger as a process and a way of communicating rather than a disease, the author sees anger as a social action. Beliefs about anger and the interpretations of the experience are also seen as important. The author expresses concern about the generalizations surrounding anger, particularly those which label an emotional response to a relatively trivial event (breaking a shoelace) or a major event (being fired) as anger without differentiating between the two types. Tavris asserts that there are different angers, processes, and consequences. The author also discusses the following basic assumptions about anger: anger and aggression are linked; anger is an instinctive response to threat or frustration, and if anger is blocked, it turns inward in depression, guilt, shame, anxiety, or lethargy. Drawing from studies in the social and biological sciences, Tavris challenges these assumptions and other basic questions about anger. The findings make fascinating reading.

Male-Female Communication

Tannen, Deborah. *You Just Don't Understand: Women and Men in Conversation.* New York: Morrow, 1990.

Linguist Tannen views male-female communication as a cross-cultural activity with men in one cultural group and women in another. According to Tannen, women seek connection whenever they communicate, while men seek independence in their interactions. In decision making women generally consult with their partner before making plans to reach a decision, whereas men may view consulting with a spouse beforehand as asking for permission. The author asserts that women speak a language of connection and intimacy, while men speak a language of status and independence. Drawing a parallel between regional dialects, Tannen coins a new term, *genderlects,* to describe this communication style. Citing research on the types of games and the language used by boys and girls when playing in same-sex groups, the author sees boys as playing games with a hierarchical structure, many rules, and the chance to demonstrate their skills. Girls play in smaller groups and often compromise to continue playing. Tannen sees these patterns continuing into adulthood. By making readers aware of the communication differences and how to work around them, the author gives a new perspective to the complex universe of communication.

Meaning and Happiness

Search for Meaning

Frankl, Viktor E. *Man's Search for Meaning: An Introduction to Logotherapy.* New York: Washington Square, 1968.

Psychiatrist Frankl, who survived his imprisonment at the Nazi concentration camp Auschwitz, developed a new approach to understanding human behavior. He contends that unlike psychoanalysis which focuses on the individual's past through introspection, logotherapy looks at the future and toward the meaning of the person's life. This approach does not ask individuals "What is the meaning of life?" but rather "What is the meaning of your life?" It also places the responsibility for creating and achieving meaning in one's life directly in the hands of the individual.

Self Efficacy and the Illusion of Control

Csikszentmihalyi, Mihaly. *Flow: The Psychology of Optimal Experience.* New York: Harper, 1990.

In *Flow* the author explores states of "optimal experience" when individuals report feelings of enjoyment, concentration, and deep involvement. As part of these peak experiences, individuals feel strong, alert, in control, and unselfconscious. Flow can occur as a result of many activities, including exercise, reaching a long anticipated goal, listening to music, and so forth. These optimal experiences are not just chance occurrences. With this understanding, readers can see how the process works and how it can be applied to their lives.

Seligman, Martin E. P. *Learned Optimism.* New York: Knopf, 1991.

Psychologist Seligman encourages readers to go beyond the power of positive thinking, to move from pessimism to optimism, and to change the way they think about adversity, its impact on their beliefs, and the consequences that result. The author sees pessimism as a learned behavior. As a learned behavior, it can be unlearned or changed in this case to optimistic thinking. Seligman provides a variety of techniques to develop optimism. These include challenging the evidence, searching for alternatives, and reviewing the implications as well as the role pessimistic thought patterns play in an individual's life.

Taylor, Shelley E. *Positive Illusions: Creative Self-Deception and the Healthy Mind.* New York: Basic Books, 1989.

For a number of years, mental health professionals have measured an individual's psychological health by how accurately they perceive reality. Taylor challenges this position by asserting that most people perceive themselves, the world, and the future more positively than reality would indicate. These illusions appear in three categories: self-enhancement, the perception of one's self and attributes in a more positive light; an exaggerated sense of personal control, which involves influencing events to produce positive outcomes; and unrealistic optimism about what the future holds in store. After identifying these categories, the author explores the nature of these positive illusions as well as their development. Instead of labeling these illusions as delusional, Taylor views them as adaptive behaviors that can enhance an individual's physical and emotional well-being.

NOTES

1. Stephen B. Fried, *American Popular Psychology: An Interdisciplinary Research Guide* (New York: Garland, 1994), xvii; Steven Starker, *Oracle at the Supermarket: The American Preoccupation with Self-Help Books* (New Brunswick, N.J.: Transaction, 1989), 15.
2. Fried, *American Popular Psychology,* xvii.
3. Ibid.
4. Starker, *Oracle at the Supermarket,* 63.
5. Ibid., 125, 142.
6. Martin E. P. Seligman, *What You Can Change and What You Can't* (New York: Knopf, 1994), 244–53.
7. Ibid., 246.
8. Ibid., 247.
9. Ibid., 249.
10. Carol Tavris, "The Mismeasure of Woman: Paradoxes and Perspectives in the Study of Gender," in *Psychological Perspectives on Human Diversity in America,* ed. Jacqueline Goodchilds (Washington, D.C.: American Psychological Association, 1991), 91–136.
11. Ibid., 94.
12. Ibid.
13. Ibid., 94–95.
14. Carol Tavris, *The Mismeasure of Woman* (New York: Simon & Schuster, 1992), 80.
15. Ibid., 80.

16. Carol Tavris, "Beautiful Souls and Different Voices," in *The Mismeasure of Woman*, 57–92.

17. Tavris, "The Mismeasure of Woman," in *Psychological Perspectives on Human Diversity in America*, 100.

18. Maxine Harris, *Down from the Pedestal: Moving beyond Idealized Images of Womanhood* (New York: Doubleday, 1994), 3–23.

19. Ibid., 10.

20. Ibid., 11.

21. Ibid.

22. Ibid., 13.

23. Ibid., 17–18.

24. Ibid., 18.

25. Ibid., 45.

26. Ibid., 74.

27. Ibid., 109.

28. Ibid., 154, 183, 214.

29. Stephanie Shields and Beth Koster, "Emotional Stereotyping of Parents in Child Rearing Manuals," *Social Psychology Quarterly* 52 (Mar. 1989): 44–55.

30. Harriet Lerner, "Our Mother/Her Mother/Our Self," in *The Dance of Intimacy: A Woman's Guide to Courageous Acts of Change in Key Relationships* (New York: Harper, 1989), 183–200.

31. Patrick Fanning and Matthew McKay, *Being a Man: A Guide to the New Masculinity* (Oakland, Calif.: New Harbinger, 1993), 4.

32. Ibid.

33. David Cherrington, *Organizational Behavior: The Management of Individual and Organizational Performance* (Needham Heights, Mass.: Allyn & Bacon, 1994), 533–36.

34. Matthew McKay, Martha Davis, and Patrick Fanning, *Messages: The Communication Book* (Oakland, Calif.: New Harbinger, 1983), 39–55.

35. Ibid., 41.

36. Ibid., 43–44.

37. Ibid., 44.

38. David Johnson and Frank Johnson, *Joining Together: Group Therapy and Group Skills*, 3d ed. (New York: Prentice Hall, 1987), 178.

39. McKay, Davis, and Fanning, *Messages: The Communication Book*, 14–16.

40. Ibid., 14.

41. Ibid., 16–19.

42. Ibid., 28.

43. Nancy Henley, *Body Politics* (New York: Prentice Hall, 1977), 27–42.

44. Edward Hall, "A System for the Notation of Proxemic Behavior," *American Anthropologist* 65 (Oct. 1963), 1003–26.

45. McKay, Davis, and Fanning, *Messages: The Communication Book*, 64–65.

46. Joseph DeVito, *The Interpersonal Communication Book* (New York: Harper, 1989), 250–52.

47. Ibid.

48. Paul Ekman and Wallace Friesen, "The Repertoire of Nonverbal Behavior: Categories, Origins, Usage, and Coding," *Semiotica* 1 (Feb./Mar. 1969): 49–98.

49. DeVito, *The Interpersonal Communication Book*, 229.

50. Marilynn Brewer and William Crano, *Social Psychology* (St. Paul, Minn.: West Pub., 1994), 110.

51. DeVito, *The Interpersonal Communication Book*, 238–39.

52. Henley, *Body Politics*, 108–10.

53. McKay, Davis, and Fanning, *Messages: The Communication Book*, 69–71.

54. Ibid., 71.

55. Ibid., 13.

56. Robert Alberti and Michael Emmons, *Your Perfect Right: A Guide to Assertive Living* (San Luis Obispo, Calif.: Impact Pub., 1986), 7

57. Martha Davis, Matthew McKay, and Elizabeth Robbins Eshelman, *The Relaxation and Stress Reduction Workbook*, Richmond, Calif.: New Harbinger, 1982, 133–34.

58. Ibid., 133.

59. Manuel Smith, *When I Say No, I Feel Guilty* (New York: Bantam, 1975), 49, 53.

60. Ibid., 46.

61. Alberti and Emmons, *Your Perfect Right*, 27–31.

62. Ibid., 28.

63. Ibid., 29.

64. Ibid., 31.

65. Carol Tavris, *Anger: The Misunderstood Emotion* (New York: Simon & Schuster, 1982), 123.

66. Ibid., 127.

67. Ibid., 128–29.

68. Ibid., 131.

69. Ibid., 132–35.

70. Alberti and Emmons, *Your Perfect Right*, 140–42.

71. Ibid., 143.

72. Ibid., 101–5.

73. Ibid., 104.

74. Smith, *When I Say No, I Feel Guilty*, 73–80.

75. Ibid., 323.

76. Ibid., 104.

77. Ibid., 324.

78. Ibid., 115–19.

79. Deborah Tannen, *You Just Don't Understand: Women and Men in Conversation* (New York: Ballantine, 1990), 298.

80. Tavris, "Speaking of Gender," in *The Mismeasure of Woman,* 297–301.

81. Tavris, *The Mismeasure of Woman,* 298–99.

82. Robert Carson and James Butcher, *Abnormal Psychology and Modern Life,* 9th ed. (New York: HarperCollins, 1992), 79.

83. Ibid.

84. Albert Bandura, "Human Agency in Social Cognitive Theory," *American Psychologist* 44 (Sept. 1989): 1175–84.

85. Shelley Taylor, *Positive Illusions: Creative Self-Deception and the Healthy Mind* (New York: Basic Books, 1989), 31.

86. Ibid., 49.

87. Martin E. P. Seligman, "The Optimistic Life," in *Learned Optimism* (New York: Knopf, 1990), 207–34.

88. Ibid., 218–19.

89. Ibid., 219.

90. Mihaly Csikszentmihalyi, *Flow: The Psychology of Optimal Experience* (New York: Harper, 1990), 74.

91. Dan McAdams, *The Person: An Introduction to Personality Psychology* (New York: Harcourt, 1994), 465–67.

92. Ibid., 466.

CHAPTER

6

Stress Management

Stress impacts everyone to varying degrees, resulting in a fleeting, mild anxiety for some and contributing to psychological immobilization and life-threatening disease for others. The removal of all life stress is not only an impossible goal but also an inappropriate one, since certain amounts and kinds of stress may be beneficial. Phillip Rice uses the term *stress* in three ways: (1) a stimulus which results in an individual feeling anxious or aroused; (2) an internal state of arousal; or (3) the body's physical reaction to an environmental stimulus.[1] The reader is cautioned regarding the meanings ascribed to stress since, in popular American culture, "'stress' has become a catch-all category, encompassing everything from quantifiable events in the psychophysiology laboratory to the entire scope of human unhappiness."[2]

Both negative and positive consequences to environmental stress occur. For example, conflicting demands on a job may contribute to an individual's feelings of helplessness, being overwhelmed, and a lowered sense of self-esteem. On the other hand, the same person may be "excited" as she readies for her passion:

jumping out of airplanes, for which she has trained diligently. A possibly terrifying experience for one human being may be exhilarating for another. Furthermore, a body of scientific research documents the notion that a number of psychological and physical problems are associated with either too much stress or too little stimulation, contrasted with a moderate or optimal level of arousal. Certainly an optimal level of arousal for a particular person may be far different for another. Also, people have developed differing strategies for coping with life demands, and so each individual can utilize specific strengths, attempt to compensate for personal deficiencies, or learn new and better approaches to managing stress.

Given the individualized nature of stress, any program aimed at its management should certainly be designed to fit personal circumstances. *When using self-help materials on stress management, the reader is strongly advised to determine whether the recommended strategies are generic, "a one-size-fits-all" approach, or include information which allows the reader to modify the instructions to fit her individual requirements.*

The Physical Aspects of Stress

The Fight-or-Flight Response

The fight-or-flight response, a pattern of physiological changes, occurs when a human being is presented with a stressful stimulus. The body endeavors to manage the threat through an integrated response controlled by the hypothalamus, which is located in the brain. As a reaction to a stressor, the hypothalamus directs the sympathetic nervous system to release hormones (epinephrine and norepinephrine), which move the body into arousal. Some of the resulting bodily alterations reflect in the following reactions: the muscles tense, the breathing quickens, the heart rate races, the blood pressure climbs, and the metabolism increases. Although the fight-or-flight response is highly appropriate when an individual is truly threatened, this chronic stress reaction may produce negative consequences if it is activated frequently over a prolonged period of time (for example, if individuals' neck and shoulder muscles tense at the very thought of their job). Highly readable discussions of the significant physical aspects of stress can be found in Herbert Benson and Eileen Stuart, *The Wellness*

Book: The Comprehensive Guide to Maintaining Health and Treating Stress-Related Illness, James Gordon, *Stress Management,* and in Lyle Miller, Alma Smith, and Larry Rothstein, *The Stress Solution: An Action Plan to Manage the Stress in Your Life.*

Physical Problems Associated with Stress

Chronic stress may lead to a variety of physical disorders, a factor contributing to the development of such fields as psychosomatic medicine and health psychology. Diseases which involve the interplay of both mind and body are considered to be psychosomatic. Currently, physicians and psychologists also refer to psychosomatic ailments as psychophysiological, since both bodily and mental elements may play a role in virtually all disease.[3]

The immune system has a profound impact on psychosomatic, infectious, and degenerative illness.[4] Research findings demonstrate that stress, especially recurring stress, serves to suppress the immune system, and that this suppression is in direct proportion to the magnitude of the stressor.[5]

A variety of scientific theories attempt to explain the links between stress and disease. Although the theories differ in their analysis of the reasons why a particular organ experiences dysfunction or a particular disease develops, the major perspectives are in agreement "that indeed over-stimulation and excessive wear of target organs lead to stress-related dysfunction and disease."[6]

Numerous physical ailments have been linked with human stress: headaches, elevated blood pressure, numbness and tingling in limbs, chest pain, allergies, frequent colds, skin rashes, and diabetic reactions. A number of cardiovascular, gastrointestinal, musculoskeletal, respiratory, and skin disorders are, in part, related to stress and the body's response to it. *The reader should keep in mind that although these physical symptoms may be associated with stress, they may also be signs of physical afflictions which can be exacerbated by stress. Thus, the reader is advised to seek medical assistance if any of these symptoms persist.*

Cardiovascular Disorders

Seventeen million Americans are impacted by migraine headaches resulting from the blood vessels in the brain constricting and dilating. Commonly misperceived as simply a very bad headache, in actuality, a *migraine* is a vascular disorder, usually involving one side of the head. Lasting around six hours, although the exact duration varies, typically migraines appear after a stressful period has ended, and it is quite common for migraines to occur on weekends. While medications may be of benefit in combatting some of the symptoms, psychotherapy and life-style modifications may be the most lasting of interventions.[7] Biofeedback treatment specifically designed for headache control holds considerable promise for many migraine patients.

Much has been written about the possible causal relationship between coronary heart disease and stress. Each year around three hundred thousand persons die in the United States as a result of coronary heart disease.[8] A disease of the arteries that feed into the heart, coronary heart disease results in blocked arteries that cause the heart muscle not to obtain the necessary oxygen, resulting in great pain, called *angina,* in the chest and other areas. Pains caused by blockage of the coronary arteries may result in shoulder and arm pain as well, but coronary arteries can be blocked without any noticeable symptoms. More serious than angina is *myocardial infarction,* which is the technical term for heart attack. When blood flow is blocked and causes damage to the heart's muscle tissue, a heart attack occurs.

Some of the most significant risk factors for coronary heart disease are: an elevated blood pressure, high serum cholesterol, and cigarette smoking. Chronic stress may well play a role in coronary heart disease because the body's response to stress includes increases in blood pressure and serum cholesterol as well as an accelerated heart rate. Much has been written about a possible relationship between the Type A behavior pattern and cardiovascular disease; we shall address this topic later in this chapter under the heading "Type A Personality and Stress."

Gastrointestinal Disorders

According to Jerrold Greenberg, the role of the gastrointestinal system "is to accept, break down, and distribute food, and to eliminate waste products resulting from this process."[9] The following aspects of the gastrointestinal system may be directly affected by a chronic stress response: (1) an increased supply of hydrochloric acid in the stomach and a reduction in gastric mucus shielding the stomach's lining, which can lead to the development of ulcers; (2) peristalsis, which refers to the rhythmic movements of the intestines, may be slowed down, resulting in constipation or sped up, causing diarrhea; (3) blockage of the pancreatic and bile ducts; or (4) pancreatitis, which refers to the inflammation of the pancreas.

Musculoskeletal Disorders

As part of the stress response, muscles tense. Chronically tense muscles contribute to a number of problems. For example, if an individual's nervous system frequently signals his muscles to contract, this further activates the mind, which, in turn, produces more muscle tension. Furthermore, according to Daniel Girdano and George Everly, "chronically tense muscles result in numerous psychosomatic disorders including headaches, backache, spasms of the colon and the esophagus . . ., posture problems, asthma, tightness in the throat and chest cavity, some eye problems, lockjaw, muscle tears and pulls, and perhaps rheumatoid arthritis."[10]

When muscles contract, the result is tension, sometimes referred to as *bracing*. It is possible to be bracing without realizing it. Fists may be squeezed during a conflict with one's child, mate, or parent without awareness one is doing so. Frequent bracing can contribute to a wide variety of physical disorders. *Readers who experience chronic muscle tension are encouraged to consider learning and applying some form of stress relaxation, including autogenic training, meditation, or progressive muscle relaxation.*

Those who are interested in learning more about the deleterious effects of stress on the muscular system and on the benefits of a sustained relaxation program should consult Herbert Benson's *The Relaxation Response*. A variety of stress management strategies will be addressed later in this chapter under the heading "Relaxation Training." Many sources on stress management discuss the physiological symptoms associated with stress; few focus on headaches, including migraines. Antonia van der Meer, in *Relief from Chronic Headache*, explains types of headaches, their treatment, and stress reduction techniques and exercises the reader can use to relieve symptoms. Alan Rapoport and Fred Sheftell cover much the same territory in their *Headache Relief: A Comprehensive, Up-To-Date, Medically Proven Program That Can*

Control and Ease Headache Pain but in much greater detail. Interested readers can also consult *Overcoming Migraine: A Comprehensive Guide to Treatment and Prevention by a Survivor* by Betsy Wyckoff.

Respiratory Disorders

Respiratory dysfunction can be impacted by chronic or acute stress. For example, as part of the fight-or-flight response, a person may hyperventilate, with a readiness for action which increases oxygen and decreases carbon dioxide. *Certainly, if one experiences hyperventilation on a recurring basis, it is important to seek professional assistance to manage this problem. Many psychologists and psychiatrists are prepared to assist with this concern.*

Allergies are common respiratory disorders, in which hypersensitivity to a specific antigen or agent is manifested. Even though allergies are, in fact, reactions to physical stimuli, psychological factors can impact the degree to which an individual reacts to an antigen. George Everly reports that when an allergic person is in more secure surroundings, allergic reactions may be much less severe than when the individual is faced with a more stressing set of circumstances. Asthmatic reactions to antigens can be most serious and can be greatly impacted by stress. According to Everly "In asthmatic patients, bronchial secretions increase, mucosal swelling takes place, and finally smooth muscle surrounding the bronchioles contracts leading to a great difficulty in expiring air from the lungs."[11] As a person struggles to breathe, anxiety dramatically increases, which increases a need for oxygen, which further aggravates the stress response. Stress management strategies can be a helpful adjunct to the successful treatment of bronchial asthma. In *Anxiety, Phobias and Panic: Taking Charge and Conquering Fear,* Reneau Peurifoy includes a discussion of several breathing exercises and relaxation techniques.

Skin Disorders

Stress can also lead to or exacerbate a variety of skin problems. As part of the stress response, an individual perspires, the temperature of the skin's surface decreases, the electrical conductance of the skin increases, and, because of constriction of the blood vessels, toes and fingers may feel colder. Many skin disorders may be related to stress, including eczema, acne, psoriasis, and hives.[12] *Those with skin problems are best served by consulting a dermatologist (a physician specializing in diseases of the skin), prior to seeking a psychological solution to the problem.*

Psychological Aspects of Stress

A growing body of research demonstrates strong relationships between the physiology of the stress response, illness, and a variety of psychological factors. This section examines significant psychological elements relating to stress and stress management.

One of the more exciting areas of research and clinical practice in psychology addresses the impact of personality on the perception, management, and outcome of distressors. Different people provided with similar levels of stress will most likely evaluate their environments differently and will probably react differently as well. In this section, comments will center on a few of the significant personality variables which may well account for these individual differences.

Coping

People differ in their abilities in coping with stressful life events. H. Asuman Kiyak and Soo Borson suggest several major competencies of coping: flexibility, emotional responsiveness, courage and limited cognitive distortion.[13] Flexibility refers to the ability to change one's mind; emotional responsiveness involves being able to communicate feelings; and courage and limited cognitive distortion reflect a person's skills in understanding and facing reality. Those persons who demonstrate coping competence are better able to adjust to the daily aggravations of life as well as the major crises—disappointments in love, financial concerns, illness, and the death of loved ones—that over a lifetime affect most human beings. It is probable that we learn these coping strategies through observing others and then applying various approaches to our own lives. If people are successful at employing a particular approach to coping, they will probably utilize that same strategy in additional circumstances as they occur. Furthermore, as one's competence when dealing with various stressors develops, it will influence our behavior and probably increase our self-esteem.[14] On the other hand, if one fails to adapt satisfactorily to stressful stimuli, that too may be incorporated into our view of events as well as our view of ourselves. Failure to adequately cope may increase an individual's susceptibility to additional distressors which can lead to even more negative impacts from a variety of life's problems.

Irwin and Barbara Sarason say those who successfully cope with stress have an assortment of skills, including the ability to search for relevant information, to discuss concerns with others, to redefine the problem to make it more manageable, to analyze both alternatives and consequences, and to utilize humor. The Sarasons delineate the following aids to successful coping: "Be task-oriented"; "Be yourself"; "Self-monitor"; "Be realistic about what you can achieve"; "Have a constructive outlook"; "Use supportive relationships"; and "Be patient with yourself."[15]

One important determinant of the ability to cope involves the individual's perception of the potential stressfulness of a particular event. According to Richard Lazarus and Susan Folkman, people make judgments either consciously or unconsciously as to whether an event will be stressful, positive, or neither. After determining a situation to be stressful, they may attempt to determine the available coping resources and their potential ability to use the necessary coping strategies. As a stressful experience unfolds, they may alter their perceptions, forming reappraisals of the entire situation. It is highly significant that both people's appraisals and coping resources determine their response to stress.[16] The following books give the reader ways to identify stress points, coping strategies, and other stress management techniques: *The Stress Solution: An Action Plan to Manage the Stress in Your Life* by Lyle H. Miller, Alma Dell Smith, and Larry Rothstein; *Stress Management* by James S. Gordon; and *The Relaxation Response* by Herbert Benson.

Type A Personality and Stress

Coping is an essential ingredient of effective stress management. But, in addition, people may be predisposed to behave in certain ways. Much has been written in the professional and popular literature on the consequences of the Type A behavior pattern. Researchers have followed the cases of individuals with heart disease or those who had a heart attack to determine if stress played a significant role in the development of heart trouble. They noted that distinctive patterns appeared. In *Treating Type A Behavior and Your Heart,* Meyer Friedman and Diane Ulmer describe the characteristics that distinguish a person with this prevailing style, including competitiveness, time urgency, impatience, and hostility. On the other hand, people classified as having a Type B personality are more relaxed and at peace with themselves and rarely experience hostility.

The Type A style is often associated with coronary heart disease, and this relationship is documented by a rather large body of research. People with Type A personalities suffer more coronary heart disease than those who are described as Type B, and to complicate matters further for Type A's, those viewed as Type A have higher levels of serum cholesterol and are more likely to smoke than is the case with Type B's. Curiously, Type A's are more likely than Type B's to survive a heart attack, but the reasons for this association are as yet unclear.[17] David Rosenhan and Martin Seligman offer this suggestion: "Hostility and anger may be the killing components of Type A."[18] In several longitudinal studies of Type A persons and coronary heart disease, the combination of hostility and anger were viewed as a key predictor in the development of coronary heart disease and heart attacks.[19]

Psychological Disorders and Stress

A number of psychological disorders appear to be directly linked to stress and stress management. *However, the reader is advised that it is a mistake to view every psychological problem as merely the result of stress. Everyone experiences stress but only a segment of the population suffers from debilitating psychological problems. Chronic psychological distress can be symptomatic of a serious problem and is an important motivation for seeking professional help.*

Although the majority of people cope more or less with the stressors of life, everyone faces personal anxieties of varying sorts. One of the most common psychological disturbances is the family of anxiety disorders marked by intense chronic psychic pain. Included in this category are phobias, generalized anxiety disorder, panic disorder, and posttraumatic stress disorder. A person categorized as phobic is consistently afraid of something to an extent that is totally unrelated to actual danger, for example, if that person feels compelled to escape from the situation or avoids it altogether, and if that person is consciously aware of the irrationality of the accompanying fear.

Generalized *anxiety disorder,* according to David Rosenhan and Martin Seligman, is "characterized by chronic tenseness and vigilance, beliefs that something bad will happen, mild emergency reactions, and feelings of wanting to run away."[20] Recurring panic attacks consist of such sensations as a racing heart, trembling, shortness of breath, and dizziness, all of which are characteristic of panic disorder. Those who suffer panic disorder may be terrified that they will totally lose control, and such an attack may continue for several minutes. Posttraumatic stress disorder results from a response to some catastrophic event (for example, combat, a fire, an earthquake, or rape) and is seen in the following symptoms: "(1) the person relives the trauma recurrently, in dreams, in flashbacks, and in reverie; (2) the person becomes numb to the world, and avoids stimuli that remind him of the trauma; and (3) the person experiences symptoms of anxiety and arousal that were not present before the trauma."[21]

Certainly stress plays a part in all psychological disturbance and readers are advised to seek assistance from a mental health professional if such stress is perceived as being beyond one's ability to cope. Successful treatment strategies have been developed for those with anxiety disorders and are available from skillful therapists. As an adjunct to therapeutic interventions, readers may wish to consult Don Catherall's *Back from the Brink: A Family Guide to Overcoming Traumatic Stress,* Reneau Peurifoy's *Anxiety, Phobias and Panic: Taking Charge and Conquering Fear,* Diane Hailparn's *Fear No More: A Psychotherapist's Guide for Overcoming Your Anxieties and Phobias,* Christopher J. McCullough's *Always at Ease: Overcoming Shyness and Anxiety in Every Situation,* and *Thoughts and Feelings: The Art of Cognitive Stress Intervention* by Matthew McKay, Martha Davis, and Patrick Fanning.

Two books which address concerns about teenage depression and anxiety are Michael Maloney and Rachel Krantz's *Straight Talk about Anxiety and Depression* and Susan Newman's *Don't Be S.A.D.: A Teenage Guide to Handling Stress, Anxiety and Depression.*

Many people cope with stress through the use or abuse of a variety of substances like alcohol, nicotine, stimulants, narcotics, hallucinogens, or tranquilizers. Of course, such drugs fail to alleviate the stressors and help to create additional ones brought on by physical and emotional dependence as well as addiction. *Substance abuse can be treated effectively, and readers with such concerns are strongly advised to obtain professional assistance.* Readers may wish to consult Chapter 7 of this book on psychological disorders for further information.

Life Stressors

A number of distressors occur in everyone's life. Some are unique, if not in content at least in combination with other happenings. Stressors common to many lives include those particularly related to work and family.

Stress on the Job

For some people the very thought of their job, boss, or place of employment produces an onslaught of physical or psychological symptoms ranging from head and stomach aches to anxiety and dread. Many persons are so "aggravated" by aspects of their work that they can not wait for a fantasized day when they might be able to tell their boss "to take this job and shove it." Others are so distraught or "burnt out" that they frequently discuss their plans for retirement, even though they are in their thirties or forties.

Stress may be associated with the job role, including role overload, underload, ambiguity, and conflict. Individuals are said to experience role overload if insufficient time or the necessary resources or skills to complete tasks in a satisfactory manner occur. Role underload exists when someone feels overqualified and bored with work assignments. A job is ambiguous if the employee is unclear about the expectations of employers, coworkers, or subordinates. Finally, role conflict reflects differing and possibly incompatible expectations between supervisors, peers, and subordinates.

In their practical book *Career Success/Personal Success: How to Stay Healthy in a High Stress Environment,* Christine Leatz and Mark Stolar describe structural plateauing, when no job exists within an organization for a specific employee to be promoted, and content plateauing, which happens when an individual knows all the relevant aspects of a position and gradually reaches a state of boredom. The authors suggest that current corporate managers are typically getting their last promotion at a much younger age than their parents' generation. Thus, more are "topping out" and possibly becoming "burnt out" at younger ages.

Burnout at work is characterized by a loss of interest and effectiveness. Especially prone to this problem are those persons engaged in work involving public contact (for example, those in service occupations, teachers, and law enforcement personnel). Symptoms include an inability to concentrate, loss of esteem associated with one's perception of the job, a diminished sense of humor, and a detachment from work. *Readers are advised that these same symptoms, if prolonged, may reflect depression, and that such recurring behaviors and feelings may suggest potentially underlying psychological problems. It is suggested that those with such continuing symptoms seek assistance from a mental health professional.*

Leatz and Stolar describe several additional sources of stress on the job: reductions in force (both the effects on those laid off and those who are left behind and are subsequently anxious and overloaded), promotions, relocations, travel, information overload, and workplace computerization. For each workplace stressor the authors provide specific behavioral suggestions, as does Barbara Mackoff in *The Art of Self-Renewal: Balancing Pressure and Productivity On and Off the Job.*

Stress in the Family

For many persons stress on the job is equalled or surpassed by stress in the context of the family. Relationships with spouses or children can add much to the richness of daily life, but these same relationships can also dramatically increase responsibilities and offer competing demands for personal time and involvement. Of course, stressors also exist for single people without children who may have to deal with loneliness and who must assume responsibility for all household duties.

One of the key problems affecting the stress level of families revolves around the allocation of household chores. Even though the vast majority of two-parent families are also two-paycheck families, women continue to perform the lion's share of the housework, cooking, child care, parent care, and other assorted domestic duties.[22]

It is in the interest of the entire family, especially those overburdened members, to expect the participation of other members of the family in fulfilling family obligations. In *The Art of Self-Renewal,* Barbara Mackoff addresses this point and many of the other challenges facing two-paycheck families. *Interested readers should consult our chapters on parenting, romance, love, marriage and divorce, and aging for additional material on responsibility in the family.*

Stress Management Strategies

In this section we shall explore a variety of stress management strategies. *Any stress management strategy should be tailored to the special circumstances of the individual.*

Time Management

Effective time management is available to everyone, and the principles are easily learned. The ways in which an individual utilizes time are both an expression of that person's values and interests as well as the various constraints of the environment. Enlightened time management starts with the clarification of values and goals, so that maximum effort can be directed in their pursuit. Bradley McRae, in *Practical Time Management: How to Get Things Done in Less Time,* Herbert Benson and Eileen Stuart, in *The Wellness Book: The Comprehensive Guide to Maintaining Health and Treating Stress-Related Illness,* and Tony and Robbie Fanning, in *Get It All Done and Still Be Human: A Personal Time Management Workshop,* provide a series of structured activities which can be used to clarify personal values, long-term and short-term goals, and current time utilization. After assessing personal goals, those aspiring to improve their time use are advised to keep a time log, which is a record of actual time allocation. Helpful charts and discussions on time logs can be found in McRae's *Practical Time Management* or in Alan Lakein's *How to Get Control of Your Time and Your Life.*

Through the use of time logs, an individual can identify recurring time wasters. Tony and Robbie Fanning discuss common time wasters, including errands, some telephone calls, many meetings, waiting, and drop-in visitors. Also, those seeking to maximize the attainment of goals through improved time use are advised to prioritize their activities by developing "A, B, C lists."

Those activities labelled as "A's" are urgent and important, "B's" are important but not urgent, and "C's" refer to those things that are necessary, but are not really important or urgent. Many people find it useful to make weekly or daily "to-do" lists and to keep those lists in a portable appointment book. In *Doing It Now: A Twelve-Step Program for Curing Procrastination and Achieving Your Goals,* Edwin Bliss provides practical techniques to combat procrastination and to manage one's time effectively.

Constructive Conflict Resolution

For many people, interpersonal conflict is an even greater source of stress than are time pressures and constraints. Joyce Hocker and William Wilmot define conflict as "an expressed struggle between at least two interdependent parties who perceive incompatible goals, scarce resources, and interference from the other party in achieving their goals."[23] The key issue is the perception of the disputing parties, because if an individual thinks another person is blocking attainment of a goal or competing for a limited resource like money, status, or power, hostility develops. With hostility, conflict can spiral. For example, if person A does something that is viewed as irritating by person B, B may retaliate, and so on. In some long-standing conflicts the disputants cannot recall what started the struggle, but they can list aggravating behaviors that keep the conflict alive. Of course, it is more difficult and personally threatening to recognize one's own part in such conflict spiralling. Interested readers might wish to consult the following books by Roger Fisher, William Ury, and Bruce Patton, *Getting to Yes: Negotiating Agreement without Giving In* and William Ury's *Getting Past No: Negotiating with Difficult People.* Fisher, Ury, and Patton advocate that disputants separate themselves from the problem, emphasize interests not positions, create options aimed at mutual gain, and emphasize objective criteria.

Social System Building

Certainly not all interpersonal relationships are sources of debilitating stress. In fact, friends and family members can offer solace in dealing with difficult times. Most benefit from the giving and receiving that are such central elements in close relationships. What is important is not the number of friendships but the quality of them. James Pennebaker describes the numerous benefits of confiding in other people in his highly readable *Opening Up: The Healing Power of Confiding in Others.* Drawing on his own research as well as a host of other studies, Pennebaker builds the case that inhibition presents a health threat to the individual and describes the benefits and costs of disclosing to other persons. A large body of research suggests that those persons with active support networks are far more resilient in the face of stress than their counterparts who lack such quality relationships. Of course, if people seek others for support or consolation, it is incumbent on them to be available when the need is reversed.

Hobbies and Special Interests

Relationships can provide great solace and relief from life's stressors, but so can special interests and hobbies. If all of an individual's time is filled with fulfilling responsibilities, work, or family, then life can be perceived as a struggle to keep up with obligations and as an experience devoid of fun. If one's spare time is comprised of activities that are an extension of work (for example, talking about work with colleagues, reading about one's vocation), an individual can gradually become narrow in perspective. *Readers are advised to seek out activities which are pleasurable. Those activities which are inexpensive and accessible are more likely to be pursued.* Structured activities aimed at helping individuals clarify their interests can be found in Stuart and Benson's *The Wellness Book* and in Bradley McCrae's *Practical Time Management.*

Humor

Another readily available source of stress management is humor, which provides an outlet for frustration and hostility as well as playfulness. Issues which may be too painful to deal with on a more rational basis may be handled through joking about the apparent inconsistencies and inevitabilities which affect an individual's life. Humor also offers a physical release for the body; one might feel quite refreshed after a good laugh. Certainly some people appreciate the humorous aspects of human existence more than others, so for those who fail to see the humor in some area of concern, attempts at joking by others may create more personal stress. Some persons appreciate and find much to laugh about in irony, while others may become delirious with laughter because of some physical error (for example, loud belching after a meal). For those persons blessed with an appreciation of the funnier sides of living, humor offers an inexpensive and accessible form of stress management.

Diet, Exercise, and Rest

Effective stress management reflects attention to an individual's physical needs, including diet, exercise, and rest. Because the human stress response is psychophysical in nature, a healthy body contributes to greater resistance to stress. Proper nutrition is comprised of foods from the four food groups, high fiber foods, ones low in saturated fat, cruciferous vegetables (for example, cauliflower and broccoli), and limited use of products containing caffeine (for example, coffee, cola, tea, and chocolate), sugar, sodium, and processed flour.[24]

A regular program of physical exercise produces both physical and psychological benefits. Depending on the nature of the exercise, an ongoing fitness program can contribute to increased muscular strength and endurance, agility, and flexibility. During strenuous exercise, the brain may release endorphins, which are neurotransmitters that produce the so-called runners' high, a perception of well-being that acts to decrease pain and produces a sense of euphoria. A good workout can be relaxing as the day's tension leaves the body.

Readers considering the initiation of an exercise program should first consult their physician to see if it is appropriate for their situation. Many people may eat wisely and exercise regularly, but by failing to get the necessary rest, they may be placing themselves in unnecessary psychological and physical jeopardy. It is important that those persons intent on effective stress management make sure they are getting an adequate amount of sleep.

Relaxation Techniques

A number of relaxation strategies have been developed to counter the stress response. Among the more prominent of these approaches are progressive muscle relaxation and meditation. *Readers are advised that there are some possible negative side effects to relaxation techniques.* Based on a review of relevant scientific studies, George Everly has compiled a list of possible negative effects including a loss of contact with reality, drug reactions (most notably persons taking sedatives, cardiovascular drugs, and insulin), panic states, and a release of repressed thoughts and feelings.[25] *A reader who is considering the use of a relaxation technique should check with their physician regarding the suitability of a particular strategy.*

Through progressive muscle relaxation, an individual can learn to distinguish between relaxation and tension. This strategy involves the appropriate tensing of muscles followed by a relaxation of the muscle contraction. Instructions for this approach can be found in Herbert Benson and Eileen Stuart's *The Wellness Book.* Phillip Rice recommends that anyone interested in starting a muscle relaxation program should consider elements of setting, mood, preparation and medical precautions.[26] Choosing a quiet and comfortable spot is an important first step for anyone interested in progressive muscle relaxation. Proper heating and ventilation are essential. Rice suggests a practice of relaxation exercises at about the same time twice a day. A consistent schedule for the exercises should be followed. Some people prefer to have soft music playing in the background while they engage in progressive relaxation.

In terms of mood, Rice suggests that participants "cultivate a sense of passive attention, . . . not rush, not use any drugs, and not be afraid of different feelings."[27] During the first weeks of practice, participants are advised to "review the instructions for the proper sequence of muscle groups and make the final arrangements you prefer in regard to phone, music, lighting, and so on."[28] Finally Rice cautions that the individual "should determine from your physician that it is permissible to engage in an activity that will place a moderate strain on bones and muscles."[29]

Like progressive muscle relaxation, meditation can be a highly useful stress management strategy. Dating back at least three thousand five hundred years, meditation can take one of several forms: mental repetition, physical repetition, problem contemplation, and visual concentration. Mental repetition involves the participant concentrating on a mantra, which is a word or a phrase, typically repeated silently to oneself, while physical repetition engages an individual in centering on a physical activity like breathing. Another approach, problem contemplation, engages one in analyzing an apparently paradoxical problem; in the visual concentration form of meditation, one centers on a visual image, like a scene or a candle flame.[30] A useful source of information on meditation is Herbert Benson's *The Relaxation Response* as is Reneau Peurifoy's *Anxiety, Phobias and Panic: Taking Charge and Conquering Fear.*

Summary

Stress management techniques should be tailored to fit personal circumstances, with some combination of strategies appropriate for each individual. Certainly stress is a reality in everyone's life, and its impact is seen in human behavior, emotion, and physiology. While a certain degree of stimulation is necessary for human survival and growth, excess stress can lead to psychological or physical breakdown. Practices like effective time management, conflict resolution, and structured relaxation, while not ridding a life of all stressors, can aid individuals in coping with the various hassles endemic to human existence.

RECOMMENDED TITLES

Physical Problems Associated with Stress

Benson, Herbert, and Eileen Stuart. *The Wellness Book: The Comprehensive Guide to Maintaining Health and Treating Stress Related Illness.* Secaucus, N.J.: Carol Pub. Group, 1991.

Physician Benson, author of *The Relaxation Response,* and his associate Eileen Stuart present the reader with a practical introduction to the mind/body connection in illnesses of all kinds. The authors discuss nutrition, stress management and reduction, and describe specific responses to illnesses ranging from insomnia, infertility, and cardiovascular disorders to cancer and AIDS. Through the use of case studies and work sheets in the book, the reader can apply the problem-solving techniques, where appropriate, to his or her own situation.

Rapoport, Alan M., and Fred D. Sheftell. *Headache Relief: A Comprehensive Up-to-Date, Medically Proven Program That Can Control and Ease Headache Pain.* New York: Simon & Schuster, 1990.

Rapoport and Sheftell, codirectors and cofounders of the New England Center for Headache, have written a practical guide for headache sufferers and their families. While stress can manifest itself in a variety of physical symptoms, headache is one of the most common. The authors define different types of headaches and their physical bases, describe treatments (drugs, biofeedback, and relaxation techniques), as well as changes in exercise and diet for headache control. The role of female hormonal changes in headaches, particularly migraines, is also covered. A separate chapter covers children and headaches.

van de Meer, Antonia. *Relief from Chronic Headache.* New York: Dell, 1990.

In this brief but practical guide, the reader is introduced to types of headaches, their causes, and their cures. Improved nutrition and avoidance of certain foods are seen as a primary change individuals can use in headache control. Biofeedback and other relaxation techniques are also recommended and described in detail.

Wyckoff, Betsy. *Overcoming Migraine: A Comprehensive Guide to Treatment and Prevention by a Survivor.* Rev. ed. Barrytown, N.Y.: A P.U.L.S.E book by Station Hill Pr., 1994.

Wyckoff focuses on migraine headaches, their definition, causes, and treatment. These headaches develop as the individual responds to a variety of triggers (e.g., certain food or foods, weather, medication, and fatigue among others). The author cautions readers that what serves as a trigger or series of triggers varies from individual to individual. Learning to identify and to avoid specific triggers plays an important part in stopping or reducing the likelihood of a headache before it develops. Through the use of a headache diary, the author encourages migraine sufferers to chart their headaches by observing their severity, by determining, if possible, the headache triggers, and by noting how the headache responds to treatment. The author also discusses alternative methods of treatment: biofeedback, acupuncture, homeopathy, massage, and herbal remedies. In addition, anecdotal evidence is presented and evaluated critically.

Psychological Aspects of Stress

Benson, Herbert. *The Relaxation Response.* New York: Morrow, 1975.

Physician Benson describes the deleterious physical and psychological effects of high blood pressure and stress on the body. He encourages readers to invoke the Relaxation Response through the practice of meditation. Twenty-minute sessions daily can lower physical and emotional stress, according to Benson. The author cites numerous studies which document the efficacy of meditation in reducing stress.

Gordon, James S. *Stress Management.* New York: Chelsea House Pub., 1990.

Gordon provides a basic introduction to stress by describing its physiological and emotional impact. The author also covers societal and environmental stressors, adolescent stress, and methods to identify and reduce stress. Stress reduction techniques, including hypnosis, biofeedback, visual imagery, cognitive therapy, and change in diet and exercise, are examined. The concluding chapter describes stress management programs for those with stress-related illnesses and individuals facing the ongoing stress of a chronic or life-threatening illness. A glossary, bibliography, and resource list add to the book's usefulness.

Miller, Lyle H., Alma Dell Smith, and Larry Rothstein. *The Stress Solution: An Action Plan to Manage the Stress in Your Life.* New York: Pocket Bks., 1993.

The authors offer a detailed stress inventory which outlines an individual's susceptibility to stress, sources of stress like job, family, personal, social, environmental, and financial concerns, and symptoms of stress. Using the results of the inventory, the book then guides the reader through a Stress Action Plan for self-regulating the particular stress point. Being aware of a stressor, deciding to take action, breaking free of past obstacles, using personal resources, friends, and allies, and taking action are some of the steps outlined by the Stress Action Plan. Each plan calls upon the reader to describe the problem, set a reasonable goal, outline possible actions, identify barriers to change and supports to change. Specific recommendations accompany the section on problem solving.

Psychological Disorders and Stress

Catherall, Don R. *Back from the Brink: A Family Guide to Overcoming Traumatic Stress.* New York: Bantam, 1992.

Posttraumatic stress syndrome (PTSD), often associated with Vietnam veterans, can also be seen in accident victims, victims of violent crime, and rape and incest survivors. Catherall provides clear definitions of PTSD, how it affects the persons who have it and those around them, and how it can be treated. He also includes a section on children with PTSD. Numerous examples from his practice are included as are guidelines for trauma survivors, their loved ones, and for parents if the trauma survivor is a child.

Hailparn, Diane. *Fear No More: A Psychotherapist's Guide for Overcoming Your Anxieties.* New York: St. Martin's, 1988.

In clear straightforward language Hailparn describes common characteristics of fearful individuals: creativity and imagination. Using a variety of cases, the author tells the stories of individuals who suffer panic attacks, anxiety reactions, and other adverse effects associated with phobias and anxiety. The book outlines the difference between fear, anxiety, and phobia with examples while advising the reader on steps to take to face or diffuse the anxiety. Hailparn includes information on nutrition, drugs, and exercise, and their role in reducing anxiety.

McCullough, Christopher J. *Always at Ease: Overcoming Shyness and Anxiety in Every Situation.* Los Angeles: Tarcher, 1991.

Using a variety of questionnaires, McCullough takes the reader through a structured program for overcoming social anxiety caused by fear of public speaking, meeting new people, interviews, dating, and other stressful situations. Advising the reader that these fears need not be debilitating, the author gives examples, provides journal exercises, and devises strategies to put the individual at ease in a variety of situations.

McKay, Matthew, Martha Davis, and Patrick Fanning. *Thoughts and Feelings: The Art of Cognitive Stress Intervention.* Oakland, Calif.: New Harbinger, 1981.

The authors explore two types of stress patterns and their effects. In the first, an environmental stimulus (a stress-producing event), physiological arousal, and negative thoughts result in painful emotions. In the second, an environmental stimulus, negative thoughts, and then physiological arousal are followed by painful emotions. For example, an individual has a flat tire on the way to work; the person is anxious and fearful about trying to change a tire on a busy highway; furthermore, she thinks that she will be fired for being late. McKay and his associates, in describing the dynamics of these stress responses, indicate that by intervening and changing any of the three components of the stress response individuals can break the cycle that results in a painful emotional response. This approach involves changing negative thinking patterns by helping readers identify types of distorted thinking, by providing examples of rational comebacks to these distortions, and by demonstrating how individuals can apply these rational comebacks instead of distorted thoughts to stressful situations. Through a series of exercises and questionnaires, the authors guide the readers through this change process.

Peurifoy, Reneau Z. *Anxiety, Phobias and Panic: Taking Charge and Conquering Fear.* 2d ed. Citrus Heights, Calif.: Life Skills, 1992.

Designed to be used as a workbook, *Anxiety, Phobias and Panic* explains phobia and how it can be overcome. The author describes panic attacks in great detail while giving concrete examples and problem-solving strategies for the reader. Biofeedback, relaxation, and meditation techniques are also included.

Adolescents and Stress

Maloney, Michael, and Rachel Krantz. *Straight Talk about Anxiety and Depression.* New York: Facts on File, 1991.

This practical guide aimed at teenagers discusses depression and anxiety from an adolescent's perspective through direct language and use of appropriate examples. It also includes sections on how to identify anxiety and depression, strategies to relieve symptoms, and how to get help. Deep breathing, meditation, and progressive relaxation techniques are described. A resource list and index add to the book's usefulness.

Newman, Susan. *Don't Be S.A.D.: A Teenage Guide to Handling Stress, Anxiety and Depression.* New York: Messner, 1991.

In a series of nine vignettes, Newman tells the stories of teenagers facing stress, anxiety, and depression as well as drug abuse, physical abuse, eating disorders, and single motherhood. In each chapter a section on problem-solving strategies for each case are given after the scene is set. A resource list and bibliography give teens additional help.

Type A Personality and Stress

Friedman, Meyer, and Diane Ulmer. *Treating Type A Behavior and Your Heart.* New York: Knopf, 1984.

By defining Type A behavior and its adverse effects on the body and its link to heart disease, Friedman and Ulmer educate the reader about the risks of Type A behavior. The authors identify five components of the Type A individual: hyper-aggressiveness, free-floating hostility, a sense of time urgency, inadequate self-esteem, and a drive toward self-destruction. The emphasis is placed on both identifying and changing Type A behavior. The individuals who modified their behavior found that their risk of heart disease decreased significantly. Specific steps on changing Type A behavior are described in detail.

Stress on the Job

Leatz, Christine A., and Mark W. Stolar. *Career Stress/Personal Stress: How to Stay Healthy in a High Stress Environment.* New York: McGraw-Hill, 1992.

The authors examine job stress and its impact by providing a variety of stress assessment tools for measuring personal and job stress. Emphasis on organizational culture, burnout, and rapid pace changes in the workplace have led to increased stress at work which compounds stress at home. The book covers coping strategies, stress-related illnesses and problems, and techniques to reduce stress. These include adopting a stress sensitive life style, healthy communication patterns, conflict resolution skills, and a clear set of values and goals.

Stress in the Family

Mackoff, Barbara. *The Art of Self-Renewal: Balancing Pressure and Productivity On and Off the Job.* Los Angeles: Lowell House, 1992.

As a management psychologist, Mackoff offers practical tips on balancing work and home life, particularly in the first hour after everyone arrives home. Often called the "arsenic hour" when work concerns follow one home, the author provides a refreshing look into how the common question "How was your day"? can be answered. By interspersing examples and exercises, Mackoff gives the reader numerous strategies for coping with job stress at home. Working parents with small children are included in a section entitled "Parents' Rules of Renewal."

Time Management

Bliss, Edwin C. *Doing It Now: A Twelve-Step Program for Curing Procrastination and Achieving Your Goals.* New York: Bantam, 1983.

Bliss provides practical solutions to procrastinators. Readers are asked to make four lists: one for work-related projects; one for home projects; one for personal relationships (answering letters or returning phone calls); and one for oneself. Using these lists as a basis for the rest of the book, the author encourages readers to take active steps to avoid procrastination by developing a plan which involves prioritizing tasks on each of the four lists, overcoming fear of failure or fear of success, and the role fatigue plays in procrastination. In addition, methods for developing willpower and discipline are also explored.

Fanning, Tony, and Robbie Fanning. *Getting It All Done and Still Be Human: A Personal Time-Management Workshop.* Menlo Park, Calif.: Kali House, 1990.

The Fannings offer the reader a variety of practical time management techniques based on self-assessment and goal setting. Activities include identification of time wasters, time stretchers, working as a couple, and relaxed rules of time management. The authors advise readers to define their goals and review how they use time. Planning around peak periods, delegation, and letting go of certain tasks are among the techniques discussed.

Lakein, Alan. *How to Get Control of Your Time and Your Life.* New York: New American Lib., 1989.

Lakein challenges the reader to ask continuously "What is the best use of my time now"? While cautioning the reader not to become a "timenut," the author breaks effective time management into several phases: decision making, planning, and applying the newly learned techniques. Emphasis is given to setting priorities, acting upon them, and finding quiet time to plan and reflect.

McRae, Bradley C. *Practical Time Management: How to Get More Things Done in Less Time.* North Vancouver, B.C.: Self-Counsel Pr., 1988.

Using goal setting, time monitoring, problem solving, and planning and managing leisure time, McRae guides the reader to better time management strategies. Practical suggestions for applying the new strategies and maintaining them are also included.

Creative Conflict Resolution

Fisher, Roger, William Ury, and Bruce Patton, eds. *Getting to Yes: Negotiating Agreement without Giving In.* 2d ed. New York: Penguin, 1991.

Although written for business applications and with examples from business settings, this book serves as a general guide to conflict resolution. Applying the conflict resolution strategies outlined in *Getting to Yes* can lead to successful outcomes in stress management and reduction. The authors focus on several key points: separating people from the problem, focusing on interests not positions, looking for options for mutual gain, and using objective criteria.

Ury, William. *Getting Past No: Negotiating With Difficult People.* New York: Bantam, 1991.

Ury uses examples from business, politics, and family conflicts to illustrate how individuals can negotiate a successful outcome for both participants. Negotiating occurs as a part of everyday life and runs the gamut from multimillion dollar contracts to whether one's teenager can use the family car. The author outlines five steps which can help individuals reach agreement in ways which benefit everyone involved. Ury stresses the importance of not reacting immediately, of disarming the other person by finding common interests, of reframing a position instead of rejecting it outright, of making it easy for opponents to agree, while at the same time making it difficult for them to say no to the proposal.

Social System Building

Pennebaker, James W. *Opening Up: The Healing Power of Confiding in Others.* New York: Avon, 1990.

Psychologist Pennebaker describes the healthful role confiding in others has in an individual's physical and emotional well-being. His studies with college students, trauma victims, and Holocaust survivors suggest that when individuals confided in others or wrote about their traumatic situation, their stress was reduced significantly and their immune systems appeared to be stronger. He describes techniques used in confiding and encourages readers to use journals.

NOTES

1. Phillip Rice, *Stress and Health: Principles and Practice for Coping and Wellness* (Belmont, Calif.: Wadsworth, 1987), 20.
2. Robert Woolfolk and Paul Lehrer, "Clinical Stress Reduction," in *Principles and Practice of Stress Management*, ed. Robert Woolfolk and Paul Lehrer (New York: Guilford Pr., 1984), 1–11.
3. Jerrold Greenberg, *Comprehensive Stress Management*, 4th ed. (Dubuque, Iowa: W. C. Brown and Benchmark, 1993), 39.
4. George Everly, Jr., *A Clinical Guide to the Treatment of the Human Stress Response.* (New York: Plenum, 1989), 72.
5. Ibid., 73.
6. Ibid., 59.
7. Greenberg, *Comprehensive Stress Management*, 48–50.
8. Charles Sheridan and Sally Radmacher, *Health Psychology: Challenging the Biomedical Model* (New York: Wiley, 1992), 259.
9. Greenberg, *Comprehensive Stress Management*, 30.
10. Daniel Girdano and George Everly, Jr., *Controlling Stress and Tension: A Holistic Approach*, 4th ed. (New York: Prentice Hall, 1989), 40.
11. Everly, *Clinical Guide to the Treatment of the Human Stress Response*, 70.
12. Sheridan & Radmacher, *Health Psychology*, 305–11.
13. H. Asuman Kiyak and Soo Borson, "Coping with Chronic Illness and Disability," in *Aging, Health, and Behavior*, ed. Marcia Ory, Ronald Abeles, and Paula Darby Lipman (Newbury Park, Calif.: Sage, 1992), 141–73.
14. Albert Bandura, *Social Foundations of Thought and Action: A Social and Cognitive Theory* (New York: Prentice Hall, 1986), 392.
15. Irwin Sarason and Barbara Sarason, *Abnormal Psychology: The Problem of Maladaptive Behavior* (New York: Prentice Hall, 1989), 118, 120.

16. Richard Lazarus and Susan Folkman, *Stress, Appraisal, and Coping* (New York: Springer Pub., 1984), 22–54.

17. David Ragland and Richard Brand, "Type A Behavior and Mortality from Coronary Heart Disease," *New England Journal of Medicine* 318 (Jan. 14, 1988): 65–69.

18. David Rosenhan and Martin Seligman, *Abnormal Psychology*, 2d ed. (New York: Norton, 1989), 284.

19. Karen Matthews, and Suzanne Haynes, "Type A Behavior Pattern and Coronary Disease Risk: Update and Critical Evaluation," *American Journal of Epidemiology* 123 (June 1986): 923–60.

20. Rosenhan and Seligman, *Abnormal Psychology*, 690.

21. Ibid., 218.

22. Barbara Major, "Gender, Entitlement, and the Distribution of Family Labor," *Journal of Social Issues*, 49 (Fall 1993): 141–59.

23. Joyce Hocker and William Wilmot, *Interpersonal Conflict*, 3d ed. (Dubuque, Iowa: W. C. Brown, 1991), 12.

24. Greenberg, *Comprehensive Stress Management*, 85–86.

25. Everly, *Clinical Guide to the Treatment of the Human Stress Response*, 167–68.

26. Phillip Rice, *Stress and Health*, 241–46.

27. Ibid., 243–45.

28. Ibid., 245.

29. Ibid.

30. Everly, *Clinical Guide to the Treatment of the Human Stress Response*, 171–73.

CHAPTER

7

Psychological and Substance-Related Disorders

This chapter is an exploration of the dynamics of psychological disorders frequently addressed in popular self-help literature. Specific attention will be directed to the nature of psychological problems, the issue of misdiagnosing through reading self-help books, locating a mental health professional, a discussion of various forms of psychotherapy, and a discussion of the dynamics of several types of psychological disturbance.

The Nature of Psychological Disturbance

Everyone from time to time experiences anxiety and sadness. No human life is devoid of a certain amount of worry, doubt, conflict, frustration, and whatever else places limitations on individual happiness. However, most persons much of the time are able, despite these assaults on the psyche, to utilize successful coping strategies. Contrary to some popular books, most of our families were not dysfunctional. Most persons probably would not be as adaptive as they seem to be, and most of us do not suffer from psychological "disease" manifested by codependency and the miseries of being an "adult child" of psychologically impaired parents.[1] For a helpful discussion of the inappropriate use of the term dysfunctional family, readers may wish to consult Stanton Peele, Archie Brodsky, and Mary Arnold's *The Truth about Addiction and Recovery.*[2] These writers suggest that "nearly every family has some flaw or foible that can, in some sense, be called dysfunctional. This unsurprising fact has become a pretext for labeling nearly every family as diseased."[3]

Readers are advised to avoid self-help books which paint psychological distress as rooted in terms like "codependency," "dysfunctional families," a wounded "inner child," and so forth. Certainly people may experience lingering problems based, in part, on inadequate parenting, early loss, and abuse. However, centering on one's recollections of family history to the exclusion of present circumstances and capacities may contribute to viewing oneself as a "victim." While these books may prove comforting to some readers, often they do not offer a strategy which can be applied and modified effectively to the life and concerns of the reader. Those readers continuing to wrestle with issues emanating from their early life are strongly encouraged to seek competent professional assistance.

Despite the overall emotional well-being experienced by most of us most of the time, psychological disturbance is very common. Robert Carson and James Butcher cite a 1988 study sponsored by the National Institutes of Mental Health which suggested that almost 16 percent of Americans have mental disorders or problems with substance abuse.[4]

While psychological problems are common, so are stereotypes about the people who have them. For example, research conducted in the mid-1980s found psychologically disordered persons were featured in about one in five television programs; seven out of ten times the psychologically disordered character was portrayed as criminal and/or violent.[5] Certainly psychologically disturbed persons do sometimes commit violent or criminal acts but, according to David Myers, "most disturbed people are not dangerous; instead, they are anxious, depressed, or withdrawn."[6]

People with psychological problems are not very different from other persons. Only in very extreme cases is the layperson able to differentiate between a "healthy" and a disordered person at a first meeting. Observing an individual who is "talking to himself" indicates disorder to the observer, but the severity of the subtle but much more common features of a state of anxiety is difficult for a layperson to detect. Anxiety may reflect a variety of disorders, differing dramatically in their origin, manifestation, and duration. Some problems interfere with part of an individual's life, while others may dominate one's very being, and some concerns are much easier to address and rectify than others.

The key elements of psychological disturbance are "atypical, disturbing, maladaptive, and unjustifiable behavior."[7]

Jack Engler and Daniel Goleman in their book *The Consumer's Guide to Psychotherapy* provide detailed discussions of an array of common psychological problems, as well as recommendations by therapists for the treatment of each disorder.

The Problem of Misdiagnosing

One potential concern is the possibility of a person reading a self-help book devoted to a particular psychological disorder and then concluding he does, in fact, have the disorder, which may not be the case. The reader may then apply inappropriate strategies to resolve the problem. Complicating the effective use of popular self-help psychology books is the instance of *intern's syndrome,* so named because it is common for some medical students to see themselves reflected in the diseases they study.[8] It is quite likely that lay readers could misapply psychological information, since many disorders which are quite different share some of the same symptoms. For example, the most common symptom of psychological conflict and disturbance is anxiety. Anxiety shows itself in numerous disorders ranging from phobias to depression and posttraumatic stress disorder. A reader with a depressive disorder may read a book on anxiety management and dutifully follow the prescribed techniques contained in the text, but experience no relief.

Readers who have concerns with anxiety, depression, addiction, and anything else which interferes with life adjustment and happiness should consider seeking professional help. Self-help books, even if correctly applied, are not an effective substitute for formal treatment.

Locating Appropriate Mental Health Professionals

For those readers seeking a psychotherapist, Jack Engler and Daniel Goleman provide a detailed rational approach in their practical book *The Consumer's Guide to Psychotherapy.*[9] These authors outline a four-step process: (1) know what to look for; (2) ask for referrals; (3) check credentials; and (4) contact the therapist. First the prospective client needs to consider various professional disciplines through which therapy is provided. Most notable among them are psychologists, psychiatrists, social workers, psychiatric nurses, marriage and family therapists, and licensed professional counselors.

Engler and Goleman provide descriptions of these disciplines, differences among them, credentials, information on professional licensing and certification, and so forth.[10] In order to be licensed as professional psychologists, providers typically must have a Ph.D. or a Psy.D. in clinical or counseling psychology, pre- and postdoctoral clinical supervision, a high score on a national licensing exam, and approval by a state licensing body. Psychiatrists train as physicians, receiving an M.D. degree. Following an internship in general medicine which includes some basic psychiatric principles, those seeking to become licensed psychiatrists complete a three-year residency. Psychiatric residencies often include some training in psychotherapy with the primary focus on the biochemical basis of behavior. Psychiatrists who pass a national examination can become board certified in psychiatry. This certification indicates the individual meets the standards set by specialists in psychiatry.

In most states social workers undergo a licensing process, and while most licensed social workers have an M.S.W. (a master's degree in social work), some have a D.S.W. (a doctorate in social work). Training in social work often centers on casework, and many social workers have completed field work placement in mental health organizations. While nursing is licensed or registered in all states, no specialized certification has been established for any type of nursing, including psychiatric nursing.

According to Engler and Goleman, marriage and family therapists have licensure requirements in about half of the states.[11] Typically, these therapists complete a master's degree centered on couple and family counseling, and clinical supervision, and then pass a licensing exam. However, some therapists have earned a doctorate in marriage and family therapy. In some states, therapists may earn a master's or doctorate in counseling, complete clinical supervision, pass a state exam, and become licensed professional counselors.

Engler and Goleman suggest that the specific mental health profession of a therapist is much less important than the need for the professional to be licensed, since licensure brings a therapist under standards of both a professional licensing board and a professional association.[12]

The second step in selecting a therapist is to ask for an appropriate referral. Engler and Goleman provide detailed suggestions on locating referrals through professional associations, mental health professionals, self-help groups, and so forth.[13] These authors discuss strategies for finding a therapist in private practice as well as one in a clinic setting. In asking for a referral, Engler and Goleman suggest the following: (1) "In general terms, say what you are considering therapy for"; (2) "Mention the kind of therapy you are interested in: individual, couple, marital, family, or group therapy"; (3) "Ask about the kind of approach the therapist practices or specializes in . . ."; (4) "Ask for a licensed professional"; (5) "In general terms, describe the kind of person you think you would work best with, or any personal preferences"; (6) "Give a general idea of what you think you can afford to pay"; (7) "Indicate whether you want a therapist in private practice or would be willing to consider a staff therapist in a clinic"; and (8) "Indicate where you would be willing to go for therapy."[14]

Upon receiving the referral, potential therapy clients can check on a therapist's credentials.[15] Engler and Goleman suggest that consumers check with the appropriate state licensing board or professional association; or if they prefer, they should call the therapist and ask directly about qualifications.[16]

The fourth step in the process of locating a psychotherapist is to contact prospective mental health practitioners by phone. Engler and Goleman provide a list of possible questions a consumer may wish to ask the potential therapist. If calling a private practitioner, the individual may wish to ask: (1) "How soon can the therapist see you, and will it be on a regular basis"; (2) "What hours are available?" (3) "What is the fee?" (4) "If you have medical insurance, will your particular policy cover their services?" (5) "Does the therapist charge for an initial consultation?" (6) "Does the therapist do the particular type of therapy you are considering?" and (7) "What are his qualifications?"[17]

If the consumer is calling a clinic, Engler and Goleman suggest the following questions: (1) "Do they see people who live in your area?" (2) "Are they restricted from seeing clients above a certain income?" (3) "How soon can you be seen?" and (4) "What kind of therapists are available?"[18]

The final step in locating a therapist is to request a consultation. Since most therapists charge for such a consultation, this will increase the cost. However, discussing one's situation with several therapists may provide a useful comparison for the consumer.[19] Engler and Goleman offer chapter length discussions about consulting a psychotherapist, deciding on a particular therapist, contracting with a therapist, paying for psychotherapy, and so forth. *Engler and Goleman encourage the reader to schedule consultations with several therapists before making a decision to begin therapy with one of them.*

Forms of Psychotherapy

Several ingredients are essential to successful psychotherapy, according to Robert Carson and James Butcher, who claim that the single most important factor regarding the potential for success is client motivation.[20] Therapy often involves some difficulties for clients, including facing difficult individual issues and conflicts. While seeking relief from emotional stress, psychotherapy may bring to the surface psychic pain.[21] Clients may require a great deal of motivation to tolerate such distress. A client's expectations about the potential efficacy of psychotherapy are also highly significant. A client who truly believes she will be helped is more likely to see improvement in therapy.[22] Also contributing to the effectiveness of therapy are the training, style, and personality of the therapist. Is there a good match between the client and the therapist? A therapist's techniques and style can be appropriate for some clients and be much less so for others. In their book *The Consumer's Guide to Psychotherapy*, Engler and Goleman devote an entire chapter to "Making Therapy Work."[23]

These authors offer insights into client and therapist behavior during sessions as well as client activities between sessions. Engler and Goleman advise those in therapy who wish to maximize the benefits, to do the following: (1) "[let] your therapist know as much as possible about the problems or issues you want help with"; (2) "[listen] to what your therapist says"; (3) "[learn]

to observe and listen to yourself"; (4) "[ask] questions"; (5) "keep your goals in view"; (6) "[let] your therapist know how you think things are going"; (7) "[stay] open to new ways of seeing things"; and (8) "[take] emotional risks that will let you change and grow."[24]

Types of Psychotherapy

Psychotherapy can be defined as "an emotionally charged, confiding interaction between a trained therapist and someone who suffers a psychological difficulty."[25] In practice, psychotherapy is another term for psychological counseling conducted by an appropriate professional. About 250 types of therapy exist, but about half of practicing therapists view themselves as following a blended or eclectic approach to psychological counseling, meaning they use counseling techniques from several schools of thought.[26]

Psychodynamic Therapies

Mainstream psychotherapy falls into one of several systems and formats. Ronald Comer states "a system of therapy is a set of principles and techniques employed in accordance with a particular theory of change."[27] Systems of therapy differ from formats. A system is based on a particular philosophical and scientific point of view, while format refers to whether counseling is conducted with individuals, couples, families, or other groups.

Historically, the first systems of therapy are referred to as psychodynamic. Comer suggests therapies of this variety "share the goals of helping clients to uncover past traumatic events and the inner conflicts that have resulted from them; to resolve, or settle, those conflicts; and to resume interrupted personal development."[28] Psychodynamic therapies focus on increasing a client's awareness or insight.[29] These therapies are based on the notion of transference, which refers to the belief that clients respond to their psychotherapists as if the therapist were the client's mother, father, or sibling. For example, people may, unknowingly, react to a therapist in a manner similar to the way they reacted to their parents. However, therapists may unintentionally countertransfer their own issues into the therapeutic relationship with the client.[30]

A crucial aspect of psychodynamic therapy, perhaps of all counseling, is resistance. Even though clients may sacrifice time, money, and emotion, they typically show resistance when psychologically threatened. Usually unconscious, this resistance centers on painful matters to the individual client. The main goal of dynamic counseling is insight, which can occur as a consequence of catharsis. Comer defines catharsis as "a reliving of past repressed feelings."[31]

Humanistic and Existential Therapies

Endeavoring to focus on the present life experiences of the client, humanistic and existential therapies address an individual's personal subjective world.[32] Humanists and many existentialists view people as having an innate capacity to grow and to have positive effects on those around them, and existentialists emphasize the idea that every individual is responsible for making meaningful choices in life.[33]

Person-centered therapy, initiated by Carl Rogers, is based on the necessity for therapists to display three attributes: "(1) congruence (genuineness, or realness), (2) unconditional positive regard (acceptance and caring), and (3) accurate empathic understanding (an ability to deeply grasp the subjective world of another person.)"[34] The focus of this counseling is to develop "a climate conducive to helping the individual become a fully functioning person."[35] Readers who wish to explore the basics of person-centered therapy further may benefit from reading *Carl Rogers on Personal Power: Inner Strength and Its Revolutionary Impact*.

Gestalt is another brand of therapy fitting into the humanistic/existential approach. It applies to an approach to psychotherapy developed initially by Fritz Perls and his associates. In gestalt therapy clients are encouraged to live in the present and take responsibility for themselves.[36] Therapists with a gestalt orientation are often confrontive in attempting to frustrate their "client's attempts to manipulate the therapist into taking responsibility for the client's well being."[37] Gestalt therapists are well known for their use of exercises like "I take responsibility," "rehearsals," and "May I feed you a sentence?"[38] For further exploration of this brand of therapy, readers can consult Joseph Zinker's *Creative Process in Gestalt Therapy*.

Centering on the human capacity for self-awareness, existential therapy addresses freedom, responsibility, anxiety, relationships, fear of death, and the pursuit of personal meaning.[39] According to Gerald Corey:

> Existentialism holds that there is no escape from freedom, in the sense that we can always be held responsible. We can relinquish our freedom, however, which is the ultimate inauthenticity. Existential therapy seeks to take clients out of their rigid grooves and to challenge their narrow and compulsive trends, which are blocking their freedom.[40]

Interested readers may wish to consult one of Viktor Frankl's books, particularly *Man's Search for Meaning* or *The Unheard Cry for Meaning*.

Behavioral Therapies

Behavioral therapies are based on the premise that psychological problems are often learned through conditioning.[41] Counselors from this perspective assist clients in uncovering the current factors reinforcing undesired behavior. They function in a directive fashion teaching clients to relax in order to deal with fear-arousing objects or situations (phobias), to monitor physical processes through biofeedback, to provide rewards for themselves or others when desired behaviors are demonstrated, or to develop social skills like assertiveness.[42] Behavioral methods seem to be most effective in dealing with concrete problems like phobias as opposed to more subjective concerns like perception of meaninglessness. Since behavioral methods revolve around learning new behaviors and reinforcing existing ones, such interventions can readily be adapted to a self-help framework. Two excellent examples of self-help books prepared by behavioral therapists are *Your Perfect Right: A Guide to Assertive Behavior* by Robert Alberti and Michael Emmons and *Control Your Depression* by Peter Lewinsohn and associates.

Cognitive Therapies

Another type of psychotherapy has grown dramatically in prominence in the past several decades. In *Love Is Never Enough,* a popular book for couples written by cognitive therapist Aaron Beck, the term *cognitive* "refers to the ways in which people make judgements and decisions, and the ways in which they interpret—or misinterpret—one another's actions."[43] This brand of therapy views irrational thinking as the cause, or at the least an exacerbating factor, in psychological discomfort. One of the major proponents of the cognitive perspective, Albert Ellis, argues people make themselves psychologically disturbed by constructing disturbing thoughts.[44] However, according to Ellis, they also have the ability to modify those thoughts, feelings, and behaviors.[45] Readers interested in sampling popular books written from a cognitive framework may want to read Albert Ellis' *How to Stubbornly Refuse to Make Yourself Miserable about Anything—Yes, Anything!*

Biological Therapies

While not actually psychotherapy, biological interventions are commonly used to assist in the treatment of psychological disorders. Most notable among them is psychopharmacology, which refers to the management of psychological problems through medication. Eliot Gelwan has written a most accessible chapter for lay readers entitled "If You Need Medication," which appears in *The Consumer's Guide to Psychotherapy* by Jack Engler and Daniel Goleman.[46] Gelwan cautions readers as follows:

> Finding the right medication, or the right dose, always involves trial and error. Even a diagnosis made by rigorous psychiatric criteria does not automatically imply you will benefit from medication. Patients classified under the same diagnosis may react very differently if medicated the same.[47]

Of course, medication should be taken under the supervision of an appropriate medical professional, typically a psychiatrist.

Common Psychological Disorders

This section will discuss psychological problems commonly seen by therapists. Subsections will cover anxiety disorders, mood disorders, addictive disorders, eating disorders, and attention-deficit disorder. *Readers are cautioned not to self-diagnose, but instead to use the information, if it appears personally relevant, as an impetus to securing professional help. Those readers currently in therapy may wish to utilize the popular books as an additional resource in conjunction with their current participation in a formal program of treatment.*

Anxiety Disorders

The most common psychological problems are anxiety disorders, which include generalized anxiety disorder, phobias, panic disorder, obsessive-compulsive disorder, and posttraumatic stress disorder. About eight of ten adults in the United States can be classified as suffering from one of these disorders.[48] An anxiety disorder "has an unrealistic, irrational fear of disabling intensity at its core."[49] Anxiety affects the physiological, cognitive, motivational, emotional, and behavioral systems.[50] Anxiety may show itself in muscular tension, hypervigilance (a continuing state of arousal), difficulty in maintaining attention, chronic fatigue and sleep disturbances.[51] According to Ronald Comer:

> [those] with generalized anxiety disorders experience persistent feelings of anxiety that are not associated with specific objects or situations. People with panic disorders have recurrent attacks of terror. . . . People with phobic disorders experience a persistent and irrational fear of a specific object, activity, or situation. . . . Those with obsessive-compulsive disorders are beset by recurrent and unwanted thoughts or the need to perform repetitive and ritualistic actions. . . . People with posttraumatic stress disorders are tormented by fear and related symptoms long after a traumatic event.[52]

Generalized Anxiety Disorders, Panic Disorders, and Phobias

People may develop generalized anxiety and panic disorders for several reasons. Some theorists argue many of these afflictions have a sociocultural basis, citing the prevalence of relevant symptoms tied to social change. Psychoanalytic theorists suggest that everyone endeavors to control unacceptable personal impulses and the associated anxiety through the use of a wide variety of defense mechanisms, including repression, denial, projection, rationalization, and displacement. These mechanisms of defense allow an individual to deny or distort reality to avoid dealing directly with the full force of one's anxieties. When the defenses do not function effectively, an anxiety disorder may result.[53]

The humanistic theorists claim that these disorders may result when parents and other persons significant in the life of a child do not accept him or her unconditionally, but instead place conditions of worth on them. This may lead to the child constructing overly strict standards for himself, which he may attempt to live up to through the use of psychological defenses. Existential theorists suggest that because human beings fear death or nonbeing and may confront the idea of the possible purposelessness of life, they may develop these types of disorders. If people choose to lead lives which are inauthentic and avoid taking full responsibility for their life choices, anxiety may overwhelm them.

Behavioral theorists view these disorders as caused by faulty learning. People can learn anxiety responses through association, reinforcement, modeling the responses of others, or some combination of these methods. Specifically, persons could have one negative experience with a cat or a dog as children and generalize that experience in such a way that they become afraid of all cats and dogs. Joseph and David Wolpe have written a useful self-help book from the behavioral perspective, *Life without Fear: Anxiety and Its Cure.*

Cognitive theorists claim these disorders come from maladaptive assumptions and faulty thinking.[54] Aaron Beck and his associates view persons with generalized anxiety disorder as having inaccurate and unrealistic fears that they are in danger. For example, these therapists list the following silent assumptions that people with this disorder may hold: (1) "Any strange situation should be regarded as dangerous"; (2) "It is always best to assume the worst"; and (3) "My survival depends on my always being competent and strong."[55] Some cognitive theorists suggest that panic disorder may be due to an individual's sensitivity to some stimuli and that these same persons may have a tendency to misinterpret the signals.[56]

In *The Feeling Good Handbook,* David Burns devotes seven chapters to specific cognitive techniques for overcoming anxieties and fears, and Barbara Markway and associates offer practical strategies for managing social phobias in their cognitive-behavioral guide, *Dying of Embarrassment: Help for Social Anxiety and Phobia.* Other theorists argue that generalized anxiety disorders and panic disorders are determined, at least in part, by biochemical dysfunctions in the brain.[57]

Obsessive-Compulsive Disorder

According to Robert Carson and James Butcher, "an obsession is a persistent preoccupation with a certain mental content, typically an idea or a feeling. A compulsion is an impulse to engage in some behavior experience as irresistible."[58] Estimated incidence of OCD (obsessive-compulsive disorder) is around 2½ percent of the U.S. population, or about six million people.[59] Probably everyone has experienced some persistent thoughts, like a series of numbers or a melody that is repeated over and over in one's mind, and it is rather common for people to have thoughts of engaging in some forbidden or destructive activity.[60]

What makes OCD maladaptive is that "it represents irrational and exaggerated behavior in the face of stressors that are not unduly upsetting to most people . . . such patterns reduce the flexibility of behavior and the capability for self-direction."[61] Ronald Comer views obsessive-compulsive disorders as one of the least understood of all psychological problems.[62] Fugen Neziroglu and Jose Yaryura-Tobias, in their self-help book, *Over and Over Again: Understanding Obsessive-Compulsive Disorder,* assert that many persons with this affliction are overwhelmed with superstitious or religious thoughts.[63] Neziroglu and Yaryura-Tobias describe several common secondary symptoms of OCD, including anxiety, depression, aggressivity, phobias, sexual dysfunctions, disturbances of perception, and an unusual speech pattern involving repetition, rarely in the present or future tense; often this pattern involves people talking about themselves.[64]

Psychodynamic theorists believe that OCD results from an individual's attempts to manage unacceptable impulses through the misapplication of defense mechanisms, and many of these same theorists contend those persons with OCD experienced aggressive impulses in childhood and develop a strong desire for controlling those impulses.[65] Behavioral research, centering on compulsive behaviors, suggests that these behaviors may develop through reinforcement. For example, an individual may engage in a specific set of activities in an anxiety-provoking situation resulting in anxiety reduction.[66]

Edna Foa and Reid Wilson provide a detailed self-help program, which is based on cognitive-behavioral therapy in their book, *Stop Obsessing!: How to Overcome Your Obsessions and Compulsions.* In recent years much interest in uncovering possible biological factors that may play a part in OCD has emerged, and some of this work has indicated that the basal ganglia, the frontal lobes, or the neurotransmitter, serotonin, may be involved.[67]

Posttraumatic Stress Disorder

In *I Can't Get Over It: A Handbook for Trauma Survivors,* Aphrodite Matsakis describes the symptoms often found in cases of posttraumatic stress disorder (PTSD): vigilance and scanning, elevated startle response, blunted emotions or psychic numbing, aggressive and controlling behavior, interruptions of memory and concentration, depression, generalized anxiety, episodes of rage, substance abuse, intrusive memories of the original trauma, flashbacks, insomnia, thoughts of suicide, and survivor guilt.[68]

Carson and Butcher, in summarizing research on the causes of PTSD, state that, in cases of low or moderate stress, the best predictor of the likelihood of PTSD is the individual's personality and adjustment prior to the trauma. In the most extreme traumatic experiences, the trauma itself is the best predictor, since "everyone has a breaking point, and at sufficiently high levels of stress the average person can be expected to develop some psychological difficulties."[69] Evidence suggests the idea that persons who receive strong psychological support following a traumatic experience seem less likely to suffer a long-term disorder.[70]

One form of trauma is rape, and a very strong guide to managing the traumas associated with this violent crime is *Recovering from Rape* by Linda Ledray. The author devotes attention to debunking common myths surrounding rape; the first chapter is titled "It's Not Your Fault." Subsequent chapters discuss obtaining medical care, dealing with the police and the courts, sorting out feelings, the first anniversary of the rape, and childhood sexual assault. Special information is provided for the significant other of the rape survivor.

Mood Disorders

Everyone experiences some fluctuations in mood depending on life events, relationships, and physical health. However, some persons can be diagnosed as having a mood disorder; 6 percent of American adults display a form of unipolar depression and another one-half to 1 percent exhibit a type of bipolar disorder at some point in their lives.[71] According to David Myers, "along with the phobias, depression is considered the 'common cold' of psychological disorders—an expression that well states its pervasiveness but not its seriousness. . . . Young adults and women are especially vulnerable."[72]

The most severe form of unipolar depression is called *major depression* in contrast to *bipolar disorder,* formerly called *manic depression,* where an individual experiences periods of depression and manic episodes. In *How to Cope with Depression: A Complete Guide for You and Your Family,* J. Raymond DePaulo and Keith Russell Ablow discuss the "hallmarks" of major depression: a continuing sadness, lowered self-concept, and lessening of physical and mental energy.[73] According to these authors, depressed persons often complain of aches and fatigue, changes in appetite, sleep disturbances, and a lowered sex drive.[74] DePaulo and Ablow write:

> A major feature of this group of disorders is the tendency toward recurrences and remissions. Of the people who experience major depression, perhaps a third go through only one episode and never have a serious recurrence. Others may suffer episodes of major depression, again and again. . . .[75]

Psychodynamic theorists often explain depression as the result of losses early in life. They suggest that these losses contribute to an individual's vulnerability to other losses occurring in later life.[76] Other psychodynamic theorists believe that due to early loss individuals may blend their own identity with the identity of the one they lost. This blending may turn feelings of anger toward the loved one who is lost into self-hatred, contributing to depression.

In recent years behavioral and cognitive explanations of depression have become more popular than psychodynamic ones in psychological circles. For example, Peter Lewinsohn and associates in *Control Your Depression* present a self-help program based on Lewinsohn's behavioral model of depression. Lewinsohn contends that when a person has a significant reduction in the number of positively reinforcing factors in life, an increased likelihood develops of becoming depressed. This self-help program endeavors to reinforce participation in pleasurable activities and other nondepressive behaviors.

Cognitive theorists like Aaron Beck and Albert Ellis point to negative and other maladaptive thinking as a fundamental cause of depression. Beck believes that depressed persons engage in continual negative thinking, which can be in three forms termed the cognitive triad.[77] Depressed persons "repeatedly interpret (1) their experiences, (2) themselves, and (3) their futures in negative ways that lead them to be depressed."[78] Two popular books covering depression and written from the cognitive perspective are *Feeling Good: The New Mood Therapy* and *The Feeling Good Handbook*, both by David Burns.

Some theorists argue that depression is a manifestation of a biological illness and see a genetic and biochemical basis in the depressive disorders. Ronald Fieve writes from the biological perspective in his popular book, *Moodswing*.

Finally, some theorists see a sociocultural basis to depression. For example, the incidence of depression varies dramatically from society to society, and in the United States women are significantly more likely to suffer from depression than men.[79] Writing from a sociocultural position, Ellen McGrath, in *When Feeling Bad Is Good* argues that women may be able to channel their depression into positive change.

Unipolar depression contrasts with bipolar disorder, commonly referred to as *manic-depression*. Occurring in around 1 percent of the U.S. population and affecting both genders in approximately the same numbers, bipolar disorder is particularly common among creative persons like artists, composers, entertainers, and writers.[80] In *The Feeling Good Handbook*, author David Burns describes bipolar disorder as containing two types of abnormally elevated moods—manic episodes and hypomania.[81] During the most severe mood elevations, manic episodes, people may feel an unlimited self-concept, believing themselves capable of almost anything. In the words of David Burns, these individuals "suddenly feel brilliant, alert, creative, and euphoric, a fountain of energy and ideas. They feel so good that they cannot accept the idea that there may be something wrong or that they need treatment."[82]

Some of the signs of a manic episode are grandiosity, elation, irritability if frustrated, very poor judgement evidenced by buying binges, needing very little sleep, thoughtlessness, and incessant activity.[83] Most persons with this disorder experience depression, which can last up to six to nine months, but the manic episodes typically extend for just several weeks.

The cycle of depression and mania varies with some persons going from mania to depression and back over months or years, while others experience a few depressive episodes prior to another manic one.[84] Strong evidence in the scientific community supports the genetic bases for bipolar disorder. As is the case with major depression, a number of physical disorders can produce bipolar disorder. The preferred treatment for bipolar disorder is the drug lithium coupled with psychotherapy. Because persons with this disorder may become extremely disoriented, frenzied, and hostile, hospitalization may be required.[85]

Mood disorders should be taken very seriously. All of us feel sad from time to time, but major depression and bipolar depression rob an individual of the joys of living. The most serious complication of these disorders is suicide. For these reasons it is important that those affected with these disorders obtain professional help. Since medication is often necessary as part of treatment, a psychiatrist or other medically trained professional should be consulted.

Substance Use Disorders

According to Jack Engler and Daniel Goleman, almost 9 percent of the American population abuses alcohol or other substances, and over a lifetime one-third of all families will include at least one member with such a problem.[86] In psychological language, an individual who continues a pattern of using drugs, could develop a substance use disorder. The two varieties of this disorder are *substance abuse* and *substance dependence*.[87] Substance abuse refers to a pattern of reliance in which the drug plays a central role in the user's life; substance dependence, also commonly termed *addiction*, implies both chronic abuse and physical dependence.

Whether substance abuse problems constitute an illness, addiction, or habit, controversy surrounds each of these concepts.

The great majority of people who drink or experiment with psychoactive (mood-altering) drugs do not develop an addiction.[88] Alcohol and nicotine are the most commonly abused substances.

Alcohol may serve "as a social lubricant and a means of reducing tension."[89] As alcohol is absorbed into the bloodstream, social restrains may begin to decline. According to Robert Carson and James Butcher, as a person continues to drink:

> Some degree of motor incoordination soon becomes apparent, and the drinker's discrimination of cold, pain, and other discomforts are dulled . . . the drinker experiences a sense of warmth, expansiveness, and well-being.[90]

Contrary to popular belief, alcohol is a depressant affecting areas of the brain involving judgment and self-control.[91]

As more alcohol is absorbed into the bloodstream, it depresses the central nervous system, altering an individual's mood to one of depression.[92] A great many persons who have problems with alcohol have periodic blackouts or memory lapses. The day after a period of drinking, that person may not be able to recall events from the day before. In addition, problem drinkers may have hangovers, composed of nausea, fatigue, and headache. Excessive drinking can lead to cirrhosis of the liver, malnutrition (drinking may reduce the appetite, which may interfere with the body's use of nutrients), chronic fatigue, depression, personality disorganization, accidents, lowered immunity to disease due to a decrease in white blood cells, tremors, delirium, or defects in memory.[93] Jack Engler and Daniel Goleman in *A Consumer's Guide to Psychotherapy* provide an extensive list of questions to determine if someone has a problem with alcohol.[94] In addition, these authors provide a four-item "CAGE test": (1) "Have you ever felt the need to CUT DOWN on your drinking?" (2) "Have you ever felt ANNOYED by people who criticize your drinking?" (3) "Have you ever felt GUILTY about drinking?" and (4) "Do you sometimes have an EYE-OPENER in the morning?"[95]

An individual may be dependent psychologically or physically on alcohol. According to Engler and Goleman, alcohol dependence is reflected when a person shows some of the following: (1) "Giving in to the temptation to have more than you intend or continuing to drink for a longer period. . . ." (2) "Being unable to quit drinking. . . ." (3) "Spending [much] of your day drinking or drunk, or recovering from being drunk. . . ." (4) "Being drunk or hung over when you should be working. . . ." (5) "Being drunk where you or someone else is put at risk—for example, while driving or taking care of children." (6) "Ignoring problems created by drinking. . . ." (7) "Increasing tolerance makes you need to drink more and more in order to get the same effect. . . ." (8) "Withdrawal symptoms if you try to stop drinking. . . ." and (9) "Drinking to avoid withdrawal. . . ."[96]

While alcohol is the drug of choice for many persons, others prefer sedative-hypnotics, opioids, stimulants, or hallucinogens, or other substances. Sedative-hypnotic drugs have a calming effect at low dosage, but induce sleep at higher dosages. Included in this category are antianxiety drugs and barbiturates. A second category, opioids, is comprised of opium and its derivatives, morphine and heroin. Stimulants include cocaine, amphetamines, and nicotine. Hallucinogens, which affect sensory perception, include psychedelics and cannabis.[97] It is projected that over a lifetime, around 6 percent of Americans will engage in drug abuse, but if tobacco is included, the percentage rises to around 33 percent.[98] Frequently, those involved in drug abuse engage in polydrug use. For example, some research supports that 27 percent of young adults using marijuana also use cocaine.[99]

A number of theories attempt to explain substance use disorders. Some evidence suggests that some persons are predisposed to developing problems with substance abuse and dependence.[100] However, some studies fail to support a strong genetic component. For example, Stanton Peele and associates in their popularly written book, *The Truth about Addiction and Recovery* cite numerous research studies which reject a strong link between genetics and alcoholism. Alcoholics Anonymous (AA) and other Twelve-Step groups promote a viewpoint that substance use disorders are diseases and provide structured self-help and support for those who ascribe to their tenets. AA and related groups are run by nonprofessionals, usually from a Christian framework.[101]

Psychoanalytic theorists see the abuse of substances as symptomatic of other underlying psychological problems. However, most therapy programs assume the problem is drinking or drug use and not another problem.[102] Engler and Goleman assert that it is essential to bring the drinking or "drugging" under control prior to engaging in productive therapy.[103]

Cognitive-behavioral theorists view substance abuse as learned behavior which can be modified through effective self-monitoring and the development of alternatives to using substances. Two useful books stress cognitive-behavioral approaches: *Rational Steps to Quitting Alcohol* by Albert Ellis and Emmett Veltan and *The Truth about Addiction and Recovery* by Stanton Peele, Archie Brodsky, and Mary Arnold. In *The Consumer's Guide to Psychotherapy,* Engler and Goleman provide extensive discussion of the nature and treatments available for alcoholism and other substance use disorders. In addition, the authors include a list of self-help groups, with addresses and telephone numbers, for a wide array of disorders, including those involving drugs and alcohol.

Eating Disorders

Under the rubric of eating disorders are the common problems of anorexia nervosa and bulimia nervosa.

Anorexia Nervosa

The current concern about anorexia and bulimia has its roots in earlier historical periods.[104] Robert Carson and James Butcher describe the key elements of anorexia nervosa as:

> an intense abhorrence of obesity coupled with the often absurd complaint that one is 'fat'; loss of at least 25 percent of original body weight (or in those under 18, significant weight loss . . .; and unremitting refusal to maintain weight within the lower limits of normal for age and height.[105]

Between 90 and 95 percent of anorexics are young females, usually white and from middle to upper class backgrounds, and overrepresented among first and second generation white immigrants.[106]

Anorexia is rare in males, suggesting much more pathology than when it occurs in women and girls, and is infrequently found in African-Americans and Latinos.[107] In *Dying to Be Thin,* Ira Sackler and Marc Zimmer, indicate that perhaps as many as 15 percent of those with the disorder may die as a consequence of the complications which result from starving.[108] Physical symptoms associated with starvation among females are the ceasing of menstruation, atrophying of breasts, growing a light layer of hair (lanugo) over some areas of the body like the chest and arms, developing bald spots, reacting especially to both heat and cold, becoming hyperactive, and developing a yellow cast to their skin.[109]

Bulimia Nervosa

The symptoms of bulimia nervosa include repeated patterns of binge eating followed by purging.[110] Among the methods used by bulimics to control weight gain are vomiting, laxatives, diuretics, exercise, and fasting.[111] In their useful book, *Bulimia: A Guide for Family and Friends,* Roberta Trattner Sherman and Ron Thompson discuss some of the important differences between anorexia and bulimia.[112] While the bulimic denies to others that she has a problem, she undoubtedly recognizes that her behavior is not normal. However, the anorexic typically denies the problem to herself as well as to others. A bulimic can vary from overweight to underweight, but an anorexic is at least 15 percent below the appropriate weight. Usually, the amount of body-image distortion is greater for anorexics. Also, while the goal of the bulimic is to maintain some "ideal" weight, the anorexic endeavors to lose more and more weight.

Sherman and Thompson describe a number of psychological problems common to bulimics, including the following: (1) "relentless pursuit of an ideal weight"; (2) "low sense of self-worth"; (3) "low sense of self-control"; (4) "depression, anger, and anxiety;" (5) "absolute thinking" (viewing events, ideas, or people in all-or-nothing terms); and (6) "difficulty expressing emotion in a direct manner."[113] According to Sherman and Thompson, bulimia can be caused by a combination of societal, familial, and individual factors.[114] American society prizes "thinness" in women, and communicates this message repeatedly through various media. Women are exhorted to be thin in order to be feminine and to be attractive to men. Usually bulimia starts with dieting in order to mirror a societal image of an appropriate weight and shape, but when the dieting does not achieve the desired result, an individual may develop a binge and purge relationship to eating.[115] Martin Seligman presents a strong case in his popular book, *What You Can Change and What You Can't: The Complete Guide to Successful Self-Improvement*. This work supports the notion that not only do diets not work, but they may contribute to eating disorders and, almost invariably, dieters regain weight after dieting.[116]

Family also plays a significant role in the development of bulimia nervosa. Sherman and Thompson suggest that families of bulimics often put great emphasis on such factors as attractiveness and weight, and at the same time expect the daughters to be perfect. In this type of family, a daughter may feel tremendous pressure to please her parents, to refrain from expressing her frustration and anger, and to be "thin."[117] Some bulimics may use binging and purging as ways of gaining control over their lives and in this way asserting power. Sometimes bulimia results from a situation in which an adolescent has problems becoming more independent, which may be related to the parents being overprotective.[118] Since families are such an important ingredient in the development of many cases of bulimia, family members, when possible, should be involved in any program of treatment.

Individual factors also play a key role in the development of bulimia. Sherman and Thompson view these personality factors as common among bulimics: (1) low self-esteem; (2) need for approval/dependency; (3) low tolerance for anxiety and frustration; (4) compulsiveness; (5) irresponsibility; (6) dramatic expression; and (7) difficulties in making decisions.[119]

Because of their very nature, eating disorders can be life-threatening. Readers are strongly encouraged to seek appropriate professional assistance from therapists who specialize in these disorders. Because of the possible medical complications associated with starving, diuretics, laxatives, and excessive exercise, a period of hospitalization may be required.

Attention-Deficit Disorder

In her useful book, *Your Hyperactive Child: A Parent's Guide to Coping with Attention-Deficit Disorder*, Barbara Ingersoll reports the general finding that attention deficit hyperactivity disorder (ADHD) is much more common in boys than in girls. However, Ingersoll suggests girls with this disorder are more likely to show attentional as opposed to behavioral problems, which contributes to girls being less likely to come to the attention of mental health professionals.[120] In his book *Dr. Larry Silver's Advice to Parents on Attention-Deficit Hyperactivity Disorder,* Larry Silver describes three common aspects of ADHD: hyperactivity, distractibility, and impulsivity.[121] According to Silver, some children and adolescents may display only one or two of the three, while others may demonstrate all three behaviors.[122]

Most obvious to parents and teachers are children who appear to be continually fidgeting. One of the hallmarks of ADHD that is sometimes overlooked is distractibility. For some children, staying on a task may be extremely difficult because they have trouble sorting important stimuli from unimportant ones.[123] Silver mentions some children, otherwise highly distractible, who can block out certain stimuli in order to engage in a desirable activity like playing a video game.[124] Impulsiveness is also seen in ADHD, since many of these children may get angry when frustrated and act before they think through the consequences. Sometimes this impulsiveness is reflected in specific behavioral problems such as stealing, fire setting, or bedwetting.[125]

Barbara Ingersoll asserts that most children with hyperactivity show symptoms by the age of two.[126] Some children later diagnosed with ADHD are restless, fussy, and very active as infants, but certainly many babies who show these difficulties do not become hyperactive children.[127] Preschoolers with hyperactivity often display a very high level of activity, and about half demonstrate clumsiness, which leads to a need for continuing adult supervision.[128] Tantrums and a lack of ability to handle almost any frustration are characteristics of many of these preschool children.

When children with ADHD reach elementary school, they present tremendous problems for their teachers and classmates, and many of the children find it difficult to follow the rules of the classroom. Coupled with a short attention span and chronic restlessness, many children with ADHD also display learning problems. These children are typically rejected by their peers who find them difficult as playmates.[129]

About one-fifth of all children with ADHD appear to be free of symptoms by the time they reach adolescence.[130] Adolescents with the disorder may show lower activity levels in their earlier years, but whatever problems they do have are exacerbated by the normal changes and concerns associated with adolescence. Adults who demonstrated hyperactivity in childhood and adolescence will see a decrease in symptoms, but may continue to experience difficulty with concentration, attention, and organization.[131]

Attention-deficit hyperactivity disorder appears to be biologically determined, specifically a neurological disorder.[132] Silver states that around 30 to 40 percent of children and adolescents with this disorder have a biological relative with ADHD.[133] Some research has centered on possible prenatal causes, while other studies have attempted to understand possible family and cultural determinants.[134]

Treatment often involves medication coupled with behavior management and parent education. It is essential that parents whose children or adolescents display chronic patterns of inattention, hyperactivity, and impulsiveness seek professional assistance. Their children may have ADHD or a learning disability, obsessive-compulsive disorder, oppositional defiant disorder, conduct disorder, or perhaps some other psychological problem. Psychiatrists or psychologists should be consulted so that an assessment and treatment plan can be developed. In many communities school counselors can make the necessary referrals.

Summary

Discussions in this chapter included comments on the overuse of some popular terms like *codependency, dysfunctional families*, and *inner child*, and readers are advised to avoid self-help books which rely on such vague notions and reinforce viewing the self as "victim." Psychological problems are common, but so are stereotypes about these disorders. Readers of self-help books are cautioned about the possibility of misdiagnosing themselves and thus reading books whose content is not specifically applicable to them.

Throughout the chapter readers are strongly encouraged to seek professional help and to not use self-help books as a substitute for appropriate treatment. Persons seeking mental health professionals can follow a rational approach in their selection of a therapist. Most types of therapy are considered to be psychodynamic, humanistic/existential, behavioral, cognitive, biological, or eclectic. Some of the more common psychological disorders for which self-help books are available include the anxiety disorders, mood disorders, substance abuse disorders, eating disorders, and attention deficit hyperactivity disorder. Such disorders are described in detail in the self-help books.

RECOMMENDED TITLES

Nature of Psychological Disturbance

Bruno, Frank J. *Psychological Symptoms.* New York: Wiley, 1993.

Psychologist Bruno provides readers with an overview of common psychological disorders by describing the symptoms, causes, and recommended coping strategies for each. The author also compares the various therapeutic approaches used by mental health professionals and describes how these approaches are applied to specific disorders. Each chapter outlines a disorder so readers can turn directly to their particular concern. A detailed glossary defines psychological and psychiatric terms.

Engler, Jack, and Daniel Goleman. *A Consumer's Guide to Psychotherapy.* New York: Simon & Schuster, 1992.

In a thorough, well-written, and informative sourcebook on psychotherapy, the authors describe what individuals should know about the therapeutic process. Issues covered include: what to expect from a therapist, types of therapy available, and what individuals can expect from therapy. The authors surveyed nearly one thousand psychiatrists, clinical psychologists, and clinical social workers, asking them about the forty most common reasons individuals come to therapy and what types of treatment were most effective. Engler and Goleman examine a variety of psychological disorders in detail: problems in everyday living (e.g., marital problems; relationship problems; parent-child conflict); emotional and behavioral problems of childhood and adolescence; and other psychiatric disorders. Each section discusses the condition in general, signs to watch for, and recommended types of therapy. This title was also annotated in Chapter 2 under marriage and family therapy.

Seligman, Martin E. P. *What You Can Change and What You Can't: The Complete Guide to Successful Self-Improvement.* New York: Knopf, 1994.

Psychologist Seligman explores the conflict between biological psychiatry, which contends that genetic predisposition and brain chemistry underlie most disorders making them difficult if not impossible, to change, and the self-improvement movement, which asserts that all behavior can be changed. In this examination the author describes what individuals can change, which types of interventions are most effective, and what cannot be changed. Conditions that could be changed with considerable success are outlined. The author also describes what cannot be changed, concluding that dieting over time rarely ever works, and that changing sexual identity and sexual orientation is difficult, if not impossible, to do. He asserts that treatment programs for alcoholism are no better that the natural course of recovery, and that adult personality problems are not improved by reliving childhood trauma.

Anxiety Disorders

Phobias and Panic Disorders

Markway, Barbara G. and others. *Dying of Embarrassment: Help for Social Anxiety and Phobia*. Oakland, Calif.: New Harbinger, 1992.

The authors define and describe a variety of social phobias. These fears characteristically are persistent and involve the fear of criticism, rejection, or embarrassment. Individuals may be uncomfortable in any social situation or may be successful public speakers, but may be extremely anxious when dating. Common sources of social phobia can be public speaking, taking tests or writing in public, eating in public, using public rest rooms, and dating. The authors examine the physical, cognitive, and behavioral components of social phobias. Irrational or maladaptive thinking can accompany the physical symptoms (e.g., "I sound stupid").

Behavioral changes involve complete or partial avoidance of social situations. The authors also examine what causes social phobias, how individuals can identify anxiety-producing events, and how to set realistic goals and objectives to reduce their anxiety. Through a series of exercises and questionnaires, readers can determine what events cause them to be most anxious, moderately anxious, slightly anxious, or completely comfortable.

In addition, relaxation techniques are discussed as an effective method to combat the physical and cognitive symptoms of social phobias. The authors also include strategies to maintain and improve social confidence, to overcome stress, and to acknowledge the role that depression, substance abuse, and other anxiety disorders may play in reducing social anxiety.

Wolpe, Joseph, and David Wolpe. *Life without Fear.* Oakland, Calif.: New Harbinger, 1988.

Psychiatrist Wolpe and his son, a writer and actor, focus on behavior therapy and its efficacy in treating anxiety. The authors distinguish between useful and useless fears by identifying as useful those fears that warn an individual of impending danger (e.g., an ambulance's siren). Useless fears develop from a single event or series of events, which can lead to a generalized fear. After an automobile accident, an individual may drive more carefully, or may avoid driving altogether.

Using fear hierarchies, the Wolpes identified anxiety-producing situations and asked clients to rank them in order from the least to the most stressful. The authors recommend that individuals can reduce their anxiety by setting a specific short-term goal which can be met easily. They find that for each positive experience they can continue to reduce useless fears. The authors also recommend that individuals may benefit from psychotherapy to treat their anxiety disorders.

Obsessive-Compulsive Disorder

Foa, Edna B., and Reid Wilson. *Stop Obsessing!: How to Overcome Your Obsessions and Compulsions.* New York: Bantam, 1991.

Psychiatrist Foa and clinical psychologist Wilson find that persons with obsessive-compulsive disorder are troubled by persistent, repetitious, worrisome thoughts; are concerned that something catastrophic has happened or will happen to them; are upset when things are not perfect; and repeat tasks again and again without reason. Furthermore, these individuals seek reassurance repeatedly from friends and family. Their worries are constant, repetitive, and anxiety-producing. Additionally, the individual is usually unsuccessful in dismissing these thoughts. To forestall the catastrophic outcome that the person fears, repeated rituals are performed. Individuals with obsessive-compulsive disorders can be characterized as washers and cleaners, checkers, repeaters, orderers, hoarders, thinking ritualizers, worriers, and pure obsessionals. After identifying the characteristics of persons with OCD, the authors discuss the causes of obsessive-compulsive disorder, the behavioral and cognitive techniques that have been effective in treating OCD, and when medical treatment is appropriate.

Neziroglu, Fugen, and Jose A. Yaryura-Tobias. *Over and Over Again: Understanding Obsessive-Compulsive Disorder.* Lexington, Mass.: Lexington Bks., 1991.

Most obsessive-compulsive behavior originates in response to superstitious belief or unfounded fears. An individual who fears contamination or germs from the outside world may spend hours at a time cleaning the house, and follow this up with repeated bathing to ward off any germs. The authors describe the basis of obsessive-compulsive behavior and its behavioral, medical, and biological treatment. Psychotherapy is seen as an effective treatment when accompanied by medication tailored to the individual's needs. Family members play a role in either encouraging the person with the disorder to seek treatment or, conversely, helping the individual continue the obsessive-compulsive behavior. The authors offer suggestions for friends and families who are coping with a person with this disorder. An appendix of one hundred commonly asked questions on obsessive-compulsive disorder is included.

Posttraumatic Stress Disorder

Ledray, Linda E. *Recovering from Rape.* New York: Holt, 1986.

Rape survivors, their significant others, and family members will find their concerns addressed in a thorough discussion of the trauma of rape and its aftermath. Ledray discredits many of the myths about rape, and in doing so emphasizes repeatedly that the rape survivor is not at fault for the attack. In straightforward language, the author describes what to expect from the police and hospital staff. While individual emotional responses may differ, rape survivors often experience shock, disbelief, depression, anger, and fear. Ledray recommends a number of effective strategies for coping with these emotions.

Matsakis, Aphrodite. *I Can't Get Over It: A Handbook for Trauma Survivors.* Oakland, Calif.: New Harbinger, 1992.

In this informative guide, the author describes posttraumatic stress disorder as a normal reaction to an abnormal amount of stress usually produced when facing a life-threatening episode (e.g., war, rape, violent crime, earthquake, and other natural disasters among others). When facing the traumatic event or events, individuals develop survival skills appropriate for the dangerous situation. Although these skills help the individual cope during a traumatic episode, using the same skills when one is not in a life-threatening situation can be inappropriate or harmful. For example, a combat veteran who would take cover while under an attack may automatically dive under a table when a car nearby backfires.

In the introduction, the author advises readers that if they experience certain reactions while reading the book they should get professional help IMMEDIATELY, and that a physician should be consulted before proceeding further. While promising no magic solutions, Matsakis describes posttraumatic stress disorder and its causes. The author explores effective coping strategies for those with PTSD, the biochemical effects involved, and the emotional and cognitive reactions to the trauma. Certain events can trigger flashbacks and other symptoms. By identifying these triggers, individuals can develop specific strategies to cope with them. While triggering events vary from person to person, two common emotional reactions to trauma appear: anger and grief. Several chapters give readers insight into the role each of these emotions plays in the healing process.

Mood Disorders

Depression

Burns, David D. *Feeling Good: The New Mood Therapy.* New York: New American Lib., 1980.

Burns, David D. *The Feeling Good Handbook.* New York: Plume Book, 1989.

In *Feeling Good* psychologist David Burns advocates using cognitive therapy as the treatment for depression. This approach, originally developed by researchers at the University of Pennsylvania School of Medicine, focuses on changing the illogical, and often, negative thought patterns found in depressed or anxious individuals. After introducing the key concepts of cognitive therapy, the author describes the results he and his associates observed in treating individuals with depression. When compared to conventional psychotherapy and some drug therapies, cognitive therapy reduced the symptoms of depression more rapidly. The author is quick to point out that it is not a "quick fix."

Burns guides readers through a variety of written exercises which assist in identifying common characteristics of anxiety and depression, their severity, and in so doing advises whether individuals can use this book independently or in conjunction with professional treatment. In addition, techniques for understanding and changing cognitive distortions or illogical thinking are provided.

The *Feeling Good Handbook* continues and broadens the use of cognitive therapy beyond depression and anxiety to personal relationships. A discussion of psychoactive drugs and their effectiveness is also included.

DePaulo, J. Raymond, and Keith Russell Ablow. *How to Cope with Depression: A Complete Guide for You and Your Family.* New York: McGraw-Hill, 1989.

Physicians DePaulo and Ablow define depression and bipolar disorder, formerly called manic depressive illness, explore their causes, and treatment. By incorporating a variety of perspectives, including the role personality, behavior, and one's life history play in depression, the authors present an excellent overview of mood disorders. Treatment alternatives include a variety of psychotherapeutic methods, drug therapy, and electroconvulsive therapy. Future trends in the treatment of depression are also discussed.

Klein, Donald F., and Paul H. Wender. *Do You Have a Depressive Illness?: How to Tell, What to Do.* New York: New American Lib., 1988.

The authors, both psychiatrists, identify two distinct forms of depression: psychological and biological. Their focus is on the biological form which centers on biochemical imbalance. Once the biological form is diagnosed, Klein and Wender assert that this type of depression responds well to drug therapy.

Lewinsohn, Peter M., and others. *Control Your Depression.* Rev. ed. New York: Prentice Hall, 1986.

The authors, all clinical psychologists, work from a social learning framework which contends that most behavior is learned and, as such, can be unlearned. Drawing on cognitive therapy, the work presents techniques for recognizing depression, for relaxing, for engaging in pleasant activities, for overcoming depression, and for determining when professional help is needed. Lewinsohn and his associates recommend strategies for maintaining the positive changes over time.

McGrath, Ellen. *When Feeling Bad Is Good.* New York: Holt, 1992.

Clinical psychologist McGrath addresses concerns surrounding depression and its effect on women. The author distinguishes between healthy and unhealthy depression. Unhealthy depression is characterized by an individual's inability to function in one or more aspects of daily life—work, relationships, eating and sleeping, the ability to enjoy activities, the ability to concentrate or remember. This condition is characterized by exaggerated or distorted thinking and by a biochemical imbalance. It is also seen as a debilitating illness which can require professional help.

Healthy depressions result from realistic feelings of pain, sadness, and disappointment which occur in response to trauma, loss, discrimination, unfair treatment, and unresolved issues in a woman's experience. McGrath examines six forms of healthy depression: victimization depression; relationship depression, age rage depression, depletion depression, body image depression, and mind-body depression. The author provides effective strategies for resolving healthy depressions.

Rosenthal, Norman E. *Seasons of the Mind: Why You Get the Winter Blues and What You Can Do about It.* New York: Bantam, 1989.

Seasonal affective disorder affects nearly ten million people in the United States who have significant shifts in energy, sleep and eating patterns, as well as mood in the winter or summer months. While this disorder affects four times as many women as men, individuals in their twenties through forties are more likely to develop the disorder than older or younger persons.

Rosenthal and his colleagues at the National Institute of Mental Health found a link between melatonin, a hormone released during each night until dawn, and seasonal affective disorder. This hormone signals the duration of darkness. As part of a larger study on cyclical depression, the author explored methods to suppress the release of melatonin by the use of light therapy. Persons with seasonal affective disorder sat in front of light boxes which simulated bright sunlight or dim light. Individuals exposed to the simulated sunlight reported a significant improvement in their symptoms. The author reports that behavior and drug therapy can also accompany light therapy.

Substance Abuse Disorder

Ellis, Albert, and Emmett Velten. *When AA Doesn't Work for You: Rational Steps to Quitting Alcohol.* Fort Lee, N.J.: Barricade Bks., 1992.

Psychologist Albert Ellis and his colleague advocate the use of Rational-Emotive Therapy as an effective alternative to Alcoholics Anonymous (AA) or other Twelve-Step programs in reducing or eliminating problem drinking. These strategies can be used in combination with AA or other Twelve-Step programs. Rational-Emotive Therapy (RET), which was developed by Ellis as a cognitive as well as a behavioral therapy, encourages individuals to set goals (in this case, to give up problem drinking) and to examine how their self-defeating thoughts, their emotional reactions, and their behavior can influence their drinking patterns. The authors also challenge the disease model of alcohol addiction and the labeling of "alcoholics" as counterproductive to positive change.

The central tenet of Ellis and Velten's approach focuses on individuals taking responsibility for their problem drinking. Using an ABC system to describe the Activating Events, Beliefs, and Consequences surrounding one's alcohol consumption, readers can recognize rational responses, beliefs, and consequences as well as irrational ones. The authors assert that AA and other Twelve-Step programs concentrate on the person's admission that they are powerless in the face of the addiction. This detracts from the clients' personal responsibility for their actions. Additionally, the authors demythologize family drinking patterns, the genetic basis of alcoholism, and groups at special risk for alcoholism.

Peele, Stanton, Archie Brodsky, with Mary Arnold. *The Truth about Addiction and Recovery: The Life Process Program for Outgrowing Destructive Habits.* New York: Simon & Schuster, 1991.

The authors challenge the disease model of addiction and the effectiveness of Twelve-Step programs. While some individuals may benefit from participation in groups like Alcoholics Anonymous, Peele and his associates cite research which indicates that other means of treatment may be as effective, if not more so. In the Life Process Program, addiction is not seen as a disease process, but as a means of coping with one's life and the world in general. This approach stresses the importance of the individual analyzing her strengths and weaknesses, learning new coping skills, and changing her environment. As part of this analysis, the authors found that individuals were not addicted to a substance per se but to the experience and its accompanying emotions. According to Peele, the problematic behavior can be abandoned or reduced when a person feels it is no longer beneficial. Additionally, individuals are responsible for their behavior, addictive or otherwise. The authors provide practical suggestions to individuals who want to learn new coping techniques, to build upon personal strengths and values, and, in so doing, to create support networks which render the former habit undesirable and unnecessary.

Eating Disorders

Kolodny, Nancy J. *When Food's a Foe: How to Confront and Conquer Eating Disorders*. Rev. ed. Boston: Little, 1992.

In this practical guide to eating disorders, Kolodny, a psychiatric social worker, links poor self-image, poor body image, and low self-esteem as risk factors for developing anorexia or bulimia. In some cases, an individual may be anorexic and bulimic at the same time. *The author emphasizes that both anorexia and bulimia can be fatal as starvation and purging take their toll.* Eating disorders occur more often in young women than young men. Both anorexia and bulimia center around individuals' relationship with food and their self-image. It may start when they change their eating habits to lose weight. Once they reach their ideal weight, they believe that they will be happier if they lose even more weight.

While most persons see food as a life-sustaining part of their existence, persons with eating disorders view food as a deadly enemy. Anorexics restrict their food intake to the point that starvation and the devastating toll it takes on the body result. Bulimics have a love-hate relationship with food. Common characteristics of bulimia include eating excessive amounts of food (often foods high in sugar) followed by purging, which involves vomiting or using laxatives to eliminate the food they have just eaten. Bulimics assume that they can eat as much as they want without gaining weight if they vomit or purge immediately after eating. After describing the symptoms of both disorders, Kolodny provides recommendations on how to stop eating disorders before they start, how to get professional help, and what friends and family can do to help in this situation.

Rodin, Judith. *Body Traps: Breaking the Binds That Keep You from Feeling Good about Your Body*. New York: Morrow, 1992.

Psychologist Rodin asserts that for many men and women appearance, good looks, and fitness have taken on a preeminent role in determining their social worth. With the increased emphasis on how one looks, mass media focuses on a single, often unattainable, perfect look. The author describes a variety of "body traps" and their impact on an individual. They include traps involving vanity, shame, competition, food, dieting rituals, fitness, and success. By exploring each one of these traps, the author provides techniques for avoiding them.

Sacker, Ira M., and Marc Zimmer. *Dying to Be Thin.* New York: Warner, 1987.

Using a wide variety of case studies of young men and women with eating disorders, the authors explore the nature and origins of anorexia and bulimia. In addition, the rituals surrounding each disorder are described. Sacker and his associate use the voices of their patients to tell their compelling stories. The authors advocate the use of biofeedback, and, if necessary, hospitalization in a facility equipped to treat eating disorders. Several chapters focus on what parents, other family members, and teachers can do to help persons with anorexia and/or bulimia.

Sherman, Roberta Trattner, and Ron A. Thompson. *Bulimia: A Guide for Family and Friends.* Lexington, Mass.: Lexington Bks., 1990.

This practical guide to bulimia helps readers understand the role of the family, the role of societal values about beauty as well as the role individual factors play in this disorder. The authors also describe the behaviors, thoughts, and emotions surrounding bulimic behavior. Their discussion of these key issues is followed by a section on entering and successfully completing treatment for the psychological and medical aspects of this eating disorder. A resource list is also provided.

Attention Deficit Disorder

Ingersoll, Barbara. *Your Hyperactive Child: A Parent's Guide to Coping With Attention Deficit Disorder.* New York: Doubleday, 1988.

In Ingersoll's analysis of attention-deficit hyperactivity disorder (ADHD), the focus is on children who have a short attention span, who have trouble concentrating, and who often act impulsively without regard to the consequences of their actions. Hyperactivity or excessive motor activity results from a child's inability to concentrate on one activity at a time. After spending a day with an energetic two-year-old, parents often wonder if their child is hyperactive. The author describes ADHD, its causes, its diagnosis, and its treatment. In addition, Ingersoll examines the effectiveness of medical and psychological treatment. Also discussed are practical strategies for parents, teachers, and other family members as well as the special problems that children with this disorder face.

Kennedy, Patricia, Leif Terdal, and Lydia Fusetti. *The Hyperactive Child Book: A Pediatrician, a Child Psychologist, and a Mother Team Up to Offer the Most Practical, Up-to-Date Guide to Treating, Educating, and Living with Your ADHD Child.* New York: St. Martin's, 1993.

This practical guide approaches attention-deficit hyperactive disorder from the perspective of a parent, a physician, and a psychologist. The authors concentrate on the interrelationships of these views in treating, educating, and living with a child with ADHD. Especially helpful is the section emphasizing the parents' role in the child's education. In some cases parents serve as advocates for their child with the school system. In addition, this work also explores the challenges that persons with ADHD face as adolescents and adults.

O'Leary, K. Daniel. *Mommy, I Can't Sit Still!: Coping with Hyperactive and Aggressive Children.* Rev. ed. New York: New Horizon Pr., 1989.

Psychologist O'Leary tells readers about attention-deficit hyperactivity disorder from a child's point of view. On the basis of examples from his practice and research, the author includes drawings and handwriting samples from children, which graphically illustrate the differences between those persons with ADHD and those who do not have the disorder. The origins of attention-deficit hyperactivity disorder can be traced to physiological, biological, or social causes. Readers are advised not to dwell on the origin of the disorder, but rather to focus on its treatment. O'Leary covers a number of alternatives which include medication, dietary changes, and psychological counseling.

Paltin, David M. *The Parents' Hyperactivity Handbook: Helping the Fidgety Child.* New York: Plenum Bks., 1993.

Paltin, a psychologist specializing in the treatment of attention-deficit hyperactivity disorder, explores, as most works on this topic do, its causes and treatment. One of the challenges facing parents, teachers, and other family members involves developing effective strategies in disciplining a child with ADHD. The author encourages parents to talk to their child about the disorder and provides a question-and-answer guide for this purpose.

Silver, Larry B. *Dr. Larry Silver's Advice to Parents on Attention-Deficit Hyperactivity Disorder.* Washington, D.C.: American Psychiatric Pr., 1993.

Psychiatrist Silver discusses the link between attention-deficit hyperactivity disorder and learning disorders in children. By recognizing the importance of this link, the author provides the reader with insight into which strategies work and which do not. Legal issues involved in ensuring that children receive the educational benefits guaranteed by state and Federal laws are also described.

NOTES

1. Wendy Kaminer, *I'm Dysfunctional, You're Dysfunctional: The Recovery Movement and other Self-Help Fashions* (Reading, Mass.: Addison-Wesley, 1992), 9–28.

2. Stanton Peele, Archie Brodsky, and Mary Arnold, *The Truth about Addiction and Recovery* (New York: Simon & Schuster, 1991), 334–35.

3. Ibid., 335.

4. Robert Carson and James Butcher, *Abnormal Psychology and Modern Life,* 9th ed. (New York: HarperCollins, 1992), 16.

5. David Myers, *Exploring Psychology,* 2d ed. (New York: Worth, 1993), 397–408.

6. Ibid., 408.

7. Ibid., 380.

8. David L. Rosenhan and Martin E. P. Seligman, *Abnormal Psychology* (New York: Norton, 1984), 21.

9. Jack Engler and Daniel Goleman, *The Consumer's Guide to Psychotherapy* (New York: Simon & Schuster, 1992), 71–102.

10. Ibid., 72–82.

11. Ibid., 77.

12. Ibid., 81.

13. Ibid., 83–86.

14. Ibid., 89–90.

15. Ibid., 92–95.

16. Ibid., 92.

17. Ibid., 95–96.

18. Ibid., 96–98.
19. Ibid., 102.
20. Carson and Butcher, *Abnormal Psychology and Modern Life,* 631.
21. Ibid.
22. Ibid.
23. Engler and Goleman, *A Consumer's Guide to Psychotherapy,* 192–223.
24. Ibid., 208.
25. Myers, *Exploring Psychology,* 545.
26. Ibid., 414.
27. Ronald Comer, *Abnormal Psychology* (New York: Freeman, 1992), 134.
28. Ibid., 136.
29. Ibid.
30. Ibid., 137–38.
31. Ibid., 138.
32. Ibid., 140.
33. Ibid., 140–41.
34. Gerald Corey, *Theory and Practice of Counseling and Psychotherapy,* 4th ed. (Pacific Grove, Calif.: Brooks/Cole, 1991), 207.
35. Ibid., 209.
36. James Prochaska, *Systems of Psychotherapy,* 2d ed. (Homewood, Ill.: Dorsey Pr., 1984), 128–31.
37. Ibid., 134.
38. Ibid., 135–36.
39. Corey, *Theory and Practice of Counseling and Psychotherapy,* 179–84.
40. Ibid., 184–85.
41. Ibid., 146.
42. Ibid., 146–50.
43. Aaron Beck, *Love Is Never Enough* (New York: Harper & Row, 1988), 2.
44. Corey, *Theory and Practice of Counseling and Psychotherapy,* 329.
45. Ibid.
46. Eliot Gelwan, "If You Need Medication," in Jack Engler and Daniel Goleman, *The Consumer's Guide to Psychotherapy* (New York: Simon & Schuster, 1992), 606–39.
47. Ibid., 607.
48. Comer, *Abnormal Psychology,* 178.
49. Carson and Butcher, *Abnormal Psychology and Modern Life,* 183.
50. Aaron Beck, Gary Emery, and Ruth Greenberg, *Anxiety Disorders and Phobias: A Cognitive Perspective* (New York: Basic, 1985), 4.

51. Frank Bruno, *Psychological Symptoms* (New York: Wiley, 1993), 31.

52. Comer, *Abnormal Psychology,* 178.

53. Ibid., 191–94.

54. Ibid., 198–99.

55. Aaron Beck, Gary Emery, and Ruth Greenberg, *Anxiety Disorders and Phobias: A Cognitive Perspective* (New York: Basic Books, 1985), 63.

56. Comer, *Abnormal Psychology,* 205.

57. Ibid., 200.

58. Carson and Butcher, *Abnormal Psychology and Modern Life,* 189.

59. Ibid.

60. Ibid., 190.

61. Ibid.

62. Comer, *Abnormal Psychology,* 211.

63. Fugen Neziroglu and Jose A. Yaryura-Tobias, *Over and Over Again: Understanding Obsessive-Compulsive Disorder* (Lexington, Mass.: Lexington Bks., 1991), 4.

64. Ibid., 7–12.

65. Comer, *Abnormal Psychology,* 211.

66. Ibid., 212.

67. Neziroglu and Yaryura-Tobias, *Over and Over Again,* 76–77.

68. Aphrodite Matsakis, *I Can't Get Over It: A Handbook for Trauma Survivors* (Oakland, Calif.: New Harbinger, 1992), 8–27.

69. Carson and Butcher, *Abnormal Psychology and Modern Life,* 159.

70. Comer, *Abnormal Psychology,* 218.

71. Ibid., 288–89.

72. Myers, *Understanding Psychology,* 393.

73. J. Raymond Depaulo and Keith Russell Ablow, *How to Cope with Depression: A Complete Guide for You and Your Family* (New York: McGraw-Hill, 1989), 3.

74. Ibid., 4.

75. Ibid., 4–5.

76. Comer, *Abnormal Psychology,* 266–70.

77. Ibid., 273.

78. Ibid.

79. Carson and Butcher, *Abnormal Psychology and Modern Life,* 407.

80. Myers, *Exploring Psychology,* 394.

81. David Burns, *The Feeling Good Handbook* (New York: Signet/New American Lib., 1980), 58.

82. Ibid.

83. Engler and Goleman, *A Consumer's Guide to Psychotherapy,* 480.

84. Ibid., 478–83.

85. Ibid., 484–86.

86. Ibid., 416.

87. Comer, *Abnormal Psychology,* 428.

88. Engler and Goleman, *A Consumer's Guide to Psychotherapy,* 434.

89. Carson and Butcher, *Abnormal Psychology and Modern Life,* 306.

90. Ibid., 299.

91. Ibid.

92. Engler and Goleman, *A Consumer's Guide to Psychotherapy,* 420.

93. Carson and Butcher, *Abnormal Psychology and Modern Life,* 299–304.

94. Engler and Goleman, *A Consumer's Guide to Psychotherapy,* 420–21.

95. Ibid., 421.

96. Ibid., 423.

97. Comer, *Abnormal Psychology,* 434–46.

98. Engler and Goleman, *A Consumer's Guide to Psychotherapy,* 435.

99. Comer, *Abnormal Psychology,* 446.

100. Ibid., 477.

101. Engler and Goleman, *A Consumer's Guide to Psychotherapy,* 426.

102. Ibid., 427.

103. Ibid.

104. Joan Jacobs Brumberg, *Fasting Girls: The History of Anorexia Nervosa* (New York: Penguin, 1988), 2–7.

105. Carson and Butcher, *Abnormal Psychology and Modern Life,* 243.

106. Brumberg, *Fasting Girls,* 12–13.

107. Ibid., 12.

108. Ira Sackler and Marc Zimmer, *Dying to Be Thin* (New York: Warner, 1987), 19.

109. Ibid., 20–24.

110. Roberta Trattner Sherman and Ron Thompson, *Bulimia: A Guide for Family and Friends* (Lexington, Mass.: Lexington Bks., 1990), 3.

111. Ibid.

112. Ibid., 4–5.

113. Ibid., 10–11.

114. Ibid., 17–20.

115. Ibid., 18; Martin E. P. Seligman, *What You Can Change and What You Can't: The Complete Guide to Successful Self-Improvement* (New York: Knopf, 1994), 174–97.

116. Ibid., 197.

117. Sherman and Thompson, *Bulimia: A Guide for Family and Friends,* 36–37.

118. Ibid., 40–41.

119. Ibid., 50–59.

120. Barbara Ingersoll, *Your Hyperactive Child: A Parent's Guide to Coping with Attention-Deficit Disorder* (New York: Doubleday, 1988), 7–8.

121. Larry B. Silver, *Dr. Larry Silver's Advice to Parents on Attention-Deficit Hyperactivity Disorder* (Washington, D.C.: American Psychiatric Pr., Inc., 1993), 15–26.

122. Ibid., 15.

123. Ibid., 15–16.

124. Ibid., 16–17.

125. Ibid., 18.

126. Ingersoll, *Your Hyperactive Child,* 8.

127. Ibid., 8–9.

128. Ibid., 10.

129. Ibid., 8–14.

130. Ibid., 16.

131. Ibid., 16–19.

132. Silver, *Dr. Larry Silver's Advice to Parents on Attention-Deficit Hyperactivity Disorder,* 115.

133. Ibid., 116.

134. Ibid., 115–22.

CHAPTER

8

Coping with Chronic Illness, Disability, and Death

Eventually most of us are faced with problems associated with illness, disability, and death. Chronic illness affects many persons, including most older adults, and disabilities impacting daily functioning alter the lives of millions of American families. The inevitability of death is part of everyone's life. The central focus of this chapter is on coping strategies that individuals and their families employ as they attempt to manage the physical, psychological, and social effects of disease and disability in order to maximize their life satisfaction, and the strategies individuals use in their attempts to understand death and dying.

Chronic Illness, Disability, Loss, Self-Concept, and Self-Esteem

According to Debra Hymovich and Gloria Hagopian, chronic illness refers to:

> A long-term health problem or condition leading to actual or potential interference with a (body) system's level of functioning.[1]

Furthermore, Hymovich and Hagopian view chronic illness as interfering with "physical, psychological, or social functioning."[2] J. M. Perrin is more specific in defining chronic illness as "a condition that interferes with daily functioning for more than three months a year, causes hospitalization of more than one month a year, or, [at the time of diagnosis] is likely to do either."[3]

On the other hand, disability, according to the World Health Organization, refers to "any restriction or lack resulting from an ability to perform an activity in the manner or within the range considered normal for a human being."[4] *It is very important to understand that persons with such illnesses and disabilities represent the entire range of humanity, just like their healthier counterparts. With that fact in mind, readers should consider the variation in responses to the issues surrounding continuing medical care, changes in levels of functioning, strategies in managing institutions, contacts with health care providers, changes in appearance, and so forth.*

It is important to note that illness and disability represent a threat. While change is a natural and continual aspect of life, chronic illness and disability threaten to bring negative alterations, which may stress the functioning of individuals and their families. Donna Falvo lists the following potential threats: (1) "to life and physical well-being"; (2) "to body integrity and comfort. . . ."; (3) "to independence, privacy, autonomy, and control"; (4) "to self-concept and fulfillment of customary roles"; (5) "to life goals and future plans"; (6) "to relationships with family, friends, and colleagues"; (7) "to the ability to remain in familiar surroundings"; and (8) "to economic well-being."[5]

One of the threats is to a person's self-concept. Self-concept, Falvo says, refers to "perceptions and beliefs about his or her own strengths and weaknesses, as well as others' perceptions of them."[6] Because an individual's self-concept can initiate responses from others, it has a profound effect on interpersonal relationships. For example, a person who projects a negative self-image may contribute to negative reactions or distancing from other people.[7]

A significant component of self-concept is body image, which Falvo describes as "an individual's perception of his or her physical appearance and physical function."[8] For persons with disabilities, body image can expand to include items like canes and wheelchairs. Specific bodily changes brought on by disease, such as hair loss or disfigurement, may prove very stressful. Interestingly, the degree of physical change does not appear to be the key issue in regards to body image. For instance, Hymovich and Hagopian report on research findings that suggest children with such diseases as hemophilia, juvenile rheumatoid arthritis, partial deafness, and partial sightedness have more psychological difficulties if the condition is mild or moderate rather that severe.[9] The authors suggest that children with milder disabilities may experience "a duality of self." While they wish to be "normal," they do have a disability. In addition, persons with milder disabilities do not ordinarily elicit the amount of support received by those with more severe conditions.

In *Building a New Dream: A Family Guide to Coping with Chronic Illness and Disability,* Janet Maurer and Patricia Strasberg encourage those with chronic problems and their families to express their feelings about changes in self-image and self-esteem to deal with loss and grief. Maurer and Strasberg believe close friends want to talk about the person's illness or disability or that of his family member, and the person with the problem can facilitate the process by speaking openly about it. But it is important not to dwell on the illness to the exclusion of other matters. If an illness is the constant topic of conversation, friends may tire and withdraw from further contact.[10]

Stereotyped Attitudes toward Chronic Illness and Disability

Coping strategies used by those with chronic conditions and their families are influenced to a large extent by the social environment.[11] Stereotypes regarding persons with illness and disability abound. At the same time, those afflicted with various physical limitations are said to be both "dependent" and "super people." If such persons demonstrate a genuine need for assistance (e.g., lacking the strength to open a door), they may be viewed as "poor, frail cripples." If on the other hand, these same people with chronic conditions maintain, as much as possible, work and family responsibilities, they may be proclaimed to be heroes of almost mythic proportions. Heroic labels are frequently attached to their family caregivers as well. Patronizing behaviors like patting those adults in wheelchairs as if they were children or speaking about a person with disabilities in the third person in the presence of that individual are, of course, demeaning. Also, expecting people with chronic conditions or their caregivers to never complain, get depressed, or frustrated is unrealistic and potentially damaging. Besides reflecting societal values regarding disabilities, other possible explanations for an individual using a stereotyped response include a lack of tolerance for that which is different or ambiguous, childhood experience, anxiety, and so forth.[12]

With the passage of the Americans with Disabilities Act, an increased awareness of some aspects of discrimination which affect employment, accessibility, and other issues now exists. For more information, readers may want to consult *The Americans with Disabilities Act Handbook* by Maureen Harrison and Steve Gilbert.

Persons with chronic illness and/or disability and their families may experience additional problems when they are perceived in stereotypical ways. Certainly those persons with disabilities and their significant others represent the entire scope of humanity. Like all descriptors, an illness does not define the entire person. Well-meaning friends and family members can make a difficult situation much worse through their inadvertent but condescending attitudes and behavior.

A Typology of Chronic Illness and Disability

Illness and disability should be viewed in the context of family. Family may be defined as "two or more people in a committed relationship from which they derive a sense of identity as a family."[13] From this perspective John Rolland developed a conceptual model of chronic and life-threatening illness and the family. Since illnesses, individuals, and families may differ widely, the model should be taken as a general framework for understanding rather than an explanation of any specific individual or family's behavior. However, some general issues facing many individuals and families may be understood by using Rolland's model.[14]

Psychosocial Typology of Illness

In *Mainstay: For the Well Spouse of the Chronically Ill,* Maggie Strong describes briefly John Rolland's typology of chronic and life-threatening illnesses.[15] Rolland believes that "every illness raises four questions. How fast did it come on? Will it hold itself in abeyance, come in bouts, or simply worsen relentlessly? Will it be fatal? How disabling will it be?"[16] Rolland also describes the impact of a specific illness on an individual and his or her family through the onset, course, outcome, and the degree of incapacitation involved.

Onset

Illness may be either diagnosed quickly or over a long period of time. An illness or disability may be understood as acute onset if symptoms appear suddenly, which is the case with a stroke. Gradual onset disorders like arthritis usually present symptoms over a long period of time prior to a diagnosis. Because of the nature of acute onset illness or disability, families are called upon to adjust rapidly to the changes. Rolland suggests that because diagnosis is often made after a longer period of time, the amount of anxiety for the individual and her family may be greater.

Course

According to Rolland, the course of a chronic illness may take one of three forms: (1) progressive; (2) constant; or (3) relapsing/episodic. A disease is more or less progressive if an individual is consistently symptomatic, and accompanying disabilities become increasingly severe. An example of a progressive course is that taken by a person with emphysema.

A disease can be categorized as constant if following a particular event, the course stabilizes (e.g., spinal chord injury or stroke). Following an initial recovery period, one is often left with a clearly defined set of deficits (e.g., loss of speech or paraplegia).

The third course of illness, relapsing/episodic, is descriptive of such disparate illnesses as migraine headaches, asthma, multiple sclerosis, and some forms of cancer in remission. Rolland states:

> The distinguishing feature of this kind of disease course is the alternation of stable periods of varying length, characterized by a low level or absence or symptoms, with periods of flare up."[17]

Families may be able to normalize behaviors, but the specter of reoccurrence is ever present. Rolland believes that stresses on individuals and families may be greatest with relapsing illnesses. Though relapsing disorders may necessitate less caretaking than other types of illness, these disorders strain individuals and their families by requiring them to shift coping styles with each new transition of the illness.

Outcome

In Rolland's model of chronic illness, outcome refers to the likelihood that a given condition will lead to death and whether it will shorten an individual's life span. Rolland believes that a very important element is the "initial expectation" held by an individual and his family regarding the possibility of death.[18] Disorders can be viewed on a continuum, with those which ordinarily do not affect life span, like blindness, on one end, and others which typically lead to death, like AIDS, on the other end. Also, some diseases occupy a middle area and are more unpredictable in their outcome. Included in this category would be certain forms of cardiovascular disease.

Rolland suggests that a major issue regarding outcome is the experience of anticipatory grief.[19] Both the individual and the family may grieve the expectation of future loss depending on perceived outcome. People may isolate themselves, experience debilitating sadness, and so forth. *Readers who experience chronic illness or disability in their family may benefit from a support group or from professional counseling. It is certainly "normal" to feel afraid, angry, guilty, or a host of other emotions. Living with chronic illness and disability brings difficulties to the entire family. Some families may benefit from professional assistance.*

Incapacitation

When illness impairs thinking, sensation, movement, or energy, or leads to disfigurement or some other form of stigmatization, degrees of incapacitation result. Different types of incapacitation require differing forms of adjustment. While some disorders cause only periodic incapacitation, disability increases over time in others. Citing a body of research, Rolland suggests that the family's expectations of the member who is disabled is a crucial factor. Rolland writes:

> An expectation that an ill family member continue to have responsible roles and autonomy was associated with both a better rehabilitation response and successful long-term integration into the family.[20]

Time Phases

The model proposed by Rolland also addresses time as an important dimension. The three major time phases considered are crisis, chronic, and terminal. The period prior to an actual diagnosis is the crisis phase. Ill persons and their families are faced with a number of important tasks, including dealing with pain and other symptoms, dealing with the hospital or clinic environment, and developing productive relationships with health care personnel. During this phase many families attempt to come to grips with the illness and its meaning in their lives so they can perceive a "sense of mastery over their lives and their competency."[21] Families begin to grieve for what their family was like before the illness began to alter their lives, and they may rally to combat the prevailing crisis.

The period between an initial diagnosis and family readjustment and a third phase characterized by terminal illness is the chronic phase. The length of this phase varies depending on the nature of the disease. For example, if an illness progresses rapidly toward death, the phase may be very brief and occur together with the terminal period. On the other hand, some diseases progress slowly, lasting decades. During the chronic phase, ill people and their families must figure how best to manage the daily challenges of living with disabilities. In *Be Sick Well: A Healthy Approach to Chronic Illness,* Jeff Kane details psychological strategies that can be employed by those with chronic conditions in adapting to changing physical functions. Effective strategies employed by children and adolescents with physical disabilities are presented in Jill Krementz' *How It Feels Living with a Physical Disability.* Successful tactics used by siblings of children with disabilities are explored in *Living with a Brother or Sister with Special Needs: A Book for Sibs* by Donald Meyer and associates. Maggie Strong discusses effective strategies for coping with a chronically ill spouse in *Mainstay.*

The terminal phase of an illness covers the time when family members see death as inevitable and this awareness takes hold of family life. According to Rolland: "This phase includes the central issues surrounding separation, death, grief, resolution of mourning, and eventual resumption of 'normal' family life."[22]

Common Emotional Reactions to Chronic Illness and Disability

Emotional reaction to illness and disability varies with individual personalities, families, values, and perceived severity of the condition. Also emotions may change as individuals and their families develop adaptive strategies. Mark Batshaw in *Your Child Has a Disability: A Complete Sourcebook of Daily and Medical Care* describes the initial feelings parents may experience as they begin to understand that their child has a disability.[23] Regardless of when a diagnosis is provided, Batshaw says, it is a shock to parents who often experience a combination of grief, denial, depression, hopelessness, helplessness, anger, and guilt. The grief reaction may resemble the reaction if a loved one were actually to die. Batshaw states: "Some parents say the grief never really ends, although it comes and goes as the child grows and changes."[24]

The degree of denial and depression can vary with the severity of the condition. A child with severe disabilities may well dominate the life of the entire family, which can reinforce feelings of sorrow and hopelessness. Anger may be targeted at the child, other family members, healthy children and their families, health care providers, or a supreme being. Parents may blame themselves, worrying that they were responsible through behavior or genetics for their child's condition.

Complicating concerns for the child are financial and marital problems. Batshaw writes that "the incidence of divorce is higher for parents of special-needs children than for the general population."[25] Single parents may quickly become overwhelmed, and Batshaw suggests they endeavor to solicit the support of extended family or friends.[26]

Respite care, even if it amounts to getting someone to babysit once in a while, is essential for the emotional needs of the parent. Involvement in parents' groups may be of great value. Not only is it important to understand that other people experience some of the same frustrations and fears, but association with such groups can open the way to more knowledge of a particular condition as well as increased awareness of available services.

Eventually most parents come to accept their child's disability. However, psychological pain and loss may continue to impact the family as they are faced with the complications and accommodations which accompany transitions, like the child's entrance into school, adolescence, and other transitions. While families which include children with disabilities are, indeed, special, they may well be highly functional and nurturing for all their members.

One problem common to all families is child behavior management. Some parents may have difficulty managing issues related to disciplining children who have disabilities. To the extent possible, based on age and level of development, all children need limits and the expectation that they will abide by family rules. John Parrish has contributed a useful chapter entitled "Love and Discipline: Managing Behavior" to Mark Batshaw's *Your Child has a Disability.*[27] In *Whole Parent Whole Child: A Parent's Guide to Raising a Child with a Chronic Illness,* Patricia Moynihan and Broatch Haig[28] offer practical tips for "asserting discipline while communicating love."[29] For additional information, see Chapter 4 on parenting.

Individual responses to chronic conditions vary with one's age.[30] In describing the role of developmental stages in comprehending a person with an illness or disability, Donna Falvo writes: "The stage of life serves not only as a guideline in assessing the individual's functional capacity, but also as a guideline to determine potential stressors and reactions."[31] Certainly, the experience of a chronic condition may severely alter the ways in which people attempt to complete developmental tasks. For example, persons with some kinds of disabilities may modify their career plans in adolescence or young adulthood, and middle-aged persons who, through accident or disease, may no longer be able to perform their chosen vocation may choose different forms of work.

Adults with chronic illness and disability are faced with potential relationship problems as well. The responsibilities of marriage and parenthood which can be difficult endeavors for everyone (see Chapter 2 on romance, love, marriage, and divorce and Chapter 4 on parenting), can become especially problematic for those with disabilities. Child care activities, formerly provided by both partners, may become more the daily fare of the well individual.

Sexual relationships may be affected adversely by factors which are physiological, psychological, and/or social in nature.[32] Leslie Schover and Soren Jensen discuss several useful methods for couples faced with health issues. These authors suggest concepts that reinforce effective coping, including the following: (1) role flexibility; (2) avoiding a parent-child interactive style; (3) scheduling adult time; (4) respecting each other's boundaries; (5) agreeing on relationship rules; and (6) allocating sexual roles and agreement on sexual rules.[33] Maggie Strong's *Mainstay* is an excellent resource for couples dealing with chronic illness and disability and its effects on their marriage and family life.

Pain Management

One of the most troubling aspects of chronic illness is the physical pain associated with it. Many chronic conditions bring with them a great deal of ongoing discomfort which can interfere with the quality of life. Illnesses as diverse as arthritis, migraine headaches, muscular dystrophy, cancer, and AIDS can bring with them debilitating pain. In *Pain Relief: How to Say No to Acute, Chronic, and Cancer Pain!*, Jane Cowles discusses the psychological aspects of pain, stating:

> The more passively a patient copes with chronic pain (feeling overwhelmed, helpless, that nothing can be done to control the pain, etc.), the worse the pain becomes and the higher the level of suffering overall.[34]

Cowles cites a study of 361 patients with rheumatoid arthritis in which the subjects' coping strategies were assessed. Those persons who used more passive approaches to coping were more depressed and reported a greater degree of pain as well as a lowered sense of control. The passive approach includes little, if any, participation on the part of the patient in treating the illness. On the other hand, patients who used more active approaches were less depressed, less functionally impaired, and perceived themselves to have more control.[35] The active patients learned about their disease and participated in exercise or pain reduction programs.

Some forms of pain can be managed actively through appropriate exercise, massage, and a variety of stress management strategies, including systematic relaxation and visualization (for more information see Chapter 6 on stress management). Material on guided imagery can be found in Ken Dachman and John Lyons,' *You Can Relieve Pain: How Guided Imagery Can Help You Reduce Pain or Eliminate It Altogether.* A balanced analysis of a wide variety of pain management techniques is included in *Defeating Pain: The War against a Silent Epidemic* by Patrick Wall and Mervyn Jones.

Readers experiencing pain should seek appropriate medical help. Pain can signal alterations in disease and should be brought to the attention of one's physician. Knowledge of a patient's symptoms can assist physicians in prescribing necessary treatments and in making referrals to other health care providers.

Death and Dying

In this section we shall emphasize attitudes toward death and death anxiety, stages in the process of dying, advanced directives, hospice care, and grief.

Death Anxieties and Attitudes toward Death

Many people fear death; others fear the process of dying.[36] The prospect of death and dying may include a sense of both physical and psychological suffering.[37] Richard Schulz and Robert Ewen discuss the reasons people may fear death: (1) the fear of physical suffering; (2) the fear of isolation and loneliness; (3) the fear of nonbeing; (4) the fear of cowardice and humiliation; (5) the fear of failing to achieve important goals; (6) the fear of the impact of death on one's survivors; (7) the fear of punishment or the unknown; and (8) the fear of the death of others.[38]

Using relevant research findings, Schulz and Ewen address important questions about death anxiety. These authors suggest that for healthy persons, no significant relationship exists between aging and death anxiety. In other words, fear of death does not automatically increase with age. However, for adults with significant health problems, death anxiety does appear to increase with age. For healthy adults Lewis Aiken found the following:

> cross-sectional surveys of adults are fairly consistent in showing that fear of death is more common and more intense during middle age than in later life. . . . This fear . . . is precipitated by the individual's awareness of his or her declining health and appearance, coupled with unfulfilled dreams and unattained goals.[39]

In this context, many people deny their actual fear of death and dying.[40] Schulz and Ewen report that a majority of studies support the idea that "increased faith was significantly related to decreased [death] anxiety."[41]

Children may experience a great deal of anxiety about death if they are seriously ill, or if a significant other is very ill or has died. It is important for parents to deal with their children's fears at each child's age level.[42] In *Talking about Death: A Dialogue between Parent and Child,* Earl Grollman offers concrete assistance for parents in communicating with their children on the subject of death and discussing the ever-present nature of death in children's lives. Pets, grandparents, parents, siblings, teachers, and others die, and children do react in many of the same ways as adults: denial, grief, crying, anger, and guilt. Grollman states:

> For every child, the meaning of death is reexamined as life changes. The concept of death undergoes a continuous process of maturation.[43]

Phases of Dying

Although several popular models of the dying process are present in the literature, little scientific evidence exists to support "the existence of any . . . stages or schedules that characterize terminal illness."[44] While any set of dying stages should not be viewed as a required path, a model can provide increased understanding of the dying process.

The most widely known model of the phases of the dying process has been developed by Elisabeth Kübler-Ross. Based on years of work with dying persons and their families, Kübler-Ross postulated the following phases of dying: (1) denial and isolation;

(2) anger; (3) bargaining; (4) depression; and (5) acceptance. For interested readers, Kübler-Ross's book, *On Death and Dying* contains a thorough discussion of the five phases. *Readers are cautioned not to try to fit a particular dying person or themselves as grievers into a particular phase and expect the individual to precede in lockstep order through the phases. The phases are useful as descriptors of issues and feelings, but are not necessarily consistent with the dying process of any individual.*

Another prominent theoretical view of the process of dying was developed by E. Mansell Pattison. According to Pattison, the three phases of dying are the acute phase, the chronic living-dying interval, and the terminal phase. The acute phase begins with the understanding that death is imminent. Anxiety and often fear and anger are present during the acute phase. In the chronic living-dying interval, Pattison postulates an initial lessening of anxiety, then the emergence of other emotions occurs. During this interval dying persons may experience some of the following emotions: sorrow, fear of the unknown, loneliness, loss of self-control, loss of body image (e.g., shame due to physical decline), suffering and pain, and loss of identity. During the terminal phase the individual withdraws. Although the emotions present in the second phase will still be present, an obvious withdrawal from others is occurring.[45]

Another way to view the process of dying is through the concept of a "dying trajectory."[46] The "dying trajectory" or course of dying occurs over time, and it has a particular pattern or shape. Several kinds of trajectories seem to exist. One is "certain death at a known time" (e.g., some accidents).[47] Another is "certain death at an unknown time," often the case in chronic fatal illness.[48] A third form is "uncertain death but a known time when the prognosis will be made." In this case it is necessary that an individual undergo radical surgery after which a prognosis will be available.[49] A fourth trajectory applies to "uncertain death and an unknown time when certainty can be known" (e.g., multiple sclerosis and AIDS).[50]

Glaser and Strauss suggest that dying persons experience seven junctures: (1) a person is labeled as dying; (2) family and institutional staff make death preparations; (3) decisions are made that there is nothing more to be done medically; (4) a final descent to death begins; (5) the last hours of life occur; (6) followed by "the death watch"; and (7) the actual death.[51]

Norman Cousins in *Anatomy of an Illness as Perceived by the Patient: Reflections on Healing,* describes how his approach to his own illness dramatically altered a dying trajectory.

Near-Death Experiences

Popular books and articles report on what are termed near-death experiences. Many of these reports have a strong religious tone, suggesting that these experiences provide clear evidence of an afterlife. Strong opinion is offered on both sides of the argument regarding the reality of such experience. According to Cynthia Dougherty, near-death experiences "are difficult to describe scientifically and virtually impossible to reproduce."[52] However, Dougherty views near-death experiences as major life transitions, which function to reorient an individual's goals and perceptions of death, and move the individual toward personal growth. Several experiences are reported by persons who believe themselves close to death, including depersonalization, out-of-body experience, and transcendence. Dougherty continues:

> Depersonalization consists of an altered perception of time, a feeling of unreality, altered attention, a sense of detachment, panoramic memory, loss of control. . . .[53]

Survivors recall losing track of time, but time itself appeared to slow down. Reports of fleeting memories that serve as a life review are also mentioned. Some persons report their

> attention was heightened but narrow in perspective. Loss of control of the body and mind was experienced as though the mind was taken to a special place while the body was left behind. . . . As the mind traveled through a tunnel, a bright light or heavenly place with much love and brightness was seen.[54]

Mental communication with deceased relatives and a supreme being are mentioned by some persons.

Out-of-body experiences, in which individuals feel both calm and detached, often include a sense of floating above their own bodies, while observing medical personnel in their attempts to revive them. Some persons recall improved sensory perception.

Also, people recall that their minds literally transcend an earthly context, giving the experience a clearly mystical flavor, sometimes containing very bright light and communion with God. Sabom found that survivors often showed a lessened degree of death anxiety, a reorientation to life, a renewed spiritual faith, and a greater concern for others.[55]

While people report numerous cases of near-death experiences, the acceptance of the phenomenon is far from complete. Since such experiences are by their nature clearly subjective, they are virtually impossible to validate scientifically. One interesting study examined the possibility some persons reporting near-death experiences may not have actually been near death. Ian Stevenson and his colleagues found that many of the patients in their study who had reported near-death experiences were, according to medical records, not actually near death. These researchers conclude that "it seems likely that an important precipitator of the so-called near-death experience is the belief that one is dying—whether or not one is close to death."[56]

When reading personal recollections of near-death experiences as reported in popular books, readers should endeavor to maintain an objective point of view. As of the writing of this book, no clear scientific evidence of much of what these personal accounts suggest exists. However, a number of persons do report similar experiences. Personal religious values will influence readers' perceptions as they encounter this material.

Coping through Grief

Clearly the pain associated with the death of a loved one is for most persons a most difficult aspect of life. The profound sadness felt when a person who has been a key part of our life dies should not be understated. In this section we shall present material on the following topics: diversity and grief; models of the grieving process; symptoms of grief; "abnormal" grief; grieving the death of a child, parent, or spouse; and support groups and grief counseling.

Diversity and Grief

The forms which bereavement takes are mediated by culture, gender, religion, social class, region, and a host of other factors representing diversity of values and life styles. Human beings grieve in widely differing ways depending on various cultural factors. For example, the death of a loved one may signal an initiation into everlasting life in the presence of a supreme being, the loved one's living on through his or her good deeds, nothingness, or countless other possibilities as well. *Readers desiring consolation and support from those sharing their particular spiritual outlook may wish to consult the appropriate publishers of religious books. Members of support groups sponsored by religious organizations may be able to recommend helpful reading material.*

Men and women may also handle bereavement in different ways. In *How to Go On Living When Someone You Love Dies,* Therese Rando discusses gender differences in mourning. According to Rando, men grieve as profoundly as women, but the expression of their grief is often a product of sex-role conditioning. Such conditioning may discourage men from communicating feelings of sadness through verbalization and crying.[57] Rando offers several suggestions for assisting traditional men with grief: (1) give the man "permission" to feel and express his emotions; (2) convey . . . that the expression of emotion in mourning is normal; (3) help the man find comfortable ways to work through his emotions; and (4) "keep in mind that the traditional man is in a 'no-win' situation as a mourner. If he gives in to his grief, he loses. . . . If he doesn't give in . . ., the unresolved grief will cause him to lose. . . ."[58] On the other hand, because of their sex-role conditioning, women may have more problems with anger as it manifests itself in the grieving process.[59]

Models in the Grieving Process

Most models of bereavement allow for the fact that mourners differ in the expression and timing of their grief. Although different, those who grieve do have some things in common. In *Living through Mourning: Finding Comfort and Hope When a Loved One Has Died,* Harriet Sarnoff Schiff writes: "While the ages and relationships of those who grieve may vary, there are common threads that bind us all: the thread of pain, the thread of confusion, and the thread of isolation."[60]

In his textbook, Lewis Aiken briefly describes several stage models of bereavement.[61] Gorer discusses three stages of grief: initial shock, intense grief, and a gradual reawakening of interest in the world. Glick, Weiss, and Parkes also recognize three stages:

a few weeks of disbelief and then crying, several weeks to one year of repetitious review, and a recovery period of about a year. Parkes postulates a four-stage approach: numbness, pining, dejection, and recovery. Also, Kavanaugh views grief as a seven part process: shock; disorganization; volatile emotions; guilt, loss, and loneliness; relief and reestablishment."[62]

Based on their analysis of the relevant literature, Barbara Backer and associates see grief as consisting of three phases: shock and numbness; intense grief; and reintegration.[63] Upon learning of the death of a loved one, an individual may experience a period of psychological numbness and unreality, which serves as a defense against the full understanding of the loss. One may appear composed, perhaps too composed to others. According to Backer and associates: "This stage works as emotional anesthesia, for to allow the feelings of grief at this point would be totally overwhelming."[64]

Following several hours or days of shock and numbness, the mourner begins a phase of intense grief. During this phase thoughts are on the lost loved one. In the beginning of this intense period, "there is continued pining and searching for the deceased."[65] Backer and associates, citing a 1975 study by Rees, claim that many mourners may hallucinate both visually and auditorial during this phase. Often a great deal of anger is additionally directed at God, health care personnel, or the deceased loved one. For many mourners experience a profound sense of guilt in this phase. This period of intense grief is marked by psychological disorganization, with aimlessness, apathy, and emptiness often present.[66]

While the bereaved may never totally transcend the grief, most mourners enter a third and final phase after a year or so. During the reintegration phase, as bereaved persons gradually reestablish themselves through role changes, their sadness typically dissipates. Occasionally, an intense sadness reappears, especially on anniversaries, birthdays, and holidays.

Factors Impacting Grief

According to Therese Rando, the three major categories of factors that influence the character of a person's grief are psychological, social, and physical ones.[67] Psychological elements impact bereavement through the qualities of the lost relationship, the mourner's personality, and the circumstances surrounding the death.

Rando describes a number of specific psychological elements, including: (1) "the unique nature and meaning of your loss and the relationship that has been severed"; (2) "the role and functions that the deceased filled in your family or social system"; (3) "the amount of unfinished business between you and your loved one"; (4) "your perception of the deceased's fulfillment in life"; (5) "your coping behaviors, personality, and mental health"; (6) "your past experiences with loss and death"; (7) "your social, cultural, ethnic, and religious/philosophical backgrounds"; (8) "your sex-role conditioning"; and specific circumstances like (9) "the timeliness of the death"; and (10) "sudden versus expected death."[68]

Social factors influencing the particular nature of grief involve an individual's support system, sociocultural background, status, and death rituals (e.g., wakes and funerals).[69]

The final set of factors involve such physical elements as the mourner's use of medications, quality of nutrition, rest, exercise, and overall physical health.[70]

Bereavement and Different Types of Death

Whether the death of a loved one has been anticipated as a result of illness or is sudden may have a significant impact on the grieving process. If a death results from a terminal condition, loved ones may have begun to grieve long before the individual dies. Anticipatory grief may afford an individual the opportunity to begin to deal with the loss long before a loved one actually dies. However, Barbara Backer and associates point out that the research on anticipatory grief suggests mixed results.[71] Based on a review of relevant studies, they conclude that while some studies demonstrate the value of anticipatory grief, others do not. Backer and her coauthors believe that such contradictory findings may be due to differing definitions of anticipatory grief and because they center on varying age groups.[72] Also, it is important not to assume that forewarning equates with anticipatory grief. Backer and her colleagues write that "the bereaved may have denied the oncoming death."[73]

Therese Rando argues that a great deal of emotional pain for survivors exists, regardless of whether the death of a loved one is sudden or anticipated.[74] She contends it is ludicrous to debate whether one type of death is worse than the other:

> Although it is unwise to compare different types of death, bereaved individuals seem sometimes to point out the special problems they have as a result of the type of death their loved one experienced.[75]

The cause of death can dramatically affect the nature of the grieving process. Rando devotes an entire chapter of her popular book, *How to Go on Living When Someone You Love Dies,* to a discussion of special issues surrounding bereavement and accidental death, homicide, suicide, and acute and chronic illness. Frequently, bereaved survivors of persons killed through accident or homicide ruminate on whether the death was preventable.[76] Rando suggests survivors fare better once they ascertain that the death was not preventable, as opposed to a death that results from human error (e.g., an airplane crash), thus avoiding blame and responsibility. However, according to Rando:

> Losing a loved one from a natural accident or disaster has its own type of stress because it may be difficult for you to cope with having no one to blame, no particular target to focus upon. . . . Some people actually assume the blame themselves because they find it easier to deal with a traumatic event's being their responsibility, . . . than to cope with the fact that it was a truly random event. . . ."[77]

Death by homicide or suicide presents special difficulties for survivors. Concerns over preventability and the knowledge of a loved one's probable suffering complicate bereavement. Feelings of helplessness, guilt, and anger may overwhelm those who grieve. *Because of the psychological trauma which typically is associated with grieving for a loved one who has died because of homicide or suicide, survivors may greatly benefit from professional counseling and/or participation in a specialized support group.*

Grieving a Family Member

Certainly the nature of bereavement is affected by the type of relationship the survivor had with the deceased. The death of a spouse or lover may be qualitatively different than the death of one's parent, child, or sibling. In *When Parents Die: A Guide for Adults,* Edward Myers discusses the special concerns of those millions of Americans whose parents die each year. According to Myers, the dynamics of parental loss are tied to attachment, various social dimensions, and the ages and genders of the parent and the child.[78] Feelings of attachment toward parents, which children continue to hold into adulthood, explain part of the trauma associated with parental death. A significant factor in understanding the reaction to the death of parents is the age of their children.[79] Carol Staudacher states in *Beyond Grief: A Guide for Recovering from the Death of a Loved One* that several special variables influence an individual's grief reaction to the death of a parent. These variables include: (1) "believing that your parent is immortal"; (2) "feeling closer to death"; (3) "losing your home"; (4) "longing"; (5) "needing to blame"; and (6) "death as a catalytic agent for unfinished business."[80] Staudacher recommends several strategies for coping with the loss. Bereaved persons are advised to "memorialize your parent in some way [and] enjoy a healthy identification with your mother or father, which includes keeping a few personal possessions of your parent. . . ."[81]

For the vast majority of couples, widowhood is inevitable.[82] With widowhood come numerous changes in identity, since most people in long-term relationships come to define themselves, in large part, through their mate.[83] Staudacher describes common feelings of those grieving the loss of a spouse like "I feel as if I have lost my best friend," "I am angry," "I feel guilty about something (or many things) I did," "Now I think about my own death more frequently," "I am afraid," "I worry about money," and "I feel relieved after the death."[84]

Rando provides suggestions for adjusting to widowhood. She recommends that the bereaved consider personal strengths and weaknesses. Does the bereaved need to develop new occupational, financial, or social skills? Many widows and widowers feel stressed at managing alone tasks they shared with their spouse.[85] The ages of the survivor, their children (if they are parents), ethnicity, their financial status, and other factors influence the quality and magnitude of the adjustment process. In spite of all the problems associated with widowhood, the majority of widows and widowers do make an adequate adjustment to their loss.[86] *For those persons who have continuing difficulties dealing with the death of a spouse, participation in counseling or a support group may provide necessary relief.* Interested readers may wish to consult Chapter 9 on aging.

For most adults, the death of a brother or a sister produces grief reactions. Exacerbating the grief can be the fact that others may not comprehend the feeling of loss experienced by surviving siblings.[87] A sibling's death can raise a great many feelings about the past, self-identity, and one's position in the family.[88] In addition, an adult may now find himself the oldest living child or only surviving one with additional responsibilities for helping to care for aging family members.[89]

Perhaps no more devastating experience happens to parents than the death of their child. Parents expect to die before their children as a manifestation of the natural cycle of life. Around forty thousand infants die in the United States each year.[90] Parental grief over the loss of a baby was largely ignored by self-help books until the 1970s, even though the grief can seem overwhelming.[91] According to Harriet Schiff:

> When a young child dies there are multiple small deaths that accompany the tragedy . . . you feel cheated of all that might have been. Perhaps your child lived long enough to walk and talk and enjoy the friendships of other youngsters. Then he died and you still see those youngsters outside laughing and playing.[92]

The younger the child who has died, the fewer memories parents may have of him. A lack of memories may interfere with the parent's grieving process.[93] Therese Rando describes the death of a child as an assault on a parent's identity.[94] Parents believe they must protect their children so they may feel a sense of failure with the death of their offspring.[95] If the death resulted from genetically based disease, a parent may experience profound guilt.[96] Obviously the death of a child will adversely affect the entire family unit. *Those persons who experience the death of a child are encouraged to join a support group or seek individual or family counseling in an effort to adapt to this dramatic loss.*

Of course, children mourn the loss of those to whom they are bonded emotionally: be they parents, siblings, grandparents, friends, teachers, pets, or others. Earl Grollman, in *Talking about*

Death: A Dialogue between Parent and Child, describes children's responses to the death of a loved one, and offers specific tips for handling the child's trauma with each type of loss.[97] How children manage the loss is related to the behavior of other family members.[98] If parents are suffering, it is difficult to attend to their child's grief as well. However, parents should not minimize the possible effect of a death on the child and a parent should make a concerted effort to listen to the child and offer the appropriate support. *If children experience lingering grief which interferes with their adaptive capacities and daily functioning, parents should seek assistance. Children can greatly benefit from counseling or from participation in appropriate support groups, which are available in many communities.*

Summary

This chapter has centered on issues surrounding the psychological management of chronic illness, disability, and death. Sections covered topics of self-concept and self-esteem as they relate to chronic illness and disability, a typology of illness, emotional reactions to chronic illness and disability, and principles of pain management. In addition, material was included on death anxiety, attitudes toward death, phases of dying, near-death experiences, coping with grief, diversity and grief, models of grieving, the psychological, social, and physical elements of grief, grieving for different types of death, and mourning the death of family members.

RECOMMENDED TITLES

Chronic Illness, Disability, Loss, Self-Concept, and Self-Esteem

Maurer, Janet R., and Patricia D. Strasberg. *Building a New Dream: A Family Guide to Coping with Chronic Illness and Disability.* Reading, Mass.: Addison-Wesley, 1989.

Physician Maurer and her psychologist colleague describe the many, and often complex, issues facing individuals with a chronic illness or disability and the issues facing their family.

After the initial shock of discovering that one has a chronic illness, the authors encourage readers to learn as much as they can about their illness, to raise questions about the particulars of their illness or disability, and to participate as actively as possible in its treatment. Practical strategies for coping with a progressive illness or recurring medical crises are provided. Chronic illness and disability both can carry significant emotional stress and social consequences for individuals and their families. Common emotional responses include anger, blaming oneself or others, depression, and mourning the losses that result from illness or disability. These responses can come from the individual or from family and friends. Numerous examples and the practical recommendations provided by the authors can aid readers who face similar situations. Each chapter ends with a summary of the major points. Appendixes include a list of organizations related to specific illnesses and an annotated reading list.

A Typology of Chronic Illness and Disability

Cousins, Norman. *An Anatomy of an Illness as Perceived by the Patient: Reflections on Healing and Regeneration*. New York: Norton, 1979.

In 1964 Cousins, during a hospital stay for the treatment of a debilitating collagen disorder, approached his physician with an alternative treatment plan. The plan Cousins developed was based on the belief that the patient should be a partner with his physicians. After reading a number of articles about collagen disorders, Cousins decided to take an active role in his recovery. He discovered that the adrenal and endocrine systems reacted negatively to emotional stress. Both these systems played an instrumental role in making the collagen disorder worse.

In contrast, Cousins asked his physician if positive emotions or activities could strengthen these systems. He embarked on a program of either watching humorous films or reading humorous books on a daily basis. He also found that he could recuperate better outside the hospital. Cousins concentrated on a nutritional approach by increasing his vitamin C intake. In the book, he repeatedly emphasizes the importance of the patient believing in the ability to recover fully, in the ability to participate in the healing process, and in looking at the entire person, physically, emotionally, and nutritionally.

Kane, Jeff. *Be Sick Well: A Healthy Approach to Chronic Illness*. Oakland, Calif.: New Harbinger, 1991.

Physician Kane emphasizes the importance of the mind-body connection in healing. Distinguishing the difference between sickness, disease, and illness, the author views sickness as the combination of disease and illness. Disease refers to the physical and measurable aspects of a particular ailment. Illness is a subjective experience unique to each individual. By focusing on illness, the author explores the myths surrounding chronic illness, encourages readers to play an active role in their treatment, and presents exercises at the end of each chapter, which involve techniques individuals can use to play that active role. Kane asserts that the importance of an individual's attitude, whether positive or negative, influences how illness affects that person. Relationships with family, friends, and physicians, and in developing a support system also have an impact.

Krementz, Jill. *How It Feels Living with a Physical Disability.* New York: Simon & Schuster, 1992.

Photographer and journalist Krementz interviewed and photographed twelve young people ages six through sixteen with a variety of disabilities. Each child tells his or her story evocatively, with stark, yet touching, photographs accompanying each chapter. The children describe in straightforward language the nature of their disability, their medical treatment, their families, and their friends. These children are not idealized but speak realistically about how they feel about their physical disability. Written for young people in an engaging style, the book speaks emotionally to their parents as well.

Meyer, Donald J., Patricia F. Vadasy, and Rebecca R. Fewell. *Living with a Brother or Sister with Special Needs: A Book for Sibs.* Seattle, Wash.: Univ. of Washington Pr., 1985.

Written for children, the authors answer many basic questions children raise about their brother or sister. Readers learn about specific disabilities and their causes. Children can read the book on their own or with their parents, because it may raise questions in the family. In addition to sections about individual disabilities, the authors talk about how children may be teased about their sibling, how others may make cruel remarks about their sibling in their presence, or how to cope with jealousy when parents spend more time with their sibling. An age-appropriate reading list is also included.

Strong, Maggie. *Mainstay: For the Well Spouse of the Chronically Ill.* Boston: Little, 1988.

Strong describes her own experience in caring for her husband, who has multiple sclerosis, and in alternating chapters the experience of other families. The work of authorities in the field and practical recommendations are included. The author explores the emotional toll chronic illness takes on partners, their children, their families, and their friends. Spouses find themselves redefining their relationship on the basis of illness. The well spouse may take on responsibilities formerly handled by the husband or wife. Balancing one's own responsibilities at home and at work, taking care of one's spouse, children, and other tasks can seem overwhelming at times. The author addresses many of these concerns as well as the financial issues associated with decreased income if the ill spouse can no longer work and the increased expenses involved in medical treatment.

Common Emotional Reactions to Chronic Illness and Disability

Batshaw, Mark L. *Your Child Has a Disability: A Complete Sourcebook of Daily and Medical Care.* Boston: Little, 1991.

Batshaw, a physician, provides parents and other interested readers a practical guide to children with disabilities. Written in direct language, the book explores the causes of developmental disabilities. The emotional impact on the parents can include denial, anger, helplessness and hopelessness, guilt, and depression. Fear can also play a role when parents feel they may not be able to take care of a child with special needs. Factors to consider when selecting a physician are also described. Genetic counseling is explored for couples whose child may have an inherited disorder.

In a section covering developmental disabilities, the author includes information on the following topics: developmental norms for a special needs child; mental retardation; Down syndrome; seizure disorders; cerebral palsy; hearing impairment; communication disorders; autism; vision disorders; and neuromuscular disorders. In a section on approaches to treatment, the author examines love and discipline; nutrition and dental care; physical therapy; occupational therapy; and commonly used medications. Educational opportunities and acquiring vocational skills are also discussed.

Goldfarb, Lori A., and others. *Meeting the Challenge of Disability or Chronic Illness: A Family Guide.* Baltimore: Paul H. Brookes Pub., 1986.

Based on the common experiences most families face when someone they care for is chronically ill or disabled, Goldfarb and associates present a practical approach to identifying underlying family beliefs as well as available emotional, physical, social resources. The authors explain how to build on existing family strengths. After identifying these resources, readers are introduced to a variety of problem-solving techniques, including improved communication, problem definition, brainstorming, weighing alternatives, and taking action. A series of written exercises in each section helps readers assess their family's resources and their problem-solving capabilities.

Moynihan, Patricia M., and Broatch Haig. *Whole Parent Whole Child: A Parent's Guide to Raising a Child with a Chronic Illness.* Wayzata, Minn.: DCI Publishing, 1989.

The authors examine many of the basic issues for parents of chronically ill children: how to balance a wide variety of roles; how to build their own self-confidence as parents as well as how to bolster their child's self-confidence; and how to identify age-appropriate developmental stages. Specific concerns involve sibling rivalry, discipline techniques, and working effectively with babysitters, day-care workers, teachers, and other school staff. A resource list of organizations and recommended reading is also included.

Register, Cheri. *Living with Chronic Illness: Days of Patience and Passion.* New York: Free Pr., 1987.

Register, who has a rare liver disorder, examines her own experience and that of others facing chronic illnesses. From the initial diagnosis and treatment to accepting the challenges and limitations set by one's illness, the author explores how this affects an individual's self-esteem and identity. A common concern is that one's identity is always tied to, and in some cases subsumed by, one's illness. The role of friendship and its importance are stressed as an effective coping strategy. The role of work, employment, or being useful to others is also seen as a valued attribute. One woman reported great satisfaction in being able to serve as a resource person for someone else who had been newly diagnosed with the same condition she had. The impact of chronic illness on children is also discussed, whether they or their parent have an illness. The role marriage plays in chronic illness is examined in considerable detail.

Turnball, H. Rutherford, III, and others. *Disability and the Family: A Guide to Decisions for Adulthood.* Baltimore: Paul H. Brookes, 1989.

A common concern of parents whose child has a developmental disorder is what will happen to their son or daughter when he or she reaches adulthood. Will their child be able to work? In what kind of setting? Can their son or daughter live independently or in a group home? This practical guide assists parents and other family members in planning for their child by describing the steps in determining what decision-making skills the young person has. Is he or she mentally competent? Should a guardian be appointed? What other alternatives exist? Government programs which assist the developmentally disabled are also explored. Parents and other family members are encouraged to explore their adolescent's preferences when planning vocational, recreational, and residential choices. In addition, family members can learn how to serve as advocates for their children with existing social services.

Pain Management

Cowles, Jane. *Pain Relief: How to Say No to Acute, Chronic, and Cancer Pain!* New York: Mastermedia Limited, 1993.

Through the use of questionnaires, pain charts, and pain diaries, the author encourages individuals to seek the pain relief available to them. Cowles finds that most types of pain are undertreated; as a result, successful recovery is hampered. Advocating patient participation in pain management, the author emphasizes the importance of keeping pain charts and describing pain accurately. Readers can learn about effective pain control and treatment for infants, children, adolescents, adults, the elderly, and the terminally ill. Groups with special pain concerns (cancer patients and those with HIV- and AIDS-related pain) are also discussed.

Dachman, Ken, and John Lyons. *You Can Relieve Pain: How Guided Imagery Can Help You Reduce Pain or Eliminate It Altogether.* New York: Harper, 1990.

The authors encourage people with chronic pain to add guided imagery as part of their medical treatment. Readers are advised to use this technique *in conjunction with, not as a replacement to, current medical treatment.* Other methods for treating pain and their effectiveness are also outlined. Readers are introduced to guided imagery exercises in general, for pain control, and for relaxation. Case studies of individuals who have found relief with this technique are also described. A resource list of support groups and other organizations interested in pain relief is included as is a reading list.

Marcus, Norman J., and Jean S. Arbeiter. *Freedom from Chronic Pain: The Breakthrough Method of Pain Relief Based on the New York Pain Treatment Program at Lenox Hill Hospital.* New York: Simon & Schuster, 1994.

Marcus and his associate develop a chronic pain relief program which includes physical and emotional explanations for pain patterns. Guiding readers through a combination of exercises, relaxation methods, stress management, and guided imagery sessions, the authors identify a variety of techniques to reduce pain. Pain-killing drugs are discussed in detail; the authors encourage individuals to reduce their reliance on them for pain control as part of the overall program. *Readers are advised to consult with their physician before reducing the amount of medicine they take to control pain.*

Wall, Patrick D., and Jones, Mervyn. *Defeating Pain: The War Against a Silent Epidemic.* New York: Plenum, 1991.

British physician Wall and his associate explore changes in how the medical profession treats pain. In the past, pain was seen as an external symptom of an injury or disease process. However, the authors note a paradox; as medical advances have been made, the occurrence of chronic pain has increased. Individuals with injuries or diseases that would have been fatal in the past are surviving. Causes of pain, pain behavior, and the methods of controlling pain are examined. These methods include the use of drugs, surgery, biofeedback, hypnosis, and psychotherapy among others.

Death and Dying

Anderson, Patricia. *Affairs in Order: A Complete Resource Guide to Death and Dying.* New York: Collier Bks., 1991.

This guide concentrates on the medical, legal, and financial aspects of death and dying. In a section on planning ahead, wills, funeral plans, and advanced medical directives are discussed, as are other health care issues. The author also covers many of the complex aspects of the dying process: when and where death occurs, bioethical concerns, euthanasia, and hospice care. Anderson outlines the practical matters surrounding the death: obtaining a death certificate, notifying insurance companies, and filing the will, among others. The emotional aspects of grief and bereavement complete this practical exploration of death and dying.

Grollman, Earl. *Talking about Death: A Dialogue between Parent and Child.* 3d ed. Boston: Beacon, 1990.

Grollman begins with a story for children about death. The story is followed by a narrative to assist parents in discussing the death of a pet (often the child's first loss), the death of a grandparent, parent, or sibling. Grollman encourages parents to give children honest, straightforward answers about death rather than clichés and euphemisms. For example, a child who has been told that Grandma is sleeping a long peaceful sleep can suddenly and understandably develop a fear of going to sleep. When a death occurs, Grollman emphasizes the importance of reassuring the child that she is not responsible for the death, and that sadness, crying, and missing the person are all normal feelings. Whenever possible, the child should attend the funeral or memorial service. The author found that children who had not been to the service felt a profound loss and felt that they had not said goodbye. A resource list of organizations and age-specific books and films about death are also included.

Kübler-Ross, Elisabeth. *On Death and Dying.* New York: Macmillan, 1969.

Based on a seminar for medical students about dying patients, the author explores the cultural basis of the fear of death in American society, particularly in the medical community. When the original seminar was conducted, Kübler-Ross found that death was rarely discussed in the medical school curriculum, and that students had little experience with dying patients. Through the seminar students meet with dying patients and their families, explore their feelings about dying, and learn to accept death as a natural process rather than an enemy to fight at all costs. The author finds that while each patient is unique, dying patients and their loved ones experience the following emotions: denial, anger, depression, bargaining, and finally, acceptance.

Coping through Grief

Myers, Edward. *When Parents Die: A Guide for Adults.* New York: Viking, 1986.

Rising out of the experience of his parents' deaths, the author explores the special nature of the grieving process when an individual's mother or father dies. Myers distinguishes the common features of mourning for all persons. Adult children face numerous challenges when a parent dies. In some cases the parent has been in declining health for a period of time, with their children taking an active role in the parent's medical care and financial affairs. In other cases the death may come suddenly through heart attack, stroke, accident, homicide, or suicide. The author describes the differences in the grieving process, which he says depends, in part, upon the age of the individual at the time of the parent's death. Relationships between the son or daughter and the surviving parent are also subject to change. The author compares and contrasts the experiences of adult children with the death of the first parent to experiencing the death of the second. Based on in-depth interviews, questionnaires, and input from health care professionals, Myers provides the reader with a practical, yet sympathetic, approach to this topic.

Rando, Therese A. *How to Go on Living When Someone You Love Dies.* New York: Bantam, 1988.

Psychologist Rando states at the outset that while each person's loss is as unique as the reaction to it, it is important to understand that grieving and bereavement are surrounded by a number of myths. In debunking these myths, the author describes how the grieving process differs for men, women, and children. A number of factors influence the way in which an individual mourns and resolves the loss: whether the loss was expected or unexpected, the age of the loved one, the relationship within the family, and the age of the bereaved at the time of the loss. Readers can learn about the social, emotional, and physical aspects of the bereavement process. Based on research and case studies, the author explores the similar threads interwoven in this process. Normal and abnormal reactions to grief are outlined, as are steps to be taken if professional help is needed to aid the individual in coping with the loss.

Schiff, Harriet Sarnoff. *The Bereaved Parent.* New York: Crown, 1977.

After relating her own experience with the death of her ten-year old son and the experience of other parents and grandparents in similar cases, the author describes the effect the loss of a child has on mothers, fathers, grandparents, and siblings. Since most parents expect their children to outlive them, the grief surrounding the child's death may be more difficult to understand and to accept. Schiff takes readers through the painful journey from the child's death and funeral to learning how to live with the loss as an individual and as a family.

According to the author, bereaved parents may be overwhelmed by feelings of isolation, guilt, and powerlessness. Other mourners or friends expect fathers to stoically contain their grief while mothers are expected to vent theirs. Schiff found that while men and women experience many of the same emotions after their loss, the expression of their grief differs greatly. The author also discusses how the loss affects communication in the family, religious beliefs, and how bereaved parents continue their lives.

Schiff, Harriet Sarnoff. *Living through Mourning: Finding Comfort and Hope When a Loved One Has Died.* New York: Viking, 1986.

Schiff explains how parents, children, siblings, grandparents, and friends experience the loss of a loved one differently. The author provides readers with techniques for dealing with the denial, anger, depression, and powerlessness that accompanies their loss. The last section of the book outlines how to start a bereavement support group, with specifics on issues to be faced, how to facilitate the group, and how each topic should be addressed.

Staudacher, Carol. *Beyond Grief: A Guide to Recovering from the Death of a Loved One.* Oakland, Calif.: New Harbinger, 1987.

With advances in treatment and medical technology, life expectancy for most Americans has increased. As a result, for many individuals, the grieving process is less frequent. Staudacher explores the form grief takes for many people and also discusses aspects related to an individual's situation involving the loss of a spouse, a child, a parent, a sibling, or a friend. The author also notes differences based on age and gender. The circumstances surrounding the death can also affect mourners (terminal illness, accident, suicide, or homicide). In each section, Staudacher describes common emotional responses associated with the loss and common coping strategies. Further discussion of the benefits of forming or joining a bereavement support group completes this helpful guide.

Viorst, Judith. *Necessary Losses: The Loves, Illusions, Dependencies and Impossible Expectations That All of Us Have to Give Up in Order to Grow.* New York: Fawcett Gold Medal, 1986.

Author Viorst, as a result of six years of study at a psychoanalytic institute, focuses her attention on all types of loss, including death, dying, and the grieving process. Interweaving psychological insights and literary examples, the author explores the "necessary losses" each individual experiences. Beginning with separation from one's mother when an infant learns its mother is a separate person, to the final separation in death, readers learn many losses are an inevitable and integral part of life. Not all losses are negative. Viorst explores four types of loss: the losses associated with childhood by moving from the mother/child bond of infancy to the development of a separate self; the losses connected with facing one's own limitations; the losses involved in seeking the "ideal" relationship, letting go of romantic illusions, and understanding the strengths and frailties of human relationships; and, finally, the inevitable losses individuals face in the second half of their lives.

Volkan, Vamik D., and Elizabeth Zintl. *Life after Loss: The Lessons of Grief.* New York: Scribner, 1993.

Psychiatrist Volkan and his colleague identify major factors in grieving as well as barriers to mourning. These factors involve the inevitability of loss at some point in an individual's life as well as the reminder of and in some cases the reliving of earlier losses. If the loss is fully mourned, the individual can grow and learn through the process. The authors broaden this process to include all kinds of loss, in addition to that of a loved one. According to Volkan and Zintl, several factors influence one's grieving process: the emotional makeup of the survivor, the nature of the lost relationship, the circumstances of the loss, and societal norms which discourage the open expression of grief.

NOTES

1. Debra Hymovich and Gloria Hagopian, *Chronic Illness in Children and Adults: A Psychosocial Approach* (Philadephia: Saunders, 1992), 313.

2. Ibid., 19.

3. J. M. Perrin, "Introduction," in Nicholas Hobbs and J. M. Perrin, eds., *Issues in the Care of Children with Chronic Illness* (San Francisco: Jossey-Bass, 1985), 1–10.

4. United Nations, World Health Organization, *International Classification of Impairments, Disabilities, and Handicaps* (Geneva: World Health Organization, 1980), 143.

5. Donna Falvo, *Medical and Psychosocial Aspects of Chronic Illness and Disability* (Gaithersburg, Md.: Aspen, 1991), 2.

6. Ibid., 3.

7. Ibid.

8. Ibid.

9. Hymovich and Hagopian, *Chronic Illness in Children and Adults,* 154.

10. Janet Maurer and Patricia Strasberg, *Building a New Dream: A Family Guide to Coping with Chronic Illness and Disability* (Reading, Mass.: Addison-Wesley, 1989), 246–47.

11. Falvo, *Medical and Psychosocial Aspects of Chronic Illness,* 8; Barbara Hillyer, *Feminism and Disability,* Norman, Okla.: Univ. of Oklahoma Pr., 1993), 77–79.

12. Hanoch Livneh, "A Dimensional Perspective on the Origin on Negative Attitudes toward Persons with Disabilities," in Harold Yuker, ed., *Attitudes toward Persons with Disabilities* (New York: Springer Pub., 1988), 35–46.

13. Catherine Chilman, Fred Cox, and Elam Nunnally, *Chronic Illness and Disability,* vol. 2, Families in Trouble Series, (Newbury Park, Calif.: Sage, 1988), 11.

14. John Rolland, "A Conceptual Model of Chronic and Life-Threatening Illness and its Impact on Families," in *Chronic Illness and Disability,* Catherine Chilman, Fred Cox, and Elam Nunnally, eds., 17–68.

15. Maggie Strong, *Mainstay: For the Well Spouse of the Chronically Ill* (Boston: Little, 1988), 27–32.

16. Ibid., 29.

17. Rolland, "A Conceptual Model of Chronic and Life-Threatening Illness and its Impact on Families," in Catherine Chilman, Fred Cox, and Elam Nunnally, eds., *Chronic Illness and Disability,* 23–24.

18. Ibid., 24.

19. Ibid., 24–25.

20. Ibid., 26.

21. Ibid., 31.

22. Ibid., 32.

23. Mark Batshaw, *Your Child Has a Disability: A Complete Sourcebook of Daily and Medical Care* (Boston: Little, 1991), 3–6.

24. Ibid., 4.

25. Ibid., 7.

26. Ibid., 8.

27. John Parrish, "Love and Discipline: Managing Behavior," in *Your Child has a Disability,* Mark Batshaw, ed., 203–15.

28. Patricia M. Moynihan and Broatch Haig, *Whole Parent Whole Child: A Parent's Guide to Raising a Child with a Chronic Illness* (Minneapolis: DCI Pub., 1988), 117.

29. Ibid.

30. Falvo, *Medical and Psychosocial Aspects of Chronic Illness and Disability,* 11–12.

31. Ibid., 11.

32. Leslie Schover and Soren Jensen, *Sexuality and Chronic Illness: A Comprehensive Approach* (New York: Guilford, 1988), 3–13.

33. Ibid., 18–31.

34. Jane Cowles, *Pain Relief: How to Say No to Acute, Chronic, and Cancer Pain!* (New York: MasterMedia, 1993), 71.

35. Ibid., 72.

36. Barbara Backer, Natalie Hannon, and Noreen Russell, *Death and Dying: Understanding and Care*, 2d ed. (Albany, N.Y.: Delmar Pub., 1994), 25–28.

37. Richard Schulz and Robert Ewen, *Adult Development and Aging: Myths and Emerging Realities*, 2d ed. (New York: Macmillan, 1991), 391.

38. Ibid., 391–92.

39. Lewis Aiken, *Dying, Death, and Bereavement* (Needham Heights, Mass.: Allyn & Bacon, 1985), 192.

40. Schulz and Ewen, *Adult Development and Aging*, 395–96.

41. Ibid., 396.

42. Earl Grollman, *Talking about Death: A Dialogue between Parent and Child* (Boston: Beacon, 1990), 35.

43. Ibid.

44. Herman Feifel, "Psychology and Death: Meaningful Recovery," *American Psychologist* 45 (Apr. 1990): 540.

45. Jeffrey Turner and Donald Helms, *Lifespan Development*, 4th ed. (New York: Holt, 1991), 578–80.

46. Barney Glaser and Anselm Strauss, *Time for Dying* (Chicago: Aldine, 1968), 5–6.

47. Barbara Backer, Natalie Hannon, and Noreen Russell, *Death and Dying*, 29.

48. Backer, Hannon, and Russell, *Death and Dying*, 29.

49. Ibid.

50. Ibid.

51. Glaser and Strauss, *Time for Dying*, 7.

52. Cynthia Dougherty, "The Near-Death Experience as a Major Life Transition," *Holistic Nursing Practice* 4 (Apr. 1990): 84.

53. Ibid., 85.

54. Ibid., 86.

55. M. B. Sabom, *Recollections of Death: A Medical Investigation* (New York: Harper, 1982), 62.

56. Ian Stevenson, Emily Cook, and Nicholas McClean-Rice, "Are Persons Reporting 'Near-Death Experiences' Really Near Death?" *Omega* 20, no. 1 (1989/1990): 45.

57. Therese A. Rando, *How to Go on Living When Someone You Love Dies* (New York: Bantam, 1991), 63–70.

58. Ibid., 70–71.

59. Ibid., 72.

60. Harriet Sarnoff Schiff, *Living through Mourning: Finding Comfort and Hope When a Loved One Has Died* (New York: Viking, 1986), 7.

61. Aiken, *Dying, Death, and Bereavement*, 238–39.

62. Geoffrey Gorer, *Death, Grief, and Mourning* (New York: Anchor, 1967), 129; Ira Glick, Robert Weiss, and C. Parkes, *The First Year of Bereavement* (New York: Wiley, 1974), 51–53; Colin Parkes, *Bereavement: Studies of Grief in Adult Life* (New York: International Universities Pr., 1972), 7; Robert Kavanaugh, *Facing Death* (Baltimore: Penguin, 1974), 107.

63. Backer, Hannon, and Russell, *Death and Dying*, 263–65.

64. Ibid., 263.

65. Ibid., 264; W. Dewi Rees, "The Bereaved and Their Hallucinations," in Bernard Schoenberg and others, eds. *Bereavement: Its Psychosocial Aspects* (New York: Columbia Univ. Pr., 1975), 66–71.

66. Backer, Hannon, and Russell, *Death and Dying*, 264–65.

67. Rando, *How to Go on Living When Someone You Love Dies*, 47.

68. Ibid., 48–53.

69. Ibid., 54–55.

70. Ibid., 55–56.

71. Backer, Hannon, and Russell, *Death and Dying*, 273.

72. Ibid.

73. Ibid., 274.

74. Rando, *How to Go on Living When Someone You Love Dies*, 90.

75. Ibid., 89.

76. Ibid., 107.

77. Ibid., 108.

78. Myers, *When Parents Die: A Guide for Adults*, 31–60.

79. Ibid., 37–45.

80. Carol Staudacher, *Beyond Grief: A Guide for Recovering from the Death of a Loved One* (Oakland, Calif.: New Harbinger, 1987), 82–86.

81. Ibid., 89.

82. Rando, *How to Go on Living When Someone You Love Dies*, 127.

83. Ibid., 128.

84. Staudacher, *Beyond Grief*, 54.

85. Rando, *How to Go on Living When Someone You Love Dies*, 133–34.

86. Ibid., 134.

87. Ibid., 157.

88. Ibid., 153–59.

89. Ibid., 158.

90. Backer, Hannon, and Russell, *Death and Dying*, 164.

91. Wendy Simonds, and Barbara Katz Rothman, *Centuries of Solace: Expressions of Maternal Grief in Popular Literature* (Philadelphia: Temple Univ. Pr., 1992), 1.

92. Schiff, *Living through Mourning,* 13.

93. Backer, Hannon, and Russell, *Death and Dying,* 165.

94. Rando, *How to Go on Living When Someone You Love Dies,* 165.

95. Ibid.

96. Ibid., 166.

97. Grollman, *Talking about Death: A Dialogue between Parent and Child,* 62–74.

98. Ibid., 63.

CHAPTER

9

Aging

A number of problems attributed to aging are, in fact, due to psychological or physical causes. These causes are not the result of aging per se, but are associated with other factors such as disease, interactions between prescription medication, and long-term psychological dysfunctions. Other changes and losses may be a natural and unavoidable part of adulthood (e.g., gradual changes in visual acuity). Whether particular discomforts are inevitable or not, such concerns are to some extent manageable for the aging adult as well as her family and friends.

In this chapter we will examine the aging process, centering on: (1) the physical aspects of aging, including the normal physical changes which often accompany aging as well as chronic illnesses associated with aging; (2) family issues, including relationships with adult children and grandparenting; (3) life transitions, including problems associated with living arrangements, financial concerns, and retirement; (4) psychological aspects, including continuity of personality, independence and dependence, and psychological disorders; and (5) societal attitudes contributing to negative images of aging and older adults.

Common Changes

Because the aging process is universal and inevitable, efforts to stay young are fruitless. Individuals can learn to make the necessary adjustments so that many of the ramifications of aging can be managed effectively. Certainly much that changes as a result of age changes slowly, allowing time to learn appropriate coping strategies. Each person ages differently, so the adaptive patterns one employs must be tailored to fit personal circumstances. Very helpful sources of information on the physical aspects of aging have been written by James Fries in *Aging Well* and by Caroline Rob and Janet Reynolds in *The Caregiver's Guide: Helping Elderly Relatives Cope with Health and Safety Problems.*

During the late twenties or early thirties, one may begin to see the first physical changes associated with aging. For example, a person may demonstrate a reduced ability to perform athletically at previous levels. By age thirty many persons notice lines in the forehead, and during the next twenty years or so other lines are typically observed. Though a wide range exists in the amount and timing, many persons notice the greying and the thinning of their hair during their thirties and forties. There are balding adolescents as well as octogenarians with thick heads of hair, showing little or no grey. The most common form of hair loss, male pattern baldness, is caused by heredity and at present is irreversible. Several aspects of appearance change with the process of aging. With age, a gradual loss of skin elasticity occurs, often resulting in sagging and wrinkling, and age spots develop due to cells producing either too little or too much pigment. Because of this sagging and thinning and increased capillary fragility, elderly persons bruise more easily. Height decreases with age. Specifically, women lose about an inch and men lose about one-half inch between the ages of thirty and fifty and another three-quarters of an inch in the period between the ages of fifty and seventy-five. With age, many persons gain weight due to lessened physical activity as well as a slowing down of basal metabolism. Lowered metabolism means a decrease in the rate at which the body converts caloric intake into energy. Weight gain occurs when individuals take in more calories than are necessary to maintain their weight.[1]

Sensory Changes

Changes in the sensory system are associated with aging. Visual changes often occur in the forties. More difficulty in reading small print held at close range is experienced, and seeing clearly at night may become gradually more difficult, especially the adjustment to the glare of lights. Eventually most older adults require some form of corrective lenses. Many persons experience even more difficulty in adapting to hearing loss.

According to studies sponsored by the National Institutes of Aging, around 30 percent of persons aged sixty-five to seventy-four and about 50 percent of those between the ages of seventy-five and seventy-nine experience a noticeable amount of hearing loss.[2] Changes in one's ability to hear are gradual, and many persons try to accommodate such loss by asking others to repeat themselves or by turning up the volume of radios and televisions. Because many people are self-conscious about hearing loss and the possible need for a hearing aid, many middle-aged and older adults deny the existence of the problem, which may lead to further isolation and a lowering of self-esteem.[3]

Memory

One common concern of many adults involves memory. With more information available on Alzheimer's disease and other forms of dementia, older adults may worry that their own memory loss may be an ominous sign of an inevitable loss of mind and with that of independence. A number of changes in memory typically accompany aging. For example, a gradual decline with aging in one's ability to remember specifics and an increase in the time necessary for information processing occurs. Although older adults may experience more problems with memory, they may also become more frustrated with such occurrences than younger adults. Those elders who report more problems associated with memory also report more sensory deficit (for example, hearing problems) and health concerns. Sensory deficit may account for what mistakenly appears to be memory loss rather than a failure to hear properly. A great many older adults think they are incapable of managing whatever memory problems they experience, since they believe that such loss is inevitably linked to age.[4]

A variety of strategies have been developed to assist the older adult with the management of memory. In this vein, B. F. Skinner and his associate Margaret Vaughan, in *Enjoy Old Age,* have described a number of easy-to use techniques to employ when forgetting a name, how to say something, to do something, to do something at the appropriate time, where one put things, as well as appointments. Two other very useful sources for middle-aged and older readers are *Your Memory: How It Works and How to Improve It* by Kenneth Higbee and *Improving Your Memory: A Guide for Older Adults* by Lynn Stern and Janet Fogler.

Chronic Illnesses and Aging

Arthritis

Most Americans over the age of sixty-five have one or more chronic diseases; the most common is arthritis which affects approximately half the older adult population. Arthritis is the effect of the breakdown of the joint cartilage lining the ends of the bones and may cause joints to stiffen, resulting in pain and immobility. It is not part of the normal aging process. The risk of osteoarthritis, the most common form of arthritis which affects larger weight-bearing joints (e.g., knees), is related to a lack of exercise as well as to previous injury to the affected joint. More common in women than in men, rheumatoid arthritis typically begins in middle age, affects joints throughout the body, and often results in both pain and swelling. Because of the disabling effects of arthritis, proper medical treatment is essential.[5] The Arthritis Foundation is a helpful source of information on the nature, treatment, and management of the disease. Kate Lorig and James Fries have prepared a highly practical guide to the subject, *The Arthritis Helpbook.*

Cardiovascular Disease

Responsible for about one million deaths in the United States each year, cardiovascular disease can be understood as any dysfunction involving the heart or the circulatory system. Typically, cardiovascular disease is the result of atherosclerosis, the hardening and thickening of the arteries. Although a degree of atherosclerosis is inevitable in the aging process, it results in pathology when the heart does not receive the necessary blood and oxygen to perform adequately. If a segment of the heart muscle dissipates due to inadequate blood and oxygen flow, a heart attack may result. With a stroke, the supply of blood and oxygen to the brain is somewhat blocked and brain tissue is lost. The risk of cardiovascular disease can be greatly reduced through a number of behaviors, including: (1) proper diet, which involves fruit, vegetables, protein, and foods low in low-density cholesterol or LDL (foods high in LDL include egg yolks, beef, and chicken cooked in its skin,); (2) deciding not to smoke (if an individual chooses to quit smoking, the benefits to the cardiovascular as well as the pulmonary system are immediate); (3) regular and appropriate exercise; and (4) effective stress management practices (see Chapter 6).[6]

Cancer

Another chronic disorder, cancer, is simply cells which spread abnormally. Most frequently found in the lungs, colorectal area, breast, and prostate gland, cancer is typically seen in middle age or in later life. Three out of four families will experience the disease. Two out of three cancer patients are over the age of fifty-five. The most common of all cancers, that which affects the lungs, is perhaps the most preventable, because smoking is associated with the vast majority of cases.[7]

Joseph Bonner and William Harris have addressed chronic illness and the physical aspects of aging in *Healthy Aging: New Directions in Health, Biology, and Medicine.*

Alzheimer's Disease

Alzheimer's disease, another chronic condition, affects around four million Americans. It impacts more women than men. Alzheimer's disease is a neurological disorder, resulting in progressive loss in memory, eventually causing an individual to lose the ability to perform even a simple task like eating. Two changes in the brain, senile plaques and neurofibrillary tangles, are associated with the disease. Senile plaques are nerve cells that have become surrounded by a protein, while neurofibrillary tangles refer to bundles of ordinary brain filaments which have become twisted.

As of this writing, the cause of Alzheimer's disease is not known, but extensive research continues in an attempt to solve this puzzle. Researchers are exploring the role that genetics, a slow-acting virus, or pollution may play in the development of Alzheimer's; these are but a few of the possibilities under investigation. The disease's progression varies greatly from one individual to another; however, several phases have been identified. In the early phase of Alzheimer's, depression often occurs, and the symptoms of depression can mimic some of the early signs of Alzheimer's. Caring for persons with Alzheimer's is especially stressful, and many families have received support and educational information from the Alzheimer's Association, which has local chapters throughout the nation.[8] Three particularly useful guides to the disorder are: *The 36 Hour Day* written by Nancy Mace and Peter Rabins; *The Vanishing Mind: A Practical Guide to Alzheimer's and Other Dementias* by Leonard Heston and June White; and *When Your Loved One Has Alzheimer's: A Caregiver's Guide* by David Carroll. Rose Oliver and Frances Bock focus on the emotional stress involved in the Alzheimer's family in *Coping with Alzheimer's: A Caregiver's Emotional Survival Guide.*

Family Issues

Relationships with Adult Children

It is typical for adult children to argue with aging parents over a great number of issues. The aging of parents may be difficult for adult children as they view the physical, emotional, and behavioral transformations of their elders.

Separation and Individuation

Mental health specialists speak of the developmental concerns that normally affect parents and their children, the central one being separation and individuation.[9] Perhaps the major goal of human development is for children to gradually separate psychologically from their parents so that they may become their own individual selves with distinct personal identities. To move in this direction, parents prepare their children and themselves for this eventuality through appropriate child-rearing practices. However, some parents have a difficult time providing an emotional environment which fosters independence for their offspring, because many of these parents never fully separated from their own parents.

Conflicts over separation and individuation manifest themselves in numerous aspects of relationships with aging parents. In *How to Survive Your Aging Parents,* Bernard Shulman and Raeann Berman discuss the dynamics of an important aspect of this phenomenon, status patterns. According to these authors, four such basic patterns exist: status-equality, status-quo, status-conflict, and status-reversal. If an adult child is truly separated and individuated, and if that adult's parent is independent emotionally, the two parties may then relate as equals. If, on the other hand, aging parents who have not encouraged emotional independence, pass judgement on their children's life styles, and exert control through manipulation as if their adult offspring were still under their parental wing, the relationship reflects the status quo. But if the children attempt to assert their right to live as they choose, and if elderly parents perceive their own status slipping, then the relationship may be characterized by status-conflict. If parents shift into an increasingly dependent role, then the situation can be characterized as status-reversal.[10]

Relationship Patterns

Even in families riddled with conflicts, most elders and their children seem to want some form of continuing relationship. The notion that adults abandon their parents is a prevailing myth, but little evidence exists to support this idea. A great many adult children and their parents maintain an ongoing pattern of mutual assistance, with parents providing services like babysitting, while adult children may contribute through offering transportation and household repairs. Gerontologist Vincent Cicirelli reports that about 80 percent of older adults have living children, and that most of these adult children feel "close" or "very close" to their parents.[11]

Effective Communication

Effective communication styles can often help when conflicts with aged parents occur. If unresolved conflicts existed in the past, such strife may well continue and be reflected through destructive interactions. Clearly many adults are not especially effective communicators with those to whom they are connected emotionally. Through practical discussion with engaging learning activities, Donna Couper, in her book, *Aging and Our Families: Handbook for Family Caregivers,* provides specific suggestions on helpful listening as well as appropriate confrontation with older family members. In addition, *The Family Guide to Elder Care: Making the Right Choices* includes a very instructive section covering communication skills.

Grandparenting

Many adults relish the opportunity to assume the role of grandparent. Many hold images of "ideal" grandparents who gave us money, good food, and emotional support when we were children. However, there are all kinds of grandparents. Some grandparents may forge active, passive, or distant relationships with their grandchildren. Many older adults love the activities associated with grandparenting, while others loathe such experiences. Of course, grandparents develop unique relationships with each grandchild, just as parents construct a special relationship with each of their children. In some family systems grandparents may function, at least temporarily, as "parents" to their grandchildren; this role change occurs when a child's parents are not able to take care of her. *It is important that adults encourage their parents to develop meaningful relationships with each grandchild and, if divorce occurs, to foster continuing ties with both sets of grandparents. Too often following a divorce, a child's parent will attempt to "punish" in-laws as well as former spouses, resulting in additional pain and loss to grandchildren as well as grandparents.*[12] Three particularly helpful books on grandparenting are: Arthur Kornhaber's *Between Parents and Grandparents;* Robert and Shirley Strom's *Becoming a Better Grandparent: Viewpoints on Strengthening the Family;* and Selma Wasserman's *The Long Distance Grandmother: How to Stay Close to Distant Grandchildren.*

Life Transitions

Living Arrangements

Psychological conflicts may center around an older adult's living arrangements. Apparently, most people prefer to "age in place," to continue to reside in the homes in which they have lived for many years. On the other hand, some elders may decide their housing needs have changed, preferring relocation to a smaller or more accessible home. Older persons may find the physical and financial requirements of maintaining a house beyond their wishes or capabilities. It is not uncommon for aging parents and their adult children to disagree over the manageability of a home in which the former have lived for many years. Elders may perceive that if they move they are giving in to the aging process, losing their roots, and disrupting the continuity of their lives. A neighborhood can represent links to one's personal past and one's present. Vivian Carlin and Ruth Mansberg explore housing options for older adults in *Where Can Mom Live?: A Family Guide to Living Arrangements for Elderly Parents* and in Carlin's *Can Mom Live Alone?: Practical Advice on Helping Aging Parents Stay in Their Own Home.* Also helpful is John Salman's *The Do-able Renewable Home: Making Your Home Fit Your Needs,* which is a how-to book for adapting a home to the physical needs of a disabled elder.

One option available to some older adults is to stay in their homes and rely on assistance from neighbors, children, other relatives, or a variety of community services, including home nursing, homemaker, and transportation assistance. Certainly, the use of these services is dependent upon availability and cost. In *Caring for Your Aging Parents: A Sourcebook of Timesaving Techniques and Tips,* Kerri Smith provides highly practical information on home health care services. Rita Robinson's *When Your Parents Need You: a Caregiver's Guide* is also helpful.

If an older adult finds that continuing to live in a home or apartment is no longer appropriate, a variety of choices exist depending on family, finances, and availability. Some older adults prefer to live with an adult child or with another family caregiver. Traditionally, daughters or daughters-in-law have provided much of the hands-on care for many elders residing with them and their husbands and children. But this is becoming more and more difficult with the growing numbers of women employed full-time as well as bearing child care responsibilities. Many sons and other male relatives do provide much assistance to their older family members but not in the numbers associated with female caregivers. Certainly, males are as capable as females in giving such help, and perhaps with the changing female role accompanying changes in the care giving expectations for males will also change.[13]

For the healthy and affluent, retirement communities provide a welcome mix of social and recreational opportunities as well as convenient shopping and health care. Another option, assisted or congregate housing, may offer individual units with or without kitchens, and those residents without kitchens may choose to eat meals in a communal setting. Some retirement communities offer comprehensive care with residential units, assisted care facilities, and extended care facilities.

One of the most difficult decisions for many families involves nursing home placement. For the frailest of older adults, the best alternative may be a nursing home. Elders and their families may perceive the nursing home as a last stop, but for those older persons who are dependent physically such a facility can provide essential round-the-clock nursing assistance. Nursing homes differ in quality, and Georgia Barrow recommends that elders and their family members analyze the suitability of possible facilities by doing the following: (1) visit several facilities; (2) visit each facility at least twice, once during mid-morning or mid-afternoon and another time during the serving of a meal; (3) check out the food by scanning menus and asking about the availability of a registered dietician; (4) see if a registered nurse is available twenty-four hours a day; (5) check to see if other health care services are available (for example, physical therapy); (6) find out who the activities director is; and (7) investigate whether a wide variety of activities are readily available (adult education, movies, outings, and so forth).[14]

Finances

A significant source of worry for many adults is money, and a great many older adults, especially those living on a fixed income, are concerned about the spiraling cost of health care, as well as the costs to maintain homes, rent apartments, pay utilities, and buy food. Practical financial skills learned in early or middle adulthood—budgeting, saving, and investing—are the cornerstone of managing money in later years. With increased longevity, many older persons are afraid they will outlive their money, and in time become dependent on their adult children or the state. Many widows experience panic when they are forced to assume the management of their financial resources, a chore often assigned to males in previous generations. After the death of a spouse, the survivor may need to handle money matters, which she has not done previously or has not done since young adulthood.

In preparation for illness or death, it is imperative that adult children or other family members become acquainted with the financial status of their older family member. Elders may require assistance in organizing financial information, paying bills, maximizing income through prudent investing, filing health insurance claims, and handling legal matters. For those families fortunate enough to have aging parents with sufficient economic assets, Francine and Robert Moskowitz, in their book *Parenting Your Aging Parents,* detail practical tips on both voluntary (power of attorney, joint ownership, and so forth) and involuntary financial management, budgeting, pensions, investments, depleting capital, and a host of other relevant topics. Michael Levy in *Parenting Mom and Dad* offers useful advice on handling the resistance that many adult children experience when they attempt to discuss financial issues with their parents. It is essential that aging parents be encouraged to manage their own economic resources to the extent possible to maximize self-determination and self-esteem.

Retirement

Most adults look forward to retirement, and most older adults express satisfaction with their retirement. High satisfaction with retirement is associated with good health and adequate income. For many persons, retirement provides the time to do just what they want to do, to be in control of what they do and when they do it. People who have difficulty with time management or who require an imposed structure, may have some problems making the adjustment from full-time employment. A great many Americans may equate being happy with being busy, and numerous opportunities present themselves for older adults to do just that. Those persons who enjoy hobbies or interests may relish the additional time available for these activities. Perhaps the best way to prepare for one's eventual retirement is to develop engaging interests (hobbies) over a lifetime, plan financially through savings and investments (if possible), and employ a healthy life style (diet, exercise, and rest) to maximize adjustment to life after work. Tom and Nancy Biracree provide a comprehensive view of retirement, an extensive treatment of financial planning, as well as chapters covering educational opportunities, travel, sports, and hobbies in *Over Fifty: The Resource Book for the Better Half of Your Life.*

Psychological Aspects

Independence and Dependence

Conflicts with elderly family members may reflect issues of independence or dependence. Individuated adults attempt to demonstrate independence in all the spheres of life. Robert Atchley suggests four dimensions of adult independence: physical, mental, social, and economic.[15] The physical aspect is demonstrated through the capacity to manage personal needs as well as mobility. Mental independence is shown through problem-solving ability. A person is thought to be socially independent if that individual has the capacity for self-reliance. One is said to be economically self-sufficient, if one has the necessary financial resources to provide for an adequate life style.

In American society, dependent adults are assigned lower status, causing many older persons great anxiety, fearing they will, in time, lose their independence and status because of health or reliance on a fixed income. Families and friends of older adults can be of great assistance in aged persons' efforts to maintain their independence. For example, if an individual is physically capable of carrying out a particular household chore, that person should be encouraged to do so. Sometimes friends and families can be "too helpful," inadvertently encouraging dependence and helplessness. In *You and Your Aging Parent,* Barbara Silverstone and Helen Hyman provide useful suggestions on helping older adults manage their lives as independently as possible.

Continuity in Adult Personality

A great many older adults adjust quite well to the vagaries of the aging process. Apparently, there is great stability in adult personality. In other words, personality is not altered significantly by age alone. For example, Paul Costa and Robert McCrae found a great deal of stability when they examined the traits of maladjustment (neuroticism), warmth and assertion (extroversion), and willingness to try new things (openness to experience). Continuity in their subjects' personalities remained stable over time; maladjusted thirty-year-olds tended to become maladjusted seventy-year-olds, and typically extroverted twenty-five year-olds remained so with age.[16] Robert Atchley suggests that adults should make every effort to maintain consistency in their lives through continuity in behavior and thinking, and that most adults depend on the stability of their personality in coping with change.[17]

Psychological Disorders

Some older adults have difficulty adjusting to the trials of living, expressing their emotional upheaval through a variety of psychological disorders. *No specific marker between what is "normal" and what is not exists. What is "appropriate" behavior for one elderly person may not be for another.* What is adaptive in one situation, may be maladaptive in another. If feelings or behaviors impact an individual's ability to function or if the feelings or behaviors cause "undue" anxiety, it is important to consult a professional for assistance. *It is not unusual for those over sixty-five to equate seeking assistance from mental health professionals with being "crazy."* Therefore, many older adults may be more comfortable in communicating their emotional concerns to their primary care physician or clergy.

It is important that the elder's physician be aware of psychological symptoms, because behavioral and emotional disturbance can be caused or intensified by physical disorders or medications. For some older adults the level of discomfort may be so great that they may welcome the opportunity to meet with a psychologist, psychiatrist, or other mental health specialist. Although a host of psychological disorders are found in the elderly, two of the more common ones, depression and hypochondriasis, will be addressed.

Depression

Depression is one of the most common psychological disorders found among older adults. From time to time everyone feels sad, which is quite different from the intense, on-going experience of depression. The most important symptom associated with depression is anergy, or lack of energy. Other symptoms associated frequently in older adults with depression are: sleep disturbance (often awakening prior to 4 a.m.), a diurnal mood variation (experiencing sadness in the morning, but feeling markedly better with the arrival of evening), a decrease in appetite, preoccupation with physical symptoms, constipation, a loss of interest in regular activities, difficulty in concentrating, a complete lack of sexual interest, expressions of guilt, and physically slowing down. With progression, an individual may gradually stop attending to matters of personal hygiene, withdraw, and regress to a childlike state. In the most serious cases, an individual may lose contact with reality, become delusional, and express suicidal thoughts.

Sometimes older adults may show what is called *masked depression*. Masked depression may present itself as a physical complaint, which upon examination has no real physiological basis, or as pseudodementia, which looks like any other dementia, except that there appears to be no underlying physical cause. Because depression can show itself through pseudodementia, persons with Alzheimer's disease or another dementia may be misdiagnosed as depressed, or those with depression may be labeled as suffering from a progressive dementia. Also, it is not uncommon that an older person could be experiencing both a form of depression and dementia.[18] Further complicating proper diagnosis and treatment of depression among older adults is the effect of drugs. According to James Fries: "Nearly any drug can cause depression on occasion, and you should always discuss this possibility with your physician. Notoriously, codeine, sedatives, tranquilizers, and alcohol increase depression."[19] Also, genetic predisposition may play a key role in the development of many depressive disorders. In *To Be Old and Sad: Understanding Depression in the Elderly*, Nathan Billig guides the interested reader through the prevailing symptoms and treatments. Billig also discusses the differences between depression and other disorders.

Several self-help books on the market purport to assist the lay person in treating the complexities of depression among various age groups. *We strongly recommend that readers manifesting symptoms of clinical depression (a lingering sadness, anergy, and so forth) consult their family physician or a mental health professional. Self-help books may serve as a useful adjunct to professional treatment for depression, but they are not an adequate substitute.* The interested reader may wish to consult Chapter 7 on psychological and substance-related disorders for more information on this topic.

Hypochondriasis

Another psychological disorder found among the elderly is hypochondriasis, which is shown through preoccupation with one's body and excessive physical complaints. If personal concern with matters of health comes to dominate one's life, little room may be left for anything else. For some elders, hypochondriasis may be employed as a way of gaining attention. This disorder appears in virtually every age group, and it is probable that younger hypochondriacs will in time become older hypochondriacs. Hypochondriasis is, at present, difficult to treat, but family counseling can prove beneficial.[20]

Stereotyping and Ageism

Even though many persons believe that older adults typically live in nursing homes, only about 5 percent of those over sixty-five reside in such facilities. This belief is one of the many stereotypes held by countless persons, who generalize a trait for behavior as representative of the entire older population. The stereotyping of older adults reflects *ageism,* a term coined by Robert Butler. Ageism refers to "the prejudices and stereotypes that are applied to older people sheerly on the basis of their age."[21] Butler argues that we perpetuate a number of myths regarding the elderly, including those of senility, inflexibility, and serenity.

One result of ageism is a form of paternalism, which Arnold Arluke and Jack Levin term *infantilization,* that is, viewing older adulthood as a second childhood, which it is not.[22] The eventual dependence of some elders is far different from the dependence of children, who normally will grow up to a lifetime of independence. Viewing older persons as childlike is condescending and places limits on their worth. Even some of the better books on issues involving aging parents appear to suggest a touch of this notion, when their titles state that we are "parenting" our older parents. *It is imperative that older family members be treated with dignity; whenever possible, elders should be the primary decision makers when actions are considered that will significantly affect their lives.*

Youth-oriented societies, like the United States, place great emphasis on looking, thinking, feeling, and acting young. Popular culture messages from television commercials, films, and greeting cards exhort the audience to stay young, equating youth with beauty and happiness, while portraying old age as depressing, debilitating, and something to attempt to avoid at all costs. Certainly, being young is no guarantee for happiness. In fact, one's self-image may improve with age.

Summary

In this chapter the physical, psychological, and some aspects of aging were addressed. Material covered normal processes, common illnesses, and social and psychological problems, which may, but do not automatically, accompany aging. Changes associated with aging are typical, subtle, and gradual. Regardless of one's beliefs about the aging process, it is inevitable. Persons are best served by planning for their own aging and that of their family members.

RECOMMENDED TITLES

Common Changes

Belsky, Janet. *Here Tomorrow: Making the Most of Life after Fifty.* Baltimore: Johns Hopkins Univ. Pr., 1988.

The author begins this informative guide with a discussion of the physical, emotional, and psychological aspects of aging. Issues surrounding love, marriage, and sexuality are also covered. The relationships developed over time with one's children, grandchildren, and other family members and friends often play a significant role as a person ages. In addition, readers can learn about the transitions from work to retirement, from spouse to widow or widower, and from living and working in one locale to retiring to a new community. The author concludes with an exploration of common medical concerns of older adults.

Bonner, Joseph, and William Harris. *Healthy Aging: New Directions in Health, Biology, and Medicine.* Claremont, Calif.: Hunter House, 1988.

Based on Bonner's UCLA Extension course on the biology of aging, this book emphasizes the physiological aspects of aging with special attention paid to diet, nutrition, and physical fitness. The final chapter deals with issues related to death and dying. Illustrations throughout the book demonstrate many of the medical concepts presented.

Fries, James F. *Aging Well: A Guide for Successful Seniors.* Reading, Mass.: Addison-Wesley, 1989.

Staying healthy serves as the primary focus in Fries' book. Maintaining an active life style both physically and mentally, retirement planning, and long-term health care are also covered in some detail. He includes information on advanced directives, living wills, and power of attorney, stressing the importance of planning ahead before a medical crisis occurs. The last portion of the book lists solutions to a variety of health problems, and the appendix includes forms for living wills and other types of advanced directives.

Rob, Caroline, and Janet Reynolds. *The Caregiver's Guide: Helping Elderly Relatives Cope with Health and Safety Problems.* Boston: Houghton, 1991.

An excellent guide for outlining health problems common to the elderly: vision and hearing loss; respiratory, cardiac, and gastrointestinal and urinary disease; memory loss and dementia, psychological problems; and cancer. Managing medication safely is a common concern for older adults who may see a variety of medical specialists for interrelated disorders and may be taking a panoply of prescription and over-the-counter medicines. Guidelines for selecting home health care personnel are also discussed. An appendix of organizations and an in-depth index are included.

Memory

Higbee, Kenneth L. *Your Memory: How It Works and How to Improve It.* 2d ed. New York: Paragon House, 1988.

Higbee introduces readers to the nature of memory as well as to practical techniques to improve it. By exploring common myths about memory, the author provides the foundation for understanding its physiological and psychological components. Given the wide variety of memory improvement strategies included, readers can discover which approach is most effective for them. Study skills for learning new material are also included.

Skinner, B. F., and M. E. Vaughan. *Enjoy Old Age: A Program of Self Management.* New York: Norton, 1983.

Skinner and Vaughan provide a practical guide for older people. The section on memory with suggestions for improving and retaining one's memory is particularly effective. The reader is given numerous useful strategies for remembering names, appointments, and medication schedules among others. The authors write directly to the older person and focus on the adjustments that are part of normal and successful aging.

Stern, Lynn, and Janet Fogler. *Improving Your Memory for Older Adults.* Ann Arbor, Mich.: Memory Skills, 1988.

As associates at Turner Geriatric Services at the University of Michigan Medical Center, the authors describe how memory works, how it changes as one ages, and factors that affect it adversely. These factors may include not paying attention, distractions, stress, depression, and medication among others. Stern and Fogler provide readers with a series of memory improvement techniques with examples, exercises, and an opportunity to apply these techniques to specific situations.

Chronic Illness

Lorig, Kate, and James F. Fries. *The Arthritis Helpbook: A Tested Self-Management Program for Coping with Your Arthritis.* Reading, Mass..: Addison-Wesley, 1986.

Recommended by the Arthritis Foundation, this book guides the reader through exercise, pain management techniques, problem solving, diet and nutrition, drugs, and coping strategies. Illustrations throughout enhance the text.

Carroll, David L. *When Your Loved One Has Alzheimer's: A Caregiver's Guide.* New York: Harper, 1989.

Based on strategies developed by health care professionals at the Brookdale Center on Aging in New York City, the work is aimed at caregivers and their loved ones. The book is divided into sections on understanding Alzheimer's disease, developing a coping plan, and meeting caregiver needs. Effective solutions provided in books about Alzheimer's patients can also apply to other home health care situations. Carroll offers many practical solutions for caring for the Alzheimer's patient.

Heston, Leonard L., and June A. White. *The Vanishing Mind: A Practical Guide to Alzheimer's Disease and Other Dementias*. Rev. ed. of *Dementia*. New York: Freeman, 1991.

This work includes a detailed medical study of Alzheimer's and other dementias, concentrating on early medical intervention, effective treatments, and useful strategies for families caring for the person with dementia. Discussion of early symptoms and normal and abnormal memory loss are especially helpful.

Mace, Nancy L., and Peter V. Rabins. *The 36 Hour Day: A Family Guide to Caring for Persons with Alzheimer's Disease, Related Dementing Illness and Memory Loss in Later Life*. 2d rev. ed. New York: Warner, 1991.

Written by medical professionals at Johns Hopkins University, *The 36 Hour Day* is one of the earliest and still one of the best books on the subject. Aimed at families of Alzheimer's patients, the work covers the physical, psychological, and social aspects of dementing illness, including legal and financial issues. Practical solutions are offered for common problems affecting the patients, their families, and caregivers. Promising research in causes and treatment are also discussed. An extensive resources section appears in the appendix.

Oliver, Rose, and Frances A. Bock. *Coping With Alzheimer's: A Caregiver's Emotional Survival Guide*. New York: Dodd, 1987.

This book concentrates entirely on the Alzheimer's caregiver, outlining specific responses to feelings of anger, shame, self-pity, guilt, anxiety, depression, and stress. The authors use Rational-Emotive Therapy (RET) as the basis for this book. Readers are encouraged to acknowledge their feelings, to view their emotions realistically, and to respond to them in a way that is beneficial for them and the person they care for. Written in the form of a dialogue between the caregiver and the authors, Oliver and Bock provide a straightforward discussion of the physical and emotional challenges facing the Alzheimer's caregiver.

Family Issues

Relationships with Adult Children

Couper, Donna P. *Aging and Our Families: Handbook for Family Caregivers.* New York: Human Sciences Pr., 1989.

This handbook presents a straightforward approach to caregiving by family members. The caregiving role played by spouses, adult children, siblings, and other friends is detailed. The changes in family dynamics as responsibilities shift from the older person to their adult children are outlined. Helpful activity sheets at the end of each major section aid the reader in seeing what their role is in caregiving, what informal resources are available, and what formal assistance from social services agencies exists.

Couper acknowledges the stress involved in caregiving both on the giver and the recipient, and suggests several alternatives, including outside help, family meetings, and open communication with the older person. Focus is on persons receiving the care, respecting their needs and wishes in balance with those of the caregivers. The author also describes effective and ineffective patterns of communication.

Family Service America, Family Care Program. *The Family Guide to Elder Care: Making the Right Choices.* Milwaukee, Wis.: Family Service America, 1990.

This book centers on issues facing the elderly and those who care for them, especially on the stereotypes associated with aging. Family structure, family history, and their impact on caregiving are described. Creating a safe home environment so the individual can live at home as long as possible is emphasized. Community resources, alternative housing arrangements, and selecting a nursing home are also examined.

Robinson, Rita. *When Your Parents Need You: A Caregiver's Guide.* Santa Monica, Calif.: IBS Pr., 1990.

A medical writer, Robinson found herself writing about caregiving from the inside out. While she was writing the book, her father, who had been caring for her mother, an Alzheimer's patient, suffered a stroke. The author describes in detail the financial and legal aspects of Medicare, Social Security, private insurance, family relations, and how to cope with medical and insurance systems. In talking about the specifics of her situation, Robinson provides a caregiver's road map for others to use.

Shulman, Bernard H., and Raeann Berman. *How to Survive Your Aging Parents So You and They Can Enjoy Life.* Chicago: Surrey Bks., 1988.

Family interactions and how communication between parents and their adult children can be maintained and improved is the focus of this work. Shulman and Berman concentrate on family structure and how the parent-child relationship changes over time. For older adults who have been independent much of their lives, becoming dependent on their children or other family members is often difficult for both parties. The authors offer a variety of communication styles which reinforce effective techniques for both adult children and their parents.

Smith, Kerri S. *Caring for Your Aging Parents: A Sourcebook of Timesaving Techniques and Tips.* The Working Caregiver Series. Lakewood, Colo.: American Source Bks., 1992.

Designed for working caregivers, Smith provides a plan for determining the health needs of the elderly person, modifying the home environment, getting help, balancing work and caregiving, providing long-distance caregiving, handling legal and financial matters, and taking care of the caregiver's needs. At the end of each chapter, the author includes a list of timesavers and "things to do this week." The use of a caregiver notebook for keeping track of everything from symptoms to emergency numbers, medication lists, insurance contacts, and all of the other details involved, is one of the best suggestions offered in this handy guide.

Grandparenting

Kornhaber, Arthur. *Between Parents and Grandparents.* New York: St. Martin's, 1986.

With the increased emphasis on parenting guides in recent years, books on grandparenting have followed. Focusing on the strength and the necessity of the grandparent-grandchild bond, the author reviews how this relationship fits into the family at large. The positive role grandparents play for the child as heroes, cronies, and mediators is stressed. Through the use of numerous examples, the reader is shown what makes a good grandparent, how to avoid the pitfalls of interfering, spoiling, and favoritism, and how to maintain ties in adverse situations like divorce, illness, or substance abuse.

Strom, Robert D., and Shirley K. Strom. *Becoming a Better Grandparent: Viewpoints on Strengthening the Family.* Newbury Park, Calif.: Sage, 1991.

The authors focus on clarifying values and moral development in exploring the relationship between grandparent and grandchild. They look at the experience of grandparents, parents, and children in building strong and effective family ties. The Stroms discuss single parent and blended families, showing how their needs differ from the traditional family structure.

Wassermann, Stella. *The Long Distance Grandmother: How to Stay Close to Distant Grandchildren.* 2d ed., rev. Point Roberts, Wash.: Hartley & Marks, 1990.

Mobility has increased significantly in recent years so the likelihood that grandparents may be separated by considerable distance from their children and grandchildren is great. Wassermann offers a number of suggestions for staying close and making connections between grandparents and grandchildren by mail, by phone, by audiotape (reading or telling stories), by writing story books, and by sending small gifts. She gives examples throughout the book for toddlers through teenagers. A section on children with special needs centers on handicapped and gifted children.

Life Transitions

Living Arrangements

Carlin, Vivian F. *Can Mom Live Alone? Practical Advice on Helping Aging Parents Stay in Their Own Home.* Lexington, Mass.: Lexington Bks., 1991.

Carlin, Vivian F., and Mansberg, Ruth. *Where Can Mom Live?: A Family Guide to Living Arrangements for Elderly Parents.* Lexington, Mass.: Lexington Bks., 1987.

While both books cover much the same ground, each focuses on a slightly different aspect. In *Can Mom Live Alone?*, the discussion centers on the importance of the home for the older individual and his or her family. It is often the place where they raised their children, where neighborhood ties are, and where they have spent most of their lives. For widows and widowers, it may be the last tangible tie with their spouse. A variety of resources can be tapped to help the elderly remain at home. Both sources include important financial strategies like reverse mortgages, low interest home improvement loans, among others. A full array of housing alternatives are discussed with the pros and cons of each explored in detail. *Where Can Mom Live?* outlines all of the housing alternatives available with housing preference surveys for the reader's use in deciding which option is best for them.

Salmen, John P. S., *The Do-able Renewable Home: Making Your Home Fit Your Needs.* Rev. ed. Washington, D.C.: American Assoc. of Retired Persons, 1988.

A practical guide to making changes in the physical home environment, *The Do-able Renewable Home* gives guidelines for making the home safer and easier for older adults. Every area of the home is discussed with clear illustrations accompanying the text. Many of the recommended adaptations can be done with relative ease without major remodeling.

Finances

Levy, Michael T. *Parenting Mom and Dad: A Guide for the Grown-Up Children of Aging Parents.* New York: Prentice Hall, 1991.

A physician, Levy effectively uses examples, case studies, and discussion to illustrate how best to care for aging parents and oneself. Changes associated with aging—memory loss, physical frailty, loss of loved ones, and the fear of death and dying—are described. In clear prose he informs the reader about the normal effects of aging and when to seek help. In seeking help, Levy presents guidelines for defining the problem, identifying available resources from the family and the community, and determining what type and level of assistance is needed. As part of this process, caregivers can make adjustments in the amount and type of help over time. Common illnesses and various psychological disorders affecting the elderly and their treatment are described. The practical and emotional aspects of financial and legal planning are also covered. A resource section on organizations and support groups appears in the appendix.

Moskowitz, Francine, and Robert Moskowitz. *Parenting Your Aging Parents: Guidance through the Nightmare of the 90's.* Woodland Hills, Calif.: Key Pub., 1991.

Using the case study approach and personal experience with their parents, the authors review common areas of concern in basic caregiving: who should take responsibility of caring for the older person, when to take responsibility, and how to intervene if the person does not welcome the assistance. The Moskowitzes also discuss housing: Can persons stay in their present home, how can it be made safer, what resources can be used to assist the individuals (home health, meal delivery, etc.), what other housing options exist, and how to choose a nursing home. Financial security can be a major concern in caring for one's parents, and the authors include a section on how adult children can assist through the use of a variety of techniques: joint bank accounts, power of attorney, trusts, guardianships, and conservatorships. The emotional issues for parents and their adult children are addressed as are family issues. Many of these involve the losses experienced by older persons and their children's reaction to them. Family concerns center on the family's past history, changes in the family (divorce, relocation, et cetera), and how the family members participate in assisting their parents' care. The emotional and legal issues related to death and dying are also included.

Retirement

Biracree, Tom, and Nancy Biracree. *Over Fifty: The Resource Book for the Better Half of Your Life.* New York: Harper Perennial, 1991.

Appropriately titled, *Over Fifty* gives directory information on personal finances, health care, retirement, travel, and hobbies. The section on financial planning covers banking, credit cards, determining one's net worth, among other useful topics. An extensive section on consumer services and consumer protection follows in an appendix.

Psychological Aspects

Independence and Dependence

Silverstone, Barbara, and Helen Kandel Hyman. *You and Your Aging Parent: The Modern Family's Guide to Emotional, Physical, and Financial Problems.* 3d ed. New York: Pantheon, 1989.

In the third edition of this classic, the authors offer practical solutions for families and individuals caring for their older relatives with emphasis on the emotional issues for all involved. When to intervene, with what kind of care, and the costs, both emotional and financial, are considered. The impact of widowhood, divorce, and remarriage on the family and its effect on the parents and their adult children are discussed. Silverstone and Hyman see the family conference as an excellent tool for planning how best to help the older person.

Psychological Disorders

Billig, Nathan. *To Be Old and Sad: Understanding Depression in the Elderly.* Lexington, Mass.: Lexington Bks., 1987.

In a frank discussion of depression and older adults, Billig describes the signs and symptoms of depression, how it can be caused by medication or as part of other illnesses, and most importantly, how it can be treated successfully. He contends that depression is assumed to accompany aging as a matter of course. This is often not the case. Family members can use the solutions Billig offers to seek treatment for the older person. The author also discusses how symptoms of depression can resemble many of the symptoms for Alzheimer's or other psychological disorders. Techniques for overcoming resistance to treatment are also included.

Stereotyping and Ageism

Fried, Stephen B., Dorothy Van Booven, and Cindy MacQuarrie. *Older Adulthood: Learning Activities for Understanding Aging.* Baltimore: Health Professions Pr., 1993.

While this practical guide covers many of the issues associated with aging (e.g., physical and psychological aging), it includes a number of activities on perceptions and stereotypes associated with aging. Readers are asked to reflect on their attitudes toward their own aging as well as that of others. The authors examine the role American society plays in perpetuating these stereotypes in films, advertising, television, and the greeting card industry.

Fries, James F. *Aging Well: A Guide for Successful Seniors.* Reading, Mass.: Addison-Wesley, 1989.

Previously listed under the section on "Physical Aspects of Aging," this book includes a brief chapter on avoiding stereotypes, in which readers are asked to confront their own prejudiced views. The author makes the important point that older adults differ from one another to a greater degree than do younger adults, as a result of many more years of varying experiences. In this way, the stereotyping of older people is even more inappropriate than the stereotyping of younger ones.

NOTES

1. John C. Cavanaugh, *Adult Development and Aging,* 2d ed. (Pacific Grove, Calif.: Brooks/Cole, 1993), 104–106.

2. Cited in Richard Schulz and Robert B. Ewen, *Adult Development and Aging: Myths and Emerging Realities,* 2d ed. (Dubuque, Iowa: W. C. Brown, 1989), 108.

3. Ibid., 108–109.

4. John W. Rybash, Paul A. Roodin, and John W. Santrock, *Adult Development and Aging,* 2d ed. (Dubuque, Iowa: W. C. Brown, 1989), 217–18.

5. Cavanaugh, *Adult Development and Aging,* 106–108.

6. Armeda F. Ferrini and Rebecca L. Ferrini, *Health in the Later Years* (Dubuque, Iowa: W. C. Brown, 1989), 226–27.

7. Cavanaugh, *Adult Development and Aging,* 127–28, 140–42.

8. Schulz and Ewen, *Adult Development and Aging,* 360–70.

9. Gerald Corey, *Theory and Practice of Counseling and Psychotherapy,* 4th ed. (Pacific Grove, Calif.: Brooks/Cole, 1991), 111–14.

10. Bernard H. Shulman and Raeann Berman. *How to Survive Your Aging Parents* (Chicago: Surrey Bks., 1988), 41–56.

11. Victor G. Cicirelli, "Adult Children and Their Elderly Parents," in *Family Relationships in Later Life,* ed. Timothy H. Brubaker (Newbury Park, Calif.: Sage, 1983), 34.

12. Georgia M. Barrow, *Aging, the Individual, and Society,* 5th ed. (St. Paul, Minn.: West Pub., 1992), 100–102.

13. Ibid., 118–25.

14. Ibid., 197.

15. Robert Atchley, *Aging: Continuity and Change,* 2d ed. (Belmont, Calif.: Wadsworth, 1987), 85–86.

16. Paul T. Costa and Robert R. McRae, "Concurrent Validation after 20 Years: The Implications of Personality Stability for Its Assessment," in *Normal Human Aging: The Baltimore Longitudinal Study of Aging,* ed. Nathan Shock and others (Washington, D.C.: U.S. Public Health Service, NIH Publication no. 84–2450, 1984), 109.

17. R. C. Atchley, "A Continuity Theory of Normal Aging," *Gerontologist* 29 (Apr. 1989): 183–90.

18. Janet K. Belsky, *The Psychology of Aging: Theory, Research, and Interventions*, 2d ed. (Pacific Grove, Calif.: Brooks/Cole, 1990), 272–79; Harold G. Koenig and Dan C. Blazer, "Mood Disorders and Suicide," in *Handbook of Mental Health and Aging*, 2d ed., ed. James E. Birren, R. Bruce Sloane, and Gene D. Cohen (San Diego, Calif.: Academic, 1991), 380–407.

19. James F. Fries, *Aging Well: A Guide for Successful Seniors* (Reading, Mass.: Addison-Wesley, 1989), 112–13.

20. Robert N. Butler, Myrna I. Lewis, and Trey Sunderland, *Aging and Mental Health: Positive Psychosocial and Biomedical Approaches*, 4th ed. (Westerville, Ohio: Merrill, 1991), 140–41.

21. Ibid., 243.

22. Arnold Arluke and Jack Levin, "Another Stereotype: Old Age as a Second Childhood," *Aging* 346 (Aug./Sept. 1984):7–11.

INDEX

E.G. FISHER PUBLIC LIBRARY